…oyds   **Scorers** – D.E…    …Australia)

…ugalle

…inimum of 75 overs has to be bowl…
.10 p.m. - 3.30 p.m. (New ball can b…   …ay

…ustralia

	First Innings		Second Innings	
.J.L.Langer	LBW B JONES	82	B FLINTOFF	28
.M.L.Hayden	C STRAUSS B HOGGARD	0	C TRESCOTHICK B JONES (S)	31
.R.T.Ponting*	C VAUGHAN B GILES	61	C JONES (G) B FLINTOFF	0
.D.R.Martyn	RUN OUT	20	C BOLL B HOGGARD	28
.M.J.Clarke	C JONES (G) B GILES	40	B HARMISON	30
.S.M.Katich	C JONES (S) B FLINTOFF	4	C TRESCOTHICK B GILES	16
.A.C.Gilchrist+	NOT OUT	49	C FLINTOFF B GILES	1
.S.K.Warne	B GILES	8	(9) HW B FLINTOFF	42
.B.Lee	C FLINTOFF B JONES (S)	6	(10) NOT OUT	43
0.J.N.Gillespie	LBW B FLINTOFF	7	(8) LBW B FLINTOFF	0
1.M.S.Kasprowicz	LBW B FLINTOFF	0	C JONES (S) B HARMISON	20

Extras 13 b 7 lb w 10 nb   31   13 b 8 lb w 8 nb   30
          TOTAL 308   **TOTAL** 279

…ll of Wkts: 1-0 2-88 3-118 4-194 5-212   1-47 2-48 3-82 4-107 5-134
          6-262 7-273 8-282 9-308   6-136 7-137 8-175 9-220

…owling Analysis	O	M	R	W	Wd	Nb	O	M	R	W	Wd	Nb
HARMISON	11	1	48	0		2	17	3	62	2	1	1
HOGGARD	8	0	41	1		4	5	1	26	1		
JONES	16	2	69	2	1	1	5	1	23	1		
FLINTOFF	15	1	52	3		3	22	3	79	4		13
GILES	26	2	78	3			15	3	68	2		

50p

…esult – ENGLAND WON BY 2 RUNS. BLOODY HELL.

Man of the Match – FLINTOFF
68, 73, 7-131 + 2 Cts

ASHES 2005

Also by Gideon Haigh and published by Aurum:

Game for Anything
Many a Slip
Mystery Spinner

ASHES 2005

THE GREATEST
TEST SERIES

GIDEON HAIGH

First published 2005 by
Aurum Press Limited
25 Bedford Avenue
London WC1B 3AT
www.aurumpress.co.uk

Copyright © 2005 by Gideon Haigh

The moral right of Gideon Haigh to be identified as the author of this
work has been asserted by him in accordance with the Copyright,
Designs and Patents Act 1988.

Many of these pieces were first published in the *Guardian*, *Observer Sports
Monthly*, *Wisden Cricketer* or on the cricinfo website.

All photos courtesy of Graham Morris/www.cricketpix.com, except nos
2 and 14 (Corbis).

All rights reserved. No part of this book may be reproduced or utilized in
any form or by any means, electronic or mechanical, including
photocopying, recording or by any information storage and retrieval
system, without permission in writing from Aurum Press Ltd.

A catalogue record for this book is available from the British Library.

ISBN 1 84513 138 X

10 9 8 7 6 5 4 3 2
2009 2008 2007 2006 2005

Typeset in Fournier by SX Composing DTP, Rayleigh, Essex

Printed and bound in Great Britain by MPG Books, Bodmin

CONTENTS

CONTENTS

INTRODUCTION

To collect together one's day-by-day thoughts on a Test series would seem a mostly futile exercise – and a potentially embarrassing one as well. Let's face it. One of the reasons that today's newspaper is tomorrow's fish and chip wrap is that it suits the journalists responsible so well. In time, people will forget how you predicted in your column that Steve Waugh would make a surprise Test comeback at the Sydney Cricket Ground after the popularity of his appearance in the hot tub on *Big Brother*. Put it in a book and it's a blot on your permanent record.

Even more stupid, surely, would be choosing a series with more snakes and ladders than . . . well, snakes and ladders. It wasn't long before the Ashes of 2005 had become the best Ashes contest in recent memory; a little longer and it was one of the best in history; by its conclusion it was a Test match classic that will be talked about for as long as I live, which can be guaranteed, because I will be doing the talking if no one else cares to.

The Ashes, however, will never stop mattering to me. I was born in England, raised in Australia, have one parent from each country, hold passports for both. I watched my first Test in Australia thirty years ago, my first Test in England twenty years ago, and ten years ago wrote a book, *One Summer, Every Summer,* based on my experiences of following an England team getting smashed all over Australia. This, despite popular demand, is a sequel, of sorts.

A word about allegiance may here be in order too. As I explained in *One Summer, Every Summer,* I live in Australia, am proud to call myself Australian, and sincerely admire the country's cricket team. When it comes to cricket, however, I support, and have always supported, England, for reasons I no longer remember, and thus feel powerless to change. Confused? Imagine what it's like living it. As Noel Coward said, he could handle the despair; it was the hope he couldn't stand.

The structure of *Ashes 2005* is self-explanatory – or more self-explanatory than cricket anyway. The broad trajectory of each Test is described in a match report written the day after the game ended. The previews, daily reports and retrospects were otherwise composed, in the main, for the *Guardian* – and filed, I might add in pre-emptive defence, about a quarter of an hour after close of play, thanks to those ever-so-friendly *Guardian* deadlines. The coverage of each match is also interspersed with entries written for a daily diary published by *Cricinfo*, and some articles for *Wisden Cricketer*. I have not gone back and altered so much as a comma, not because I am a particularly honest soul, but because I couldn't; for reasons of expeditious publication, *Ashes 2005* was submitted and typeset in instalments, as it emerged, still smoking, from my filthy, coffee-stained, crumb-clogged G4 iBook. So I might as well make it a virtue: you hold in your hands a faithful record of the battle between two Test cricket teams, and of the battle of one man with cricket's glorious uncertainty. Cricket can be described as the winner in both cases.

It remains to me to thank those people not wearing white who made my trip memorable by their generous hospitality and cordial comradeship. First and foremost were Stephen and Prudence Fay, who provided a delightful base camp in Islington; from Stephen's journalistic wisdom I have also been a great beneficiary; thanks to Prudence, campanologist extraordinaire and stalwart of *The Ringing World*, I now know the difference between a Spliced S Major and a Bristol S Maximus. Well, I know they're different, anyway. In the north, I was welcomed into the bosom of my English family, especially by my cousin Heather Benson, her husband Andrew Hutchinson, and their daughters Jenny and Lucy. In the south, I was also taken in by my friend Lynne Truss, who lived every ball of this Ashes series, and in whose London pied-à-terre quite a bit of *Ashes 2005* was written. Norm and Adele Geras, Tanya Aldred and Andy

Wilson, Pilita Clark and Peter Wilson, Stephanie Bunbury, David Frith, Matthew Engel, Ramachandra Guha, Mike Atherton, Ken Smith, Nabila Ahmed, Emma John, Simon Rae and Professor Ian Smith either put me up or put up with me on the road. There were also the familiar friendly faces of the Yarras in (temporary) exile: Sven, Big Al, Humphrey, Robbo F. Moe, Kinger and Marty C.

A big thank you to my *Guardian* colleagues: Mike Selvey, David Hopps, Richard Williams, Lawrence Booth, Alex Brown and Paul Kelso in the press box, Ben Clissitt, Ian Prior, Adam Sills, Martin Rose, Mike Herd, Mark Redding and Matt Hancock in the office. Some strong personalities in that lot, but in two months there wasn't a disagreement, let alone an angry word; on the contrary, it wasn't just because of the cricket that I looked forward to going to work. Likewise thanks to my *Wisden Cricketer* and Cricinfo colleagues, especially John Stern, Andrew Miller and my dear friend Sambit Bal. Above all, thanks to someone who wasn't there, my girlfriend Sally Warhaft, who watched every ball of the series on television in Australia with only Trumper the cat for company: to both of them, I now have a lot of making up to do. Because of the sheer quality of the cricket, I was rapt while this series was on; because of Sal, I was glad when it was over too.

THE PHONEY WAR

A LONG-RANGE FORECAST

JANUARY 2005

Early one morning during the Boxing Day Test, I arrived at a meeting with some senior and respected members of the Australian cricket community to find them clustered round a television at the Melbourne Cricket Ground. Checking the highlights of Pakistan's innings the day before, I fancied. But no: the focus was England's first-innings collapse at Durban, which was being savoured with malicious glee.

As each English batsman was dismissed by the South Africans, so were they dismissed again by the pundits, the harrumphs being scarcely less ecstatic than the howzats. Trescothick? Overrated. Strauss? Untested. Butcher? Second-rate. Thorpe? Soft. The abiding popularity of the national pastime of writing England off, indeed, was strangely pleasing to the ear, a reminder of that line of Sir Robert Menzies: 'We [England and Australia] know each other so well that, thank Heaven, we don't have to be too tactful with each other.'

The Australian summer has been a lacklustre affair. New Zealand and Pakistan have come and gone without leaving a trace. There have even been musings, at least among the high-minded, about whether this baggy green and golden age hasn't gone a little far, that it is as edifying as watching Mike Tyson polish off the procession of punching bags that prolonged his career. 'Cricket has a problem,' Greg Chappell has complained. 'It can't afford to have any of the top nations down for long – and to have two of them,

England and the West Indies, down for ten years or more is a very unhealthy state of affairs.'

The Ashes thus seem an unusually welcome prospect. Bear in mind that Australian cricket fans have only ever seen their team beaten in home series by the West Indies (four times) and New Zealand (once) besides England; the Poms are an old and lately a rather puny enemy, but they are at least a recognizable one. The trophy, too, seems to be working its usual magic. England's run of ins has been closely followed. Six and a half months before a ball is bowled, newspapers are already producing pages of preliminary analysis. With the Channel Nine team augmented by the plummy tones and round vowels of Mark Nicholas, who sounds like Henry Higgins doing field work, it can occasionally seem as though the series has already begun.

No one has yet been found to put a buck on England – Wasim Akram has gone furthest with his assertion that the Ashes could 'go either way'. But perhaps that's because the odds are no longer of the order once so enticing to Dennis Lillee and Rod Marsh.

Jeremiahs might point out that there was a similar sense of antici-pation four years ago, as England impressively disposed of Pakistan then Sri Lanka on their surfaces, on the eve of hosting Steve Waugh's Australians. Much was heard of Nasser Hussain's general-ship, of Graham Thorpe's genius, and of coming men like Michael Vaughan and Andy Flintoff. Seldom in sport can anticipation have proved so perishable. Hussain was promptly injured in the First Test; Thorpe, Vaughan and Flintoff played one Test between them. Australia won a catchweight contest by 4 p.m. on the third day of the Third Test.

Even if you accept that the challengers are a superior outfit to four years ago, it is arguable that the same applies to the trophy holders. This time last year, fixated on the whip-around for Waugh's parting bouquet, and deprived of the injured Glenn McGrath and the internally exiled Shane Warne, Australia were struggling to hold an irrepressible India in check.

Yet the handover of the captaincy was timed to a nicety. In Sri

Lanka, Ricky Ponting dropped into the role like a penny into a slot. Thrice his team trailed on first innings; thrice it thrillingly rallied to win. In the rematches against Sri Lanka at home and India away, Australian also comfortably prevailed. The attack's keen edge has been sharpened by the returns first of Warne, then of McGrath. The disappointing deceleration of Brett Lee has been more than made up for by the stealthy advance of Jason Gillespie, who is within a few scalps of becoming Australia's fifth-highest Test wicket taker, and who since the start of the last Ashes series has also averaged 21.1 with the bat.

Under Ponting, Australia seems to have attained a new level of organic harmony. While Matthew Hayden, Darren Lehmann and even the captain himself marked time with the bat last year, Justin Langer and Damien Martyn were the world's two tallest Test run scorers, and Adam Gilchrist comfortably the fastest. Certainly, the country continues to churn out cricketers as *Neighbours* grinds out characters. Michael Clarke emerged in India in a starburst of strokes; Simon Katich, less conspicuous, was in his own serene way just as impressive. Shane Watson enjoyed a sedan chair ride in Sydney by taking guard on his Test debut at 471 for five, but such are the luxuries of playing for the world's best team. And without wishing to poop anyone's party, it is worth recalling just on whom England will rely to curb such abundant talent: six bowlers – Harmison, Hoggard, Flintoff, Jones, Giles and Anderson – whose total of twenty-three Australian Test wickets have cost 50.47 each.

For Australian cricket, however, this Ashes contest holds an unusual, even a disconcerting, significance. The barnstorming success of the XIs of Waugh and Ponting are but one indicator of the game's health here; others are not nearly so favourable. When *Cricket Australia* commissioned a new strategic plan from McKinsey six months ago, consultant Andrew Jones found some worrying evidence of a game struggling to broaden its appeal: flat attendances, diminished ratings, minimal penetration of immigrant and indigenous populations, only so-so growth in participation. A recent official cricket census – which arrived at an active junior and

4

senior player population of 436,000 – almost certainly represents a per capita decline on a decade ago.

Cricket Australia is even, for possibly the first time since the googly, appropriating an English invention by introducing the Twenty20 game to local audiences. Pakistan is pitted against Australia A at Adelaide Oval on 13 January in the first such fixture of its type here. A full-blown international against England follows six months later.

Yet very few Australians will see the latter, because this year's tour of England will be the first not to be screened, even partly, on free-to-air television – a reflection of the clout of Australian rules football and the rugby codes as they vie for the right to call themselves national games, but also of cricket's relatively diminished cachet. Once this would have invited prime-ministerial rebuke and quite possibly a royal commission; this time, it occasioned barely a murmur.

That's because Australian involvement in sport, once intensely traditional and relatively narrow, has broadened markedly. The country, for instance, had the third-largest contingent at the Olympics, competing in an unprecedented range of events. And Australians will go where the action is: there are estimated to be as many as 180 playing professional football in Europe.

Consumption of sport down under, likewise, has never been so ecumenical. No longer do Australians imagine that the Tour de France is offered by Kon-Tiki, or that Murray Walker is perhaps Max's brother. Football is making the deepest inroads. No other country celebrated Greece's July win in Euro 2004 with greater abandon, while Australian children covet replica gear and discuss the Premier League with a fluency that they used to reserve for batting and bowling averages. A new national competition, the A-League, intended to lure back some of the talent heading offshore, kicks off in August. No cricket on the telly? Very well, say this generation of Australians, let's check what's on the other channel.

Australian cricket devotees have often in recent times expressed the wish for a stronger England, but always somewhat airily and condescendingly. The need is now a good deal more urgent, not least because of the commercial imperative to continue producing attractive spectacles for broadcast. Much as my countrymen enjoyed England's setbacks at Durban a couple of weeks ago, England's spirited second innings was in its own way as welcome.

FREQUENT FLIERS

JUNE 2005

In days of yore, Australian teams arrived in England like exotic parcels in the mail bearing strange stamps and addressed in an unfamiliar hand. What could they contain? What excitements did they portend? What fun was in the offing?

The 2005 Australians arrive with the menacing familiarity of a buff envelope from the Inland Revenue. There are no Bradmanesque bolters, no mystery men like John Gleeson or mystery teens like Ian Craig – just all too well-known quantities revisiting old haunts, bent on further 'mental disintegration'.

In 128 years of Anglo-Australian cricket, only fifty-five Australian players have toured England as often as thrice. Eight of them are in this team: Shane Warne on his fourth sojourn, Ricky Ponting, Matt Hayden, Damien Martyn, Justin Langer, Adam Gilchrist, Jason Gillespie and Glenn McGrath on their third.

If rain interruptions compel the screening of archival footage this season, it may be a little difficult to tell the difference. Australia's first-choice attack – Warne, McGrath, Gillespie and Michael Kasprowicz – is the same as the one with which they began the Ashes of 1997. Five of the team also helped heft the World Cup here six years ago.

No Ashes series in recent memory has stirred such interest in

Australia. When Kerry Packer's Channel Nine ignored it, the second public network SBS, whose 'multicultural' schedule is usually stuffed with Egyptian soap operas and Danish detective series, won the undying allegiance of Anglophone Australia by filling the breach.

For the hosts, the sight of Australians swaggering around the Rose Bowl today will signal the conclusion of what might be called the Gareth Batty phase of summer, where the stiffest competition England has faced has been in the nets. Yet to dawn is what sort of power stalks the land. The last Anglo-Australian one-day and Test contests were both decided in England's favour; the fourteen consecutive limited-overs defeats, and ten Test losses for one win preceding them, have somehow receded from memory.

Well, maybe not quite. There's always the scorebook. Graham Thorpe remarked last month that his country's best hope against Australia was to 'play the men rather than the statistics'. A glance at *Playfair* suggests that this was sage advice. Ponting's Australians form a tight-packed phalanx of figures that would make any opponent quail. The captain himself averages 58.68, Gilchrist 55.65, Hayden 53.46, Martyn 51.25 and Langer 46.52 – and the last of these can scarcely be called least when he was Test cricket's tallest scorer in calendar 2004.

Among Australia's all-time Test wicket takers, meanwhile, Shane Warne, Glenn McGrath and Jason Gillespie rank first, second and fifth (two old lags, Lillee and McDermott, have been relegated to third and fourth). From their 3000 maidens can be inferred the tight grip Australia manages to exert in the field. And of this key collection of players, furthermore, all but the skipper and Hayden fare better statistically against England than all-comers.

There is a tendency to think, even in Australia, that it cannot go on forever. But evergreen as some of these names might seem, Australian cricket is also deciduous. The three oldest members of the team of 2001, the Waugh twins and Colin Miller, have gone;

likewise the unhappiest, Michael Slater, whose lips will hence-forward be brushing a microphone rather than a cap badge.

The summer that unfolds, in fact, will be a reverse of the traditional order. The unknown team will be not be Australia but England. In the If-This-Is-Wednesday-It-Must-Be-Wankhede world of modern cricket, few secret weapons stay so for long, and everyone's game pretty soon gets picked apart. Nonetheless, many of England's critical players are either total or virtual strangers to Ashes competition, despite it being barely thirty months since the countries last met on the Test field.

Andy Flintoff visited Australia in 2002–3, but had only frequent flier miles to show for his pains – which, it turned out, localized in his back. His darkest hour, however, came just before a dawn worth 1596 runs at 44.3 and 96 wickets at 23.7 since. No cricketer will exert quite the same influence this summer as Flintoff. His success will be worth more than its weight in runs and wickets to England; his failure will, likewise, be disproportionately disadvantageous.

Andrew Strauss may look familiar to Australians mainly because his left-handed poise and wells of concentration are so reminiscent of his erstwhile Middlesex team mate Langer. Like Flintoff, he has also been a touchstone of English success in his fourteen Tests, nine of his ten scores of more than fifty having come amid English victories.

Australians have seen some of Steve Harmison, but scarcely the 2004 model who inflicted on the West Indies what they had long meted out to others. It isn't two years since Harmison, withdrawing from a tour of Bangladesh, looked like a regulation English enigma in the making; he has since made a renewed bid for enigma status in South Africa. But he is the only member of Michael Vaughan's pace attack with the pace and lift to discomfort the visitors.

The other player of whom Australians have seen little is, strangely enough, one who made a century against them on debut in 1993. Thorpe has missed fourteen of the last fifteen Ashes encounters, citing a bad back then a broken heart, and perhaps also protecting a weakened will. The rekindling of his competitive fires is perhaps England's most promising leading indicator, suggesting a happier dressing room environment than has been customary.

While there is no escaping the strength in continuity that the Australians enjoy, there is something to learn from. In the last four home Ashes series, England has used no fewer than sixty different players; Australian teams have drawn on thirty-three. This is only partly explained by the country's varying degrees of success. In some ways it is an explanation of it.

Australians always look askance at the free and sometimes frantic hand with which English selectors turn their teams over, and the class of *desaparecidos* they leave in their wake. An Australian cricket enthusiast returning to England after four years finds himself asking over and over again: 'So, whatever happened to what's-his-name?'

Oh yeah, now I remember. What about those talented young batsmen Owais Shah, Usman Afzaal, Ian Ward, Ali Brown, Aftab Habib, Ed Smith, Jim Troughton and Nicky Peng, so vaunted the last time the Australians were here? How go those bright bowling prospects Alex Tudor, Chris Silverwood, Richard Johnson, Matthew Bulbeck and Richard Dawson? Oh, you don't know either.

Australians, frankly, are more frugal where talent is concerned. In this line-up, there are players challenged to improve, for those that live by the stats can die by them too. Matt Hayden's recent Test batting has been strangely free of fluency, and his last twenty-two innings worth only 662 runs at 33.10. He has still to prove he is a great player, as distinct from a good one who enjoyed an uncommon but unsustainable hot streak.

Since his meteoric arrival, including centuries on debut at home and away, Michael Clarke's average has been decidedly earth-bound, with his last eight bats yielding a meagre 128 runs at 16. Then there's Brett Lee, uncapped since the Sydney Test of January 2004 and turning twenty-nine in November – for a fast bowler, *d'un certain âge*.

Not everyone in a cricket team, however, is in form and in luck at the same time. Players off the boil, indeed, are also players with something to prove, and likely as not to grab an opportunity when it comes.

The next three months should be tough and fun. The contents of the Australian buff envelope do not suggest much possibility of the unexpected. Since losing a rain-ruined series to Sri Lanka by the odd Test there in September 1999, Australia has won fifty-three of sixty-nine Tests, while only two of its eight draws were not rain-effected.

Of the mystery packaged players destined to arrive from all over England, one can only hope that not too many will have been stamped 'return to sender' by summer's end.

THE INNER ASHES

Cricket neologisms come and go. The 'corridor of uncertainty'? A bit naff now, really. 'Back of a length'? The pretentious version of 'short of a length', innit? 'Bowling a heavy ball'? A vestige of the convict game, perhaps.

One recent idiom, however, shows a definite staying power. 'Mental disintegration' is again the *leitmotiv* of the Australian approach to this summer's Ashes series. 'Mental disintegration?' commented Ricky Ponting in response to a question on the day of his team's departure. 'That's what it's all about, really, trying to keep England under pressure from ball one of the series until the series ends. That's what our whole cricket theme, if you like, is based on.'

If we like? We like a lot. A Google search for the phrase 'mental disintegration' produces 228,000 hits. One half expects it to see it written as mental disintegration™, under licence from Steve Waugh's sports marketing company, with mental toughness™ its wholly-owned subsidiary.

Repetition, of course, has diluted it to banality, rather as it has one-day cricket. 'Mental disintegration' is now just the portmanteau version of 'pressure', which itself was probably first inserted in a soundbite by Alfred Mynn. But it didn't start out that way.

It is Allan Border who has been credited with the concept, during his pitiless 1989 campaign to regain the Ashes, when he was so famously bloody-minded to everyone that the Queen was lucky not to get an earful about the fall of Singapore. Border says, however, that he recalls its origination only at the end of the tour, in the dressing room during the Sixth Test at the Oval, and ascribes it to fellow Queenslander Carl Rackemann, who had spent the tour as a supernumerary.

The context was a conversation about a declaration on the final morning. Australia was 4–0 up and had England on the rack again. But while some players were urging a closure and setting a target, Rackemann pressed for the full Torquemada treatment. 'Full mental and physical disintegration' would only result if Australia batted longer than England expected, forcing them into the demoralising state of bowling and fielding in futility. Border was persuaded. After all, why did England, so feeble all summer, deserve a target? The proposition he proffered at lunch on the last day – 393 in 65 overs – ensured that only Australia could win. It might well have sufficed had not bad light ruled out the last twenty overs with England 143–5.

'Mental disintegration', then, originally conveyed not an expression of totality, as Ponting is now employing it, but a matter of degree, like the extra notch on Nigel's amp in *This Is Spinal Tap*. This was the way it entered Steve Waugh's lexicon four years later, when Border applied it at Headingley. Border and Waugh batted most of the second day in partnership, being 175 and 144 at the close respectively. But the former surprised the latter by batting almost another hour the next morning with the objective being to cause 'further mental and physical disintegration'. England slid quickly to 50–3, barely lasted the rest of the day, and were rounded up by an innings and 148 runs – a result that also disintegrated Graham Gooch's captaincy.

Like everything in cricket, this approach has ancient antecedents. Cricket is a game in which the act of aggression and the instinct to dominate have always operated within certain bounds of propriety and taste – something lately given actual black letter form in the 2000 revision of the MCC's Laws of Cricket. Australia, traditionally, has set those bounds a little wider than England, understanding intuitively that they need only be a little wider to represent a considerable advantage.

Perhaps 'mental disintegration's forefather is the immovable Warwick Armstrong, that roundhead in the age of cavaliers. This time a hundred years ago he was bowling outside leg stump to packed leg-side fields, disputing umpiring decisions and remonstrating with opponents – a truculence more unsettling in times more polite.

Armstrong even psyched out Jack Hobbs, when the latter benefited from an umpire's indulgence at Headingley in July 1909. 'The Australians made a rare fuss,' wrote Jack Hobbs in *My Cricket Memories*. 'They gathered together on the field and confabulated. The chief offender was Warwick Armstrong, who got very nasty and unsportsmanlike, refusing to accept the umpire's decision. This upset me. I did not know whether I was standing on my head or my heels, with the consequence that two balls later I let one go, never even attempting to play it, and it bowled me. I still bear this incident in mind against Armstrong.'

Armstrong was certainly the antipodean archetype that Percy Fender had in mind when he gave a speech to the Junior Imperial League on the eve of Australia's 1926 visit to England in which he sought to summarize the Australian way of cricket – its intensity, its lack of inhibition – which he contrasted with more staid English mores. 'We are going to see certain things in the Australian game which are not to their detriment but which are not in our game,' he forecast. 'We are up against a lot of things *which we don't do but which other people do* [my italics].' According to Fender's biographer Richard Streeton, Australians were aghast at such an imputation; the truth, of course, always hurts.

Nor is it a coincidence that the most successful of England's captains have seemed almost Australian in their combativeness and obstinacy. Fender saw Douglas Jardine as 'a man cast in the toughest Australian mould, *à la* Armstrong'; Neville Cardus thought it 'a pity his [Jardine's] opponent is not Warwick Armstrong'. Len Hutton, whose boyhood primer was *The Game's the Thing* by Armstrong's contemporary Monty Noble, drew freely on Australian inspiration: 'I admire the Australians' approach to the game; they have the utmost ability for producing that little extra, or instilling into the opposition an inferiority complex that can have, and has had, a crushing effect. Australians have no inhibitions.'

If anything, then, Border rediscovered an Australian tradition rather than establishing one – a tradition that might be felt to stretch back to the country's colonial inheritance, and the desire to shrug it off.

In perhaps the most famous essay about cricket by an Australian intellectual, 'Cricket versus Republicanism' (1977), the philosopher David Stove gave a memorably succinct explanation for the Ashes edge his country enjoyed: 'The margin of superiority is slight, but it is consistent, and therefore calls for explanation. I have heard dozens of theories advanced to account for this. My own belief is that it is due to a difference in attitude towards the opponent: that whereas the Australians hate the Poms, the Poms only despise the Australians.'

In one of the more delightful essays about cricket by a English intellectual, 'On The Boundary' (1981), Lord Bragg described his country's habitual recourse: low-level resentment. He recalled being stirred from a snooze at the screening of an Ingmar Bergman film after a particularly galling defeat and interrupting Liv Ullmann's monologue with an audible grunt of 'bloody Australians!'

The Border *risorgimento* did, however, have an additional dimension, passed down to the present. Australian teams of the last twenty years have been perhaps the most ardent apostles of the doctrine of play as 'work' – a devotion instilled by that formidable taskmaster Bob Simpson during his decade as coach.

Practice under Simpson, and later Geoff Marsh and John Buchanan, became more than a means of enhancing skills. It served purposes of building collegial feeling, and showing that the Australians meant business. 'We never talk about hard work, just valuable work that has to be done and therefore might as well be enjoyed,' explained Simpson. 'I just tell the players that it's an opportunity to show what they can do, to show off, if you like.'

It had an effect. John Wright described seeing Simpson orchestrating a fielding drill on the lawn of the hotel at Chandigarh in August 1987, the morning after Australia had beaten New Zealand in a gruelling one-day match. Wright said he knew then Australia would win the World Cup. There's no doubt that not only have Australia been stronger, fitter and better-prepared than any of their international opponents over the last two decades, but that this Stakhanovite reputation has preceded them.

In theory, the 'hard work' solution, with its underlying conviction that there are no limits to a player's potential for improvement, is accessible to all. In practice, it is a seed that often falls on stony ground. Both Simpson and Buchanan brought their philosophies to England, at Leicestershire and Middlesex respectively, and got nowhere. 'The big problem with Bob,' complained James Whittaker afterwards, 'was that he wanted us all to be Test cricketers.' As Simpson responded: 'Just fancy that!'

The difference in the belief in the capacity for continuous improvement in Australia and England has had some illuminating manifestations over the last decade or so. Consider, for example, the contrasting fortunes of Darren Gough and Glenn McGrath – not as bowlers but as batsmen.

When they first met, in Australia in 1994–5, Gough had the makings of an all-rounder – or a 'newbotham', as such players are known in England. He had all the shots, plus some of his own design, which he paraded in a bravura half-century at Sydney.

When Gough left Australia, it was with a Test batting average of 35. But over his next fifty Tests, this average dwindled to 12.5. His batting became ineffectual, even ridiculous, like an annoying comic catchphrase. More embarrassing still was Gough's indifference to his declining effectiveness; ah well, he comments airily in his autobiography, he 'never was one for keeping up an end', as there was 'no fun in that'.

At the time of that first encounter, McGrath was averaging less than 2. A box placed in front of the stumps might have done as well. This was amusing to everyone except McGrath, who never looked other than baffled and betrayed after each cheap dismissal.

McGrath, amid a certain amount of derision, took on as a coach Steve Waugh himself. The investment yielded dividends more or less immediately when McGrath lingered ten minutes at the crease in Antigua in May 1995, allowing Waugh to achieve his only Test double-hundred.

McGrath's improvement since has been steady. By the end of his next tour of England, McGrath's average had increased to just under 4. His last 450 runs have been garnered at a tick under 9. The sum may seem paltry, but in the space of 9 runs from McGrath a Gilchrist might add 30 or 40. McGrath's autobiography devotes his batting an entire, typically earnest, chapter. 'You see, the way I look at cricket is there are *eleven* batsmen in a cricket side,' he insisted. 'We all have a job to do, and we're expected to do it with a certain aplomb.'

Seldom has the doctrine of mental disintegration been so methodically enforced as at Adelaide Oval last November, when McGrath joined Jason Gillespie with their team 118 in the lead on first innings just after tea on the third day. The teams seemed close to parity as the New Zealanders contemplated their second dig in advance. But, with nothing other than orthodox stroke play, the last Australian pair made increasingly merry. They had added 93 by the close, and a record 114 by their separation, their partnership lasting longer than the eventual response of the visitors – a demoralized 76.

The interlude, nonetheless, was not merely about Australian strength. The New Zealanders were complicit in their own downfall, slack bowling and outcricket allowing the partnership to establish itself. Advantages in cricket are not always taken; sometimes they are ceded.

Such is the case with Australia's psychological edge in the Ashes: it is something they have both acquired and been given. It is, therefore, in England's power to change. And if we could get through a whole a series without any further need to talk of mental disintegration, one could almost resign oneself to occasional use of 'corridor of uncertainty' and 'back of a length'.

PORTRAIT OF THE LEG-SPINNER AS A YOUNG MAN

In the Australian team of which he is the oldest, most experienced and comfortably most famous member, Shane Warne is the great decomplicator. People tangle themselves in theories, he complains: cricket is a simple game. Batsmen should block the good ones and belt the loose ones; bowlers are there to get them out. None of John Buchanan's Sun Tzu stuff for him; he prefers eternal cricket verities. Don't force it. Back yourself. Relax.

It's when Warne is relaxing, however, that the trouble always seems to start, usually involving some combination of fag, fix, phone and *femme fatale*. No cricketer has so dominated both back and front pages of the newspapers of his time – confirming in the process the truism about the back pages chronicling only man's successes, the front only failures.

It would be inexact to say that Warne embraces fame ambivalently. On the contrary, he revels in the doors that celebrity have opened for him; he merely resents that the doors do not always close behind him, remaining ajar for a pesky press. But he can certainly attest the costs of his public misadventures, which have already guaranteed that the best Australian cricketer of his generation will not captain his country in a Test. For the stakes have only grown larger: his most recent tabloid humiliations have cost him his relationships with his wife Simone and with Kerry Packer's Nine Network, to both of whom he has been wedded for the last decade.

What is it with Warne? Over the years, I have probably interviewed Warne as much as anyone: for the first time in July 1994, most recently last year when his one-year suspension for testing positive to a banned substance ended, and on five other occasions at length in person and on the phone between times. Interviews offer only fake and superficial acquaintanceships, yet some personal impressions have stayed with me.

Our initial meeting was in a favourite bar in the Melbourne suburb of Brighton. Warne had already found fame to be dual-edged: it was a year since 'the ball of the century', and about four months since his infamous send-off of Andrew Hudson in Johannesburg. Yet he wasn't about to abandon old haunts, any more than old friends. If he had to lead an extraordinary life, he would, as much as possible, lead ordinary ways.

My first impression was of shaking Warne's hand. Warne's fingers are huge and strong, but he does not affect the bear-like grasp common among Australian sporting males. Warne's greeting has always reminded me of the description of Governor Jack Stanton's warm and intimate handshake 'with that famous misty look' at the beginning of *Primary Colors* – inspired, of course, by Bill Clinton. And there is actually more than a touch of Clinton about Warne: great in ability, vast in charm, susceptible to appetites, disinclined to responsibility.

As we began, Warne lit a cigarette. He smoked more or less continuously for the next two hours: another proclamation of normality, it seemed, although it didn't affront me as it did others because I also smoked, and we steadily filled an ashtray to overflowing. When I ran out, in fact, Warne tossed me a packet of

Benson & Hedges, then still the sponsors of Australian cricket. 'Here ya go,' he said. 'I've got heaps.' Warne clearly thought that one of the coolest things about being a Test cricketer was getting free cigarettes.

I was reminded of the gesture during Warne's match-fixing misadventure, which began, if you recall, when an unknown stranger offered to make up his losses in a casino in Sri Lanka apparently out of the kindness of his heart. Of all Warne's indiscretions, this is the one I have found hardest to abide, and the one about which in print I was harshest. Yet even I could see how vulnerable Warne would have been to such an inducement. Big time sport drenches naïve and sheltered young men in free stuff; free money must have seemed to Warne just another perquisite.

I found lots about Warne to like. He didn't duck a question. He wasn't conceited, but nor was he afflicted by that cloying 'it's all about the team' false modesty. And where one journalist wrote recently that Warne's autobiography should be called 'Whatever It Was, It Wasn't My Fault', this young Warne was still quite mortified by how he'd lashed out at Hudson in Johannesburg – mortified because he liked Hudson and respected him as an opponent. However he has treated others near to him, Warne has always been genuinely generous to the cricketers he has played with and against.

Cricket, frankly, is where it's at for Warne. He is, otherwise, a limited man, with limited interests, who would always prefer a cheese and tomato toastie to *haute cuisine*, who has travelled the world and never quite left suburban Melbourne. When we next met, in a hotel room just before the Brisbane Test of November 1996, I asked him for a self-assessment. He was no scholar, he admitted: 'But I think I'm pretty street smart.' A young, cloistered, prematurely wealthy white male – and he thought he knew the street? *Purlease*. Why, by this stage, he couldn't even walk down a street without a penumbra of fans and star spotters.

Warne isn't dumb, but nor is he notably broad. On one occasion in Sydney in January 2000, I had to wait for Warne while he filmed something for pay TV, and sat quietly reading Erik Larson's book *Isaac's Storm*. When Warne arrived, he asked what I was perusing. I explained that it was an account of the hurricane that destroyed Galveston in 1900, and its role in the development of accurate weather forecasting. Warne nodded. 'I read this book once,' he said. 'It was about UFOs.'

At the time, I winced slightly; on reflection, I found the remark endearing. Most sportsmen wouldn't have bothered asking what I was reading, let alone trying to form a reply. Warne seeks a connection with people. It has often been commented that he needs you to like him. He also, I think, wants to like you. He remains the only sportsman who has rung after an interview to ask if his swearing could be toned down, for like many Australians he effs and blinds as a kind of punctuation. But he is also the only sportsman to have rung back after an interview to see if anything else needed asking, and then talked happily for another hour.

There's no doubt that Warne is sensitive to the way he appears, and that this is partly a matter of personal vanity. But it's also, I think, an outcome of a reputation that precedes him everywhere. At the end of our first interview, Warne asked abruptly: 'Was I what you expected?' I can't remember my reply, but I recall his next comment: 'The trouble is, people I've never met think they know all about me.' He isn't, of course, the first famous person to lament that disconnect, but I have always wondered since about the impact of never meeting anyone who did not already know who one was.

The best thing about talking to Warne is that he knows cricket backwards. A biography of Warne appeared in Australia last year that presented him as an insensate blond oik who did no more than roll his golden wrist over. It was bollocks. Why was short mid-wicket straight rather than square? When should you push mid-off and mid-on back? He's got an answer and it's always an interesting one. Warne's autobiography is pretty standard, but the chapter on leg-spin is as good as anything written on the craft.

More than that, Warne is in tune with cricket. When we last spoke at length, I asked what he had missed most about cricket while suspended. To my pleasant surprise, he did not have immediate recourse to the stupefying cult of the baggy green. He said that, whether it was a Test match or a club game, the great thing about cricket was that you never knew what would happen on any given day: 'You don't know whether you're going to knock 'em over, or you're going to get slogged, whether you'll have a bad day or take a couple of screamers.'

The possibilities and uncertainties of cricket, however, rich as they are on the field, are bounded by it. In the end, one wins, loses or draws. Life is deeper, denser, darker, and not so amenable to decomplication. Even with money, fame and charm, life is not something against which to 'back yourself'. One must even be careful about the way that one relaxes.

HOME AWAY

21 July is usually noted as the anniversary of the day Neil Armstrong took his one small step for a man. This 21 July, England's cricketers will be seeking a giant leap for their country's sporting traditions by winning an Ashes Test at Lord's.

A frivolous comparison? Probably. After all, what's the big deal about the moon anyway? Lord's, meanwhile, is a cricket ground in the same way that the Sistine Chapel is a church. And Australia's is an occupation impervious to all insurgencies for seventy-one years.

England last won a Test at what the cognoscenti call 'the home of cricket' in the same month as Mussolini accepted a fascist salute at the inaugural World Cup. It was a different time with different habits. Australia's prime minister, Joseph Lyons, had eleven children. England's prime minister, Ramsay Macdonald, was a dour Scottish socialist, the illegitimate son of a ploughboy and maid. Adolf Hitler looked like a fascist dictator we could do business with.

Of the players, there is only one survivor: Bill Brown, who made a hundred in the face of the matchwinning fourteen-wicket day of Yorkshireman Hedley Verity, and turns ninety-three a few days after the Test ends.

Even then an English victory at Lord's had that single-swallow quality of not making a summer. It was the host nation's first win there since 1896. English cricket at its own headquarters could be said never to have quite recovered from the passing of Queen Victoria.

There is no lack of theories as to why Australia has traditionally prospered at cricket's sanctum sanctorum. Some believe it is because Australians still see the ground as something special, while Englishmen, who visit it on the county circuit, regard playing there as more routine. 'It is every Australian cricketer's dream to be selected to play in a Test at Lord's,' said Steve Waugh. 'Once inside this fabled arena, you always get a sense that you are in a place that is steeped in tradition. It is rightfully called the home of cricket.' Waugh averaged 115.5 here in Tests, following the example of his first skipper Allan Border, who averaged 100.6. Glenn McGrath's wickets here cost less than 13 each, Shane Warne's 22.

Others hold that the atmosphere of Lord's is too oppressive for the host country, while their colonial kin are untroubled by the same inhibitions. To be sure, the walk through the Long Room can be both daunting and confusing: walking out to make his Test debut at Lord's thirty years ago, England's David Steele famously descended an additional flight of stairs and found himself in a lavatory. The toilet is something English batting efforts have more commonly vanished down. There have been only three English Ashes hundreds at the arena in the last half a century.

The serried ranks of spectators with their ties of egg and bacon, for whom whisky sour seems somehow an attitude as well as a beverage, sometimes do not live up to the Marylebone Cricket Club's professed ideals of gentlemanly behaviour and hospitality. It is twenty-five years since members scuffled with umpire David Constant when they believed a post-rain restart was in order during the Centenary Test, while it was the silent verdict of members after dismissal at Lord's that affirmed Ian Botham in his decision to resign his country's captaincy in July 1981: 'I was made to feel like a villain as I approached the members sitting in their seats in front of the pavilion. Most of them sat unmoving, staring straight ahead, seemingly doing their best to ignore me completely . . . Whenever I looked up or about me, eyes were quickly averted . . . If my mind hadn't been made up, the attitude of the MCC members that day would have made it up for me.' In fact, much as he purported to love the ground, Botham averaged 18 with the bat and 34 with the ball there in Ashes encounters.

The First Test should test not merely the teams, but all the foregoing speculations and suppositions. Ricky Ponting's Australians come to Lord's in a position beyond imagining as little as five weeks earlier, having given a solid workout to the old truism that form is temporary and class permanent. Some players seem hardly to have left the plane; Jason Gillespie looks like he wouldn't mind being back on it.

Carted at Cardiff by Bangladesh; broken at Bristol and heavied at Headingley by Michael Vaughan's testosterone-enhanced England; taunted at Taunton by Somerset, for heaven's sake. Young men are excused inconsistency; in older men, and most members of this team have a good deal more cricket behind them than in front, failure can seem a *memento mori*. The critical siege might have been even tighter but for Shane Warne's selflessness in staging a diversionary sex scandal. He seems dedicated to proving that while you're only young once, you can be immature forever.

Australia's hold on cricket's citadel, however, has not been loosened, for it is a one-day hunting ground no less happy than in Tests, the scene of demolitions of Pakistan rewarded by the World Cup six years ago and Natwest Series four years ago, and of only two defeats in the last twenty years.

Ponting's team tied the Natwest Series final at Lord's on 2 July and won the Natwest Challenge encounter eight days later, where the captain's timely hundred was rather more in keeping with the natural order Australians have come to expect. That the series begins at this famous Australian fastness displays on the part of the England Cricket Board either an admirable disdain for superstition or a cavalier disregard of portents.

Perhaps this hegemony was foretold. The First Fleet embarked a week before the inaugural match at Lord's; Matthew Flinders affixed 'Australia' to the landmass he had devoted his life to exploring in the month that Lord's opened at its present site. In coming back to play there and win, the colonized somehow recolonizes the colonizer. As prime minister John Curtin put it in his famous speech at the ground in May 1944, in lines as resonant now as then: 'Australians will always fight for those twenty-two yards. Lord's and its traditions belong to Australia just as much as to England.'

According to *Wisden Cricketer's Almanack*, the first Australian cricketers to arrive at Lord's in May 1878 did so 'in such a quiet and unpretentious way' as to pass unrecognized, but their victory over the Marylebone Cricket Club led by W.G. Grace remains one of the least likely and most bewildering in all cricket's annals: the hosts were bustled out for 33 and 19, and the visitors prevailed in a day by nine wickets.

Australian cricketers at Lord's remain unpretentious. They are, however, almost never quiet. Hours after winning the World Cup by eight wickets in July 1999, Ponting himself led his half-cut mates into the middle, propped himself on Tom Moody's shoulders, recited some doggerel he had written some weeks earlier, then led a stirring rendition of 'Under the Southern Cross' that reverberated round the empty stands. It is hard to see such a captain giving any quarter in the Test to come. Surrender Australia's precious Lord's record? One suspects that, like Neil Armstrong, he'd sooner fly to the moon.

THE FIRST TEST – LORD'S

21, 22, 23 and 24 July 2005
Australia won by 239 runs

UP FOR IT?

'Mentally we've got them by the balls.' Ricky Ponting might have put it more neatly but hardly more clearly when he summarized Australia's attitude to playing England during the last World Cup – and at Port Elizabeth, the psychological squirrel grip proved tight indeed.

Different times, different habits. This summer, the grip has been neither so sure nor so lasting, and the captain's own *cojones* have been put to the test.

The first few weeks of this tour were as close to ruinous as any Ponting has experienced in his captaincy career. He led a listless, indolent team at Cardiff, and himself missed a direct hit run out that might have saved its face even at the last. He managed to hit the stumps at the crucial moment at Bristol but found Pietersen home by a micron, then unaccountably failed to pressure Jon Lewis in the game's closing stages

Traditionally so expert at applying pressure, Australia began showing an unusual propensity for relieving it. Darren Gough was permitted to bat as though it was his benefit match at Chester-Le-Street. Paul Collingwood and Geraint Jones were allowed to creep back into the Natwest Series final; Ponting then shunned Brad Hogg, who was conceding 4 runs an over, in favour of Michael Hussey, who went for 8.

These were captaincy calls not so much incorrect as tentative, as though following a plan rather than adapting it, trying to make sure that nothing went wrong, rather than gambling that something would go right. It was as though the Australians were so rapt in their rituals of preparation as to have played their games in advance –

reminiscent of the American commander in Iraq who complained that the engagements he was being expected to fight were not those which his soldiers had war-gamed.

In any event, nothing about these decisions would have mattered overmuch had Ponting been batting well. In fact, he began the tour hesitantly, even vulnerably, for reasons not far to seek. Ponting tends to lift his bat in the direction of second slip and bring it down in the direction of mid-on, which can cause him to scissor across that distinctive pre-emptive front foot stride. You can tell that Ponting is in good touch if he hits the ball through the covers early; when he is sweating too much on the overpitched delivery to work off his pads, his eyes can drift outside the line, as they were tending to in those first few weeks.

This would have vexed Ponting – not the technical wrinkle, which could be ironed out, but the managerial disturbance. He has neither Border's affinity for the last ditch, nor the Nelson touch that Taylor cultivated; he has only a hint of Waugh's lounging hostility. Ponting is a savvy professional with much cricket sense, but the currency of his captaincy is runs, the principal means by which he stamps his authority on his team.

Ponting's all-round consistency, and the opportunity he enjoys at the top of the order to seize the advantages he will later exploit, underpins perhaps his most important attribute as captain: unquestioned places in both Test and one-day teams.

There's no doubt that the limited-overs retrenchments of Taylor and Waugh gradually affected their Test tenures. In the later stages of their careers, they came and went like divorced fathers on uneasy access visits. Their statures were unmistakably diminished.

The first advice that Waugh gave his successor about captaincy, in fact, was to 'make sure you take care of your own game and maintain your form because everything else will follow from that'.

It's advice redolent of Waugh, who would be unbackable favourite were there such a reality television show as *Celebrity Lifeboat*; it was probably also an allusion to the Taylor years, when the captain's batting form put an Australian republic in the shade as an issue of moment. Ponting has followed the advice to the letter, and his stature visibly enhanced.

In the last fortnight, Ponting has appeared a happier man. He also holds to another old Australian dictum that 'it's a different game when you've been at the crease for half an hour', and has seen it verified.

Those first few succulent boundaries at Lord's eleven days ago during his hundred in the Natwest Challenge were a tonic to his system, and Ponting is such a swift scorer that his touch always seems to flood back after any departure from his usual standards. He rebounded from making his first three Test ducks consecutively with a score of 197; he ended a streak of 77 runs in ten innings with a handsome hundred at Headingley on the last Ashes tour.

It's no fluke that his captaincy has been more decisive, and Australia more disciplined since Ponting resumed normal service. England, however, has also seen a glimmer of possibility. Were their bowlers able to keep Ponting in check over the next two months, the results might be interesting, and mentally a whole new ball game.

MATCH REPORT – THE BITER BIT

Plans for battle are notorious for never surviving contact with the enemy. England's in this Test lasted longer than most in recent memory – a whole two sessions – but by the end of five days was as battered and bedraggled as any since 1989. England's battle plan, in truth, always looked a little dodgy. They brought to the Test a captain short of runs, numbers four and five with three Tests between them, and a big hitter making his Ashes debut. Graham

Thorpe played an excellent innings during the Test. Unfortunately it was at Guildford for Surrey.

The plan depended for its effectiveness on a lot going right, and to begin with, much did. In a hectic first session after Ricky Ponting won the toss from Michael Vaughan, Stephen Harmison tenderised Australia's top order with bowling that seldom arrived below the waist, seemed to centre on the sternum, and occasionally came for the coat of arms. The captain himself felt his ears ring like the bells of Notre Dame after being clanged on the helmet, the ball driving the grille into his cheek and drawing an impressive amount of blood.

The challenge seemed to touch off Australia's fight or flight mechanisms. They tackled the bowling with a will, scored six in ten of their runs in boundaries, but lost their way and their wickets at inconvenient intervals, including two, Justin Langer and Simon Katich, to senseless hook shots. Gilchrist's short-lived flail was curtailed by Flintoff from round the wicket – the angle England had found profitable during the Natwest Series. When Harmison came back to polish off the tail with 4–7 in 14 deliveries, it seemed like the visitors were also permanently set to one-day tempo. Ponting led Australia out with stitches in his cheek and problems on his mind, as the media centre hummed with the composition of 'Glory glory Ashes coming home' pieces.

Anything Harmison could do, however, Glenn McGrath could do better. In his fourth over, the first after tea, he removed Marcus Trescothick then Andrew Strauss with deliveries that went down the slope; in his seventh, eighth and ninth respectively, he bowled Vaughan, Bell and Flintoff. It was high quality seam bowling against batting of deepening diffidence, and the continuation of a remarkable renascence. Just over a year earlier, McGrath, with his dicky ankle, had looked a spent force at Test level, struggling to trouble the Zimbabwe 2nds. Now he made England look like the Zimbabwe 3rds. While he spoke during the game of a desire to resume county cricket, Middlesex could hardly be expected to renew his contract on the evidence before them: he would ensure that every home match finished in a day and a half.

The only batsman who exuded any sense of security was Kevin Pietersen, whose technique had been the object of such critical interrogation before the match, yet who played irreproachably straight without sacrificing any of his attacking instincts. Pietersen rallied England from its nadir of 21 for 5 with Geraint Jones, and the next morning took twice as many runs from McGrath in three deliveries as the bowler had conceded in taking five wickets the previous day, including a six into the Pavilion over mid-off. He looked to be soaking up the atmosphere, welcoming Warne into the attack with another stupendous six into the Grand Stand, before he was caught on the run by Damien Martyn trying to repeat the shot. It was Pietersen's session, in fact, for he swooped at cover in the sixth over of Australia's second dig, skilfully transferred the ball from left to right hand, and picked out the stumps at the bowler's end to evict Langer by six inches.

Pietersen's chief impact on the day, however, was to come. If not on his last legs as a Test batsman, Michael Clarke was stumbling into enigma territory, his bonny debut in India a pleasant but fading memory. His progress here should have been arrested at 21 when he punched Jones at knee height to Pietersen at short cover: Pietersen's third drop of the match, and comfortably the costliest, not only because of what it meant in the context of this match, but what it might mean for the series.

From here Clarke batted like a man without fear – as well he might have. As his partnership with the unflappable and unostentatious Martyn swelled to 155 from 208 deliveries, the limitations of England's attack were steadily exposed. Chief among these limitations was Ashley Giles, who may have been hampered by the after-effects of his recent hip operation, but who was mainly hampered here by batsmen who didn't let him get away with his normal negations. After tea, Clarke put his foot down: the fourth fifty of Australia's innings took 47 balls, the fifth 54, with Flintoff and Simon Jones also coming in for treatment. Clarke finally goose-stepped into a drive and dragged on, and Martyn was trapped next ball, but the damage was done. Australia led by 314 at the close of what, staggeringly, was still only the second day.

The game was essentially won and lost, but England made sure of defeat on the third morning by allowing Jason Gillespie and Glenn McGrath to participate in partnerships worth 95 from 162 balls with Simon Katich, bringing their total of scattered catches for the match to seven. The worst was Flintoff's indolent effort when McGrath skewered a delivery from Simon Jones to slip; Jones's precaution of a buzzcut prevented him tearing out too much hair.

England eventually needed 420 to win – or, more properly, rain – to go to Edgbaston on equal terms. Hope sprang eternal when Trescothick and Strauss batted through the afternoon with patient application, seeing off McGrath's opening sally, and playing some firm shots against Warne. But once their promising opening partnership was broken by Lee's pace and athleticism – the former causing an aborted hook, the latter conveying him to the return catch – resistance was meek. Shane Warne made the most of the incision, and surgically extracted Trescothick, Bell and Flintoff. Even the rain was pathetic, lasting only two sessions on the fourth day when England needed quantities of the kind more commonly associated with arks. The rain will have to lift its game. Can a rain academy be set up?

When play finally got under way, Geoff Boycott's campaign for four-day Tests obtained another boost as England's last five succumbed in 61 balls. There was only one disappointment for the victors. When Simon Jones missed a convulsive heave and escaped being bowled by a whisker, Warne forewent perhaps his last opportunity to get on the famous Lord's honour boards: with 4–65, he had to cope with only getting his portrait on the wall. With 4–27, McGrath completed a shut out taking fewer than 250 overs. The only home batsman to prosper was Pietersen who became only the eighth English representative – it is hard to write 'Englishman' if one believes that this is more than a matter of passport – to mark their maiden Test with twin fifties. He was bold enough to muss Warne's well-groomed figures with a few fetching slog sweeps. But, as Simon Barnes put it in *The Times*, his batting 'was like the V-sign you give the headmaster ten minutes after you've left school', making you 'feel a bit better without affecting the balance of power'.

No single game can set at nought the progress of two years, and the margin of defeat ended up flattering the visitors, but Australia were not so impressive in this match as England were acutely disappointing. Australia, basically, did just enough. England's effort was too much too soon then too little too late; there was plenty of aggression but little fight, and their tail's last writhings were agonized. If this was the first battle, one wondered what on earth the war would look like.

DAY ONE

AUSTRALIA 190, ENGLAND 92–7
(PIETERSEN 28*; 37 OVERS)

For the last five weeks, Australians have been reassuring themselves about their team's indifferent one-day form by philosophizing that Test cricket is an entirely different game. Quite right too. The irony is that England were the first to illustrate it yesterday. Fortunately for Australian blushes, Glenn McGrath gave an even better demonstration.

The staples of one-day bowling – yorkers, slower balls, the back of a length nag – were hardly to be seen. Steve Harmison, Simon Jones and Andy Flintoff reminded watchers why it is called a bowling 'attack' rather than a bowling 'defence', pitching the ball up for the sake of swing when they were not pounding it in short in search of bounce.

Cometh the hour, however, cometh McGrath. He has been an accomplished one-day bowler, if seldom an especially memorable one, tending to prevent things rather than precipitate them. It's Test cricket that reveals his full range of virtues – now 504 Test wickets' worth of them.

In a one-day game, England would have had merely 60 deliveries to withstand; McGrath might well have been rested after an exploratory five overs. Yesterday he began with a probing thirteen-over spell: he had the chance to impose his usual austerities at agonizing length, and to move the ball those half bat-widths that seem always to snag edges.

At tea, the 5–0 series scoreline McGrath has tipped so freely was sounding a little reminiscent of the 6–0 scoreline that Graham Yallop tipped for the Ashes of 1978–9 (which ended up almost reversed). About half an hour after tea, 5–0 seemed to be the analysis at which McGrath was aiming. There was so little running between wickets that it was like watching a net session.

The story goes that when McGrath first came to London ten years ago, he overheard his team mates planning a trip to Harrods. 'Harrods?' he asked. 'What's that?' He's a more worldly man today – it's arguable that he could hardly have been less – and must feel almost a native of Lord's, where his Test wickets now cost 11 runs each.

On that original visit a decade ago, McGrath was en route to the tour of the West Indies during which he first made his name, and where he routinely clocked speeds of 145kph. In recent years he has lost a yard – or perhaps that should be a 0.91m – and his comeback from serious ankle surgery in May last year was tentative indeed. Off an approach shortened to reduce the stress on his reconstructed joint, he posed even the beleaguered Zimbabweans few difficulties.

Since then, he seems to have settled into a groove at around 130kmh, but his effectiveness has returned. There are actually some advantages to a loss of knots. A ball from the speedier Lee and Gillespie that deviates off the seam will tend to beat the edge because the batsman has insufficient time to adjust. Batsmen are likelier to catch up with a ball they are trying to cover when it is moving at McGrath's lesser velocities.

While McGrath was the toast of visitors last night, there was ample food for Australian thought in the deeds of Harmison, whose analysis really needed an extra column marked 'c' for 'casualties'. His second ball buffeted Langer's unprotected upper arm; his 16th pinged Hayden's protected head; his 34th opened a cut under Ponting's eye that brought seconds from the Australian corner, albeit with butterfly tape rather than bucket and sponge.

English pace has enjoyed its days out against Australia even in this green and golden age, but seldom with such a bodycount. One half imagined a row of helmets outside the visiting dressing room last evening awaiting the attention of panel beaters.

In between times, the nicks began sticking, the shouts grew louder, and the momentum became irresistibly England's. Clarke may have been a victim of the tide of affairs, Rudi Koertzen's arm rising like a conductor's as if orchestrating the crowd's crescendo.

If the ascendancy at day's end was still in dispute, Test cricket itself chalked up a win. We saw how Test matches, without the limits and artificialities which administrators seem obsessed with foisting on other forms of cricket, punishes faulty execution and rewards technical excellence. Batsman went too hard, too early, essayed hooks that they were never in position to control, failed to move their feet, were caught out of position – and paid penalties. Bowlers harried them relentlessly – and were rewarded.

It's become a media custom to speculate, ever more elaborately, about the duelling psychologies that underlie sporting contests – and no wonder in this case, given that this series has been the most previewed event since the Second Coming.

Yesterday's proceedings were the outcome of neither mental disintegration, reintegration nor deconstruction for that matter; they were the technical shortcomings that the five-day game reveals, and the technical variety and virtuosity it permits. And McGrath is a Test cricket maestro.

DAY TWO

ENGLAND 155, AUSTRALIA 279–7
(KATICH 10*; 70.2 OVERS)

The American sociologist Neil Postman once said that all his books should properly end with the same three words: 'Or vice versa'. Such a caveat would probably also come in handy for cricket punditry.

Since the toss on Thursday, this match's best-laid plans have done what best-laid plans are apt to do – even Australian ones. Partnerships have developed, then been broken at their moment of seeming permanence. Excellent bowling has been eclipsed by better. Fielding has touched heights and plumbed depths – and that's just Kevin Pietersen.

All the while, however, the general Australian trend line has been strengthening, with only a few technical corrections between times. Michael Clarke fell nine runs short of planting a smacker where Michael Slater put one on this same ground twelve years ago, but has probably helped ensure that Lord's remains an Australian citadel for at least three-quarters of a century.

This was an intelligent, resourceful batting display. For most of the day, Australia was not following the Waugh path: the 400-a-day-or-bust batting mandated by Ponting's predecessor. Rather this was a re-creation of the patient application, respectful of conditions and opponent, that the Australians achieved in India last year, and which secured for them their first series victory there since 1969–70.

The tempo of Australian batting in this match, so frenetic and fretful on the first day, was first reset by the captain. He stretched a long way forward defensively, found profitable gaps and called decisively, one nicely judged off-side single from Hoggard taking him to 7000 Test runs. Then, as in India, it was Damien Martyn who made crease occupation into an art form, playing pendulously straight, essaying few memorable strokes but fewer false ones, and passing his own landmark of 4000 Test runs.

Martyn does not often spend two and three-quarter hours over 50, but nor does he often commence his second innings shortly after lunch on the second day. He has had to learn patience – waiting eight years from the date of your first Ashes tour until you play a Test in England will do that to you – and is at this stage of his career showing the benefit of those lessons.

India last year was also, of course, the scene of Clarke's red-blooded Test debut. But his batting pulse has been fading since, and his average would have dipped below 40 for the first time had Pietersen not himself stooped a little slowly at short cover.

Clarke introduced himself to Test cricket with sparkling foot-work and quick hands, especially against spin. He has found the going harder since, especially against pace, because of a tendency to open his shoulders and square up in defence.

This made Vaughan's decision to prescribe him such a healthy diet of slow bowling yesterday a little puzzling. When you have handled Anil Kumble and Harbajhan Singh on dusty turners in India, Ashley Giles wheeling away from over the wicket does not present the sternest challenge. Giles is a stout-hearted cricketer, who bowled well in Australia thirty months ago before he was injured. But he hardly turns the ball enough to justify operating round the wicket with a 7–2 field as he did after tea. Perhaps it was felt important to give him something to write about for the *Guardian*.

In general, England's bowlers were all too straight. All Australia's batsmen are proficient off their pads. Harmison, Jones, Flintoff and Hoggard produced testing deliveries, but the pressure was eased between times too frequently by batsmen getting off strike.

Sometimes boredom seemed to set into England's cricket – or perhaps not enough. Vaughan must have longed to stultify the Australians with some McGrathesque tedium. Jones and Flintoff are conceding more than 4.5 runs per over which, for all their commendable aggression, is too many in a Test of such paltry first innings. It was when Hoggard and Harmison finally managed to reassert a measure of control over the scoring in the last hour that the breaks finally came.

Martyn wrested one other priceless advantage for his team yesterday. Pietersen had every right to expect more from the slog sweep he played off his old mucker Warne, for it was only slightly miscued, and appeared along most of its flight path to be headed for a depopulated zone.

But Martyn capered round the boundary in front of the Grand Stand, jinking in, veering out, like a butterfly catcher on the trail of a sought-after specimen. He timed his final leap exquisitely, then absorbed the shock of re-entry in his forearms.

It wasn't quite the equal of McGrath's spring-heeled catch in the same position at Adelaide thirty months ago, which lacked only the flutter of Superman's cape, but perhaps only because it was executed so nimbly and naturally. It meant that Australia could afford the 33-run last-wicket gambol of Harmison and Jones and still start their second innings 35 to the good.

It looked for a time on Thursday that the toss might have been a good one for Vaughan to lose. With half a mind on Nasser Hussain's Gabba pratfall, he might not have had the nerve to insert Australia. Batting last here, however, will not be a boot-filling exercise, and Ponting fetched one gazunda from Harmison yesterday that left him shaping as if for French cricket. England will now need a lot of weather to avoid going to Edgbaston a Test down, and its quota of vice versa must be close to exhaustion.

DAY THREE

AUSTRALIA 384, ENGLAND 156–5
(PIETERSEN 42*, G.O. JONES 6*; 48 OVERS)

Some Tests are won, some are lost; this has been both, and as convincingly as any in the seventy-one years of Australian hegemony at Lord's. Only rain can save England – and how often have my colleagues and I written that in recent, and not-so-recent, memory?

England began the day needing to amputate the Australian tail pronto. In fact, it grew, until it was almost wrapped around their necks and tightening. The morning session was as flat and lacklustre as the previous two days have been absorbing. Well, the English component of it, anyway; the Australians just carried on as they have for fifteen years and more.

In the first innings, England had been like a beagle pack on Australia's scent; in the second, they were like Scotland Yard on the trail of Moriarty, too slow, too clumsy, and languishing a growing distance behind. Gillespie is an obstinate sticker; McGrath might still elicit a cheer when he scores a run, but he is no longer a negligible batsman at Test level. England underestimated them, and they helped Katich extend Australia's lead by 95 over two hours.

There was again some mercurial fielding, Ashley Giles at last finding a way to hit the stumps in this Test by throwing Lee out from cover. But seven chances by Australian batsmen have gone begging in this Test, none of them inordinately difficult, and the efforts yesterday savoured of insufficient concentration rather than inadequate technique, of players contemplating their second innings rather than Australia's.

When the time comes, by contrast, the Australians field brilliantly. The way some critics have written of this team, it is as though Bill Brown is ripe for a recall. So far, in fact, they have fielded better than the side in 2001, which caught fallibly, even if it was not forced to pay much of a price.

Lee's sprint to a return catch from Strauss ate up the distance in a few strides, his eyes never leaving the hovering ball. Hayden made an awkward slip catch bouncing from the rough via Trescothick's edge look deceptively simple. Ponting pulled up a snick to fine third man with an inch in it, vaulted the npower sponsors' fortification at the Nursery End, bounced off the rolled-up tarpaulin and bounded back over the signage to hurl the return to Gilchrist. Katich was adept at short leg, Clarke busy at cover point.

Warne was frustrated by the imperviousness to his entreaties of umpire Aleem Dar, who spared Trescothick on the stroke of tea from a pad-bat-pad lbw that looked set to miss off and leg but hit middle; at various times, it seemed like the only thing preventing him pulling his hair out was attention to the needs of his sponsor. Gradually, however, he got on top, and when Bell took guard, he and his catching contingent, fresh from a couple of wickets, were as noisy as a cage of cockatoos.

Once Vaughan had gone, painfully, and Flintoff, perhaps tiredly after 38 overs, the Australians had regained their strut of old, and England were thinking about their chances in 2014–15 when Test matches will probably be played on a neural network without anyone leaving home.

Deferring the inevitable fell to Kevin Pietersen which was only right seeing that his failure to catch Clarke the day before was so fundamental to the general diminution of evitability. Whatever one's criticisms, one cannot complain about his entertainment value. Hit by Lee on the knee, he fell down, then turned to watch the replay, before hoisting a retaliatory six into the Tavern. He slogged Warne against the spin to the Grand Stand, first in front of square then behind, and finally drove with the spin down the hill to the Mound Stand boundary. It was a thoroughly inclusive innings. A pity his team mates couldn't get involved.

DAY FOUR

ENGLAND 180. AUSTRALIA WON BY 239 RUNS

It has been hard to reconcile the Shane Warne of the Lord's Test with his alter ego that keeps half England's tabloid journalists employed. He has not been seen to text anyone from first slip. The only threesome he has mooted has been round the bat. He has allowed team mates to ruffle his hair without once saying: 'Hey! That's expensive!'

Yet that is somehow always the way of it. Whatever Warne's private tribulations, he leaves them hanging on the dressing room hook when he heads out the gate. He has lost himself in this Test the minute he rejoined his countrymen, and has ached for success – Aleem Dar probably ended the match a little hard of hearing. When he took the climactic catch yesterday, he threw it so high into the heavens that it might well still be coming down.

Before the Test, Warne was also reunited with his spin guru Terry Jenner, who joins him at intervals to check on Warne's mechanics, and if necessary recalibrate them. For all his casual insouciance, Warne toils hard at his craft, and has an abiding fascination with the spinning cricket ball – in fact, with any ball.

When he was a youngster at the cricket academy in Adelaide, Warne would dazzle his peers by spinning billiard balls off the cushions and into the pockets of the table at their Alberton Hotel digs: leggies, flippers, wrong 'uns, toppies. Students of cricket history will recognize the historical antecedent of B.J.T. Bosanquet playing twisti-grab on a billiard table and experiencing the eureka moment that gave rise to the googly. Warne wouldn't – but that's because he makes history instead.

Warne's weapon of choice in this Test, however, was not the monster leg-break of yore. It was a ball going straight on, delivered with a leg-break action but squirted out the front of the hand: a 'slider', to dignify it with the Benaudism of the moment. And although Warne has been bowling such a ball in Australia for many seasons, England have treated it here like a Martian death ray. They should know a bit about slow bowlers making it go straight. They do have Ashley Giles.

Ian Bell's second innings dismissal has already been replayed almost as often as the Zapruder film. But it wasn't, of course, merely about the ball that caused it: it depended on the sequence of big leg-breaks, at which Bell nodded deferentially, preceding the *coup de grâce*.

Warne also had noisy support from his close fielding convention, in whose presence Bell was made to feel a most unwelcome guest. Bell took his time between deliveries – the approved way to reduce heart-rate and achieve inner calm these days – and ended up attaining a perfection of inertia. When the ball struck his pads, he looked up as though he could not believe the world contained such deceit and cruelty.

This isn't, mind you, just a case of Warne the magician. As a trick, Warne's is a goodie, but an oldie. Perhaps its first great Australian perpetrator was Warwick Armstrong, the unsinkable Big Ship who made Douglas Jardine look as captain like a soft-hearted sentimentalist, and who hoodwinked scores of batsmen by the simple expedient of a straight ball after a series of leg-breaks.

One of the first important variations that Richie Benaud learned, meanwhile, was a skidding top spinner pushed from between his second and third fingers. In the Lord's Test of 1953, Benaud was held at bay, in some comfort, by Willy Watson and Trevor Bailey. That evening on the train to Bristol, Doug Ring plucked up an apple from a fruit bowl to demonstrate the grip of his own skidder, and encouraged him to experiment by throwing it over a short distance. When I asked Benaud to confirm my dim recollection of this story yesterday, he remembered it as if it *were* yesterday. 'It was a green apple,' he said.

So for all Warne's greatness as a bowler, it also says something that English batsmen remain so perplexed whenever they encounter him, and that they are in general such strangers to wrist spin and its variations. Such is the outcome of England's inability to produce a leg-break bowler worth the name for thirty years or more: generations of players who haven't been able to tell a leg-break from a leg-warmer. For as long as he plays, Warne will be happy to take advantage of this dearth.

The only duel which Warne has not yet convincingly won has been with his old chum Kevin Pietersen. Since it emerged that Warne had nicknamed Pietersen '600' – designating him victim of choice when that wicket landmark was attained – their relationship has been a matter of some media fascination. It has looked like a case of following Machiavelli's advice about keeping one's friends close and one's enemies closer, even if who has toyed with whom has yet to become quite clear.

Pietersen faced 63 balls from Warne in this match and scored 47 runs for once out. It can't be claimed that he played the bowling not the reputation – Pietersen might be said to have made his own special contribution to the Warne reputation – but he did tackle his task with something like relish. Warne even bowled him a bouncer yesterday in mock annoyance that may not have been so mock.

Ah, perhaps I'm being too harsh. There can't be much wrong with English cricket when it continues producing cricketers the quality of Kevin Pietersen, can there, eh?

THE BETTER YET

A wise man once said that the world's biggest room is the room for improvement. It may have been Sun Tzu. Or Confucius. Or maybe I read it on the calendar on the desk in front of me. Whoever it was, Australian players almost certainly awoke yesterday to a message of this order from John Buchanan, famous for a coaching manual owing a deeper debt to M. Scott Peck than MCC.

Yesterday, of course, Australia were enjoying the fruits of their labours: a fallow fifth day of a Test seized by 239 runs in fewer than 250 overs of a theoretical 450. But Mark Taylor used to say that the time to chide your team was after you had won; in the shadow of defeat, players feel bad anyway and criticism can seem carping. It's when they are buoyant that they are most receptive to new challenges and new ideas.

Not everything about Australia's victory, moreover, would have satisfied aficionados of *Who Moved My Cheese?* Australia's first innings was actually eight overs shorter than England's. But for Damien Martyn's happy landing when catching Kevin Pietersen on Friday, England might well have stolen a lead. But for Pietersen's hard hands on Saturday, Michael Clarke might now be praying for a flat deck at Worcester.

Andy Flintoff, if he achieved little else, also managed to spike Adam Gilchrist's guns for a Test, at the moment the Australian whackitkeeper seemed to be running into form. Darren Gough also attacked Gilchrist from round the wicket four years ago – indeed, he attacked Gilchrist from every angle except through reality TV. But thanks to bounce and youth, Flintoff has been able to keep Gilchrist pinioned.

So far anyway. Gilchrist is bound to strike sooner or later, probably the former. And if the results were not quite there for the scoreboard to see, the same looked to be true by the end of the Test for Matthew Hayden.

Hayden has been the weakest link in Australia's batting for the last year or so, with an average over his last two-dozen innings that has now dropped to less than 30. At times, he has looked too aggressive, too eager to carve the bowling into tiny pieces, like someone who's watched *Gladiator* a few too many times.

During April, a shrewd judge in Ian Healy commented that Hayden seemed to have become bored with what he was doing, and it's surprising that this explanation for indifferent form is not invoked more often. Players play so much nowadays that the experience could easily pall. The prospect of smashing Matthew Hoggard through the covers would be enough to induce ennui in anyone. Whack. 'What's it all about, eh?' Thump. 'Gotta be more to life than this, doesn't there?' Pow. 'Maybe Sun Tzu has something to say about this.'

Before he was cut short by an under-edged pull at Lord's, however, Hayden looked in ominously secure touch, the closest he has seemed to the balance between prudence and enterprise for some time. Each of his five boundaries came out of the screws, and he perished at his first mistake. Depending on the odds, he might attract smart money to be top Australian scorer at Birmingham.

Hayden has enjoyed some selectorial indulgence; so, too, in the last few weeks, has Jason Gillespie, subdued again at Lord's, and wicketless. At his best, he is a powerfully rhythmic bowler from the start of his run. At present, he appears to be doing most of his work in the last few strides, depending heavily on his shoulder, and not merely failing to get edges but scarcely beating the bat.

It is interesting in its inequity that Gillespie, Australia's fifth highest Test wicket taker, should be under pressure for his place. While there never seems too much concern about carrying a Test-quality batsmen through a few low scores, a labouring bowler soon attracts attention. This time last year a bowler was being severely scrutinized who'd returned from a series of African one-dayers with figures of 2–115. His name was Glenn McGrath.

Gillespie's barren period, however, is now something more than a short-term lull. His fourteen Test wickets since the start of Australia's series with Pakistan have cost almost 45 each, and he has been a victim in England of the itinerary. Rhythm can be elusive when one is confined to short spells under one-day conditions. The dilemma is that Gillespie needs bowling to find form, but omission now, even if it offers time to brush up on those seven habits of highly successful people, will more or less condemn him to supernumerary status for the next seven weeks.

For such problems, nonetheless, England would cheerfully kill, their room for improvement being roughly the size of the Royal

Albert Hall. One thing, too, Lord's has convincingly demonstrated. The most arresting contrast between the teams there was that the senescent Australians fielded as energetically as kids in a playground, while the youthful Englishmen stumbled round like Chelsea pensioners. *Pace* Matthew Hoggard, it never served any purpose to point out that the Australians weren't getting any younger; what mattered then, and matters now, is their capacity to get better.

DIARY

MONDAY 1 AUGUST

Andy Caddick has been missed in this Ashes series – not as a bowler, but as a writer. The tissues of self-justification he composed for his newspaper employer in 2001 were unmissable: it was always just his luck that the ball stopped swinging the moment England came on to bowl, and that the Aussies kept on making these totally arsey hundreds.

Caddick may, however, have a successor. Ashley Giles has sailed into print in the *Guardian* with a column baiting his baiters, complaining about 'hurtful' and 'unfair' critics of his bowling in the First Test. 'I am angry and I think have a right to be,' he says. 'I feel like I am pissing into the wind.' This will help his loop, but Giles is unimpressed: 'People will accuse me of being sensitive and maybe I am. Maybe I should stop reading the papers. But I'm worried that people might drag me down. It feels like a bit of a witch-hunt. I try to keep the blinkers on and keep the critics at bay, but there are only so many times that you can fend them off. I suspect that people are after me again.' He also shares an exclusive with us: he is not Shane Warne. His wife will be pleased, at any rate.

Not only because he is a *Guardian* colleague am I loath to write ill of Giles. He is an improving cricketer important to England's excellent record over the last eighteen months, by all accounts an excellent team man, and generally pretty stoical. No one becomes a bad player overnight, and it cannot be other than upsetting to be written off so peremptorily. If he gets wickets against the Australians, I will be surprised. They manhandled a superior left-arm tweaker in Daniel Vettori a few months ago, and I can't see finger spin of any ilk troubling the tourists for the next seven weeks.

But there simply aren't many options in England. There is, of course, no wrist-spin on offer unless the Ian Salisbury self-service queue is reopened.

Giles's despatch, however, is ill-advised. With a Test at Edgbaston round the corner, he might gainfully study the coverage of the corresponding game there thirty years ago, when the press erected an *auto da fé* in honour of captain Mike Denness after he inserted Australia and lost by an innings and 85 runs. Denness had been given a horrid time in Australia. He once received a letter addressed simply to 'Mike Denness, Cricketer', which read simply: 'If this reaches you, the Post Office think more of you than I do.' But at Birmingham, the local press were able to roast him over their own coals; by the time he was finished, Denness had been thoroughly charred. Even his successor Tony Greig was horrified, and swore as a result that he would always jump before he could be pushed. The recent release of Keith Fletcher's memoir reminded me, likewise, of the day ten years ago in Australia when a newspaper published the fax number of England's team hotel in Sydney and encouraged readers to register their disgust at its performances. Hotel staff obligingly filled an envelope with anatomically explicit advice and some helpful illustrations and pushed it under Fletch's hotel room door; his wife then opened it.

By these standards, the attention Giles has attracted has been the soul of kindness. He has taken two international wickets for 305 this summer. If there was not some scrutiny of his place, it would insult all other spinners in the country. Worse, Giles has revealed the kind of chink in his armour that Australian teams are expert at exploiting, and opened hostilities on a new front when all England's energies should be directed to their cricket. His captain will have to respond to it; Ponting and Buchanan will be asked to comment on it; pundits will have to stick their oar in. For the record, I hope Giles does not become the New Andy Caddick. There's only one Andy Caddick. But it would be better for all concerned if he reverted to being the Old Ashley Giles.

TUESDAY 2 AUGUST

The Australians' game with Worcestershire has ended in a draw. As a sports news item, this is nowadays something to rival Claude Cockburn's famous candidate in the competition among *Times* sub-editors for the year's dullest headline: 'Small Earthquake in Chile: Not Many Dead'. After the loss of the first day to rain, the game was a sleepy one-innings affair. The days are long gone when Australia's journey to New Road marked the beginning of its tour. Bradman famously hit centuries in the shadow of Worcester Cathedral on four consecutive occasions.

This is usually how traditionalists begin a 'Why O Why' piece about the decline of the tour match, reminiscing of the days in which the whole of the county turned out to see their heroes challenge the might of Australia, and explaining how the Aussies' game against Yorkshire used to be regarded as a 'Sixth Test'. It's a melancholy decline, I grant you, but the blame lies squarely with the counties who brought such fixtures into disrepute. As Steve Waugh complained to me five years ago: 'The last couple of tours, the county games were a waste of time anyway. You were playing teams half full of 2nd XI players, you went through your paces and won quite easily, and that to me doesn't make a good tour. You want quality games.' As they didn't get them, what was the point? The time is coming when there may not be first-class fixtures outside the Tests at all.

This will be a bad idea. But given that so many bad ideas seem to burst on us fully formed these days, it may be as well to articulate why. As a preparation for Test cricket, there is still no substitute for first-class cricket, especially where bowlers are concerned. Nets will not suffice; one-day cricket is a different game. The other factor, in England most of all, is the size of the country's Test grounds. To actually see the world's best cricket team play a Test in the flesh this season, you had to start queuing last October and take out a second mortgage, then pray that it did not rain and that England did not collapse. But if you either weren't able to or couldn't afford such an investment, there was the good second-best of seeing them play a tour match. If we take seriously the idea that actually attending games is the best way of watching cricket, rather than a season's ticket in the Couch Stand, then we should offer different varieties of this experience. We might even, one day, twig that such sub-international cricket is worth promoting. 'Best Cricket Team in World Comes to Our Home Ground' is a headline one can go places with.

WEDNESDAY 3 AUGUST

Never mind Michael Vaughan's elbow or Ashley Giles's psyche. On the eve of the Second Test, English cricket has had a timely boost from the game's appearance on the cover of the weekly hipster's bible, *Time Out*. The cover promotes an interview with Johnny Borrell of Razorlight, who poses next to the image of some stumps stencilled on a brick wall, and what we're excitedly informed is the vocalist's own bat – which, bare of stickers *à la* Steve Waugh at the Oval four years ago, suggests Borrell may be seeking a sponsor. The interview took place in the Lord's Media Centre, about which Borrell is a wild enthusiast. 'This is the coolest fucking place,' he says, having never shared one phone connection with another five correspondents.

Borrell, nonetheless, seems a genuine devotee: 'It seems that people want to mess around with sport more and more. But football is a magic sport, cricket is a magical sport, leave them alone.' He gives an impressively articulate explanation of his fandom, how it helped eat up time when he was on the dole: 'If you have back-to-back Tests,' he comments, 'that's ten days out of two weeks.' Not at the moment it's not. Come on England! You're letting down an unemployed generation! Perhaps the most interesting remark he makes – it is even slightly chilling – concerns television: 'It does worry me that this is the last Test series on terrestrial TV. If cricket had been on Sky when I was seventeen, I would never have got into it.' You're worried, Johnny? That's you and me both.

In general, this is the most positive press I have read about cricket in England this summer: cricket was probably last on the cover of *Time Out* in when W.G. gave an interview professing an admiration for Gilbert and Sullivan. The magazine has leveraged off the interview to provide a guide to cricket in the capital, although to bulk up its statutory irony quotient also burdens us with another example of the popular sub-genre of 'woman-who-does-not-understand-cricket-tells-us-that-she-does-not-understand-cricket'. Does anyone write this sort of junk about any other sport, pastime or pursuit? Would you run something headlined 'I Thought They Were Gay But It Turned Out to Be Ballet' or '10 Reasons Wallpaper Beats Art'?

There is, mind you, a slightly troubling undertone in cricket's turning up on the radar of London cool, that cricket is now seen as so quaint and anachronistic that when the lead singer of Razorlight professes to enjoy the game, it is as though he has expressed an enthusiasm for contract bridge or underwater bocce. Yet are we entitled to complain? The ECB seems to share that view, deliberately narrowing its audience by taking the Sky shilling, milking what they have rather than building on it. Still, one good turn deserves another, Johnny. I promise I'll buy the next Razorlight album.

THE SECOND TEST – EDGBASTON

4, 5, 6 and 7 August 2005
England won by 2 runs

TARGET PRACTICE

The Second Test at Edgbaston nominally involves England and Australia. But the contest, if one is to judge by recent emanations from both camps, will be as private and personal as collective and national. Ashley Giles, Marcus Trescothick, Andrew Strauss, Michael Vaughan, Ian Bell, Kevin Pietersen: there won't be so many targets seen on an English cricket ground again until Lord's hosts the Olympic archery in 2012.

The habit is so contagious that, as a patriotic Australian, I almost feel obliged to target someone in the media, perhaps crouching behind Mark Nicholas in the Channel Four commentary box and muttering: 'Reckon yer the new Benaud, do ya, cobber?'

Certainly, it's a game everyone can play. Matthew Hoggard even tried targeting the entire Australian team on the eve of the Lord's Test, but this delivery veered as wildly down the leg side as his opening spell. And master of the art is surely Glenn McGrath, to whom targeting has become such a way of life that he probably arrives at breakfast saying: 'I am targeting tea and toast this morning, and the muesli is looking very vulnerable.'

On one level, this is all pretty superficial. Does McGrath try any less hard while bowling at those members of the England team he has not specifically targeted, few as they may be? Is Adam Gilchrist any less formidable for not pinpointing any particular opponent? It's not as though Shane Warne has begun bombarding his opponents with texts about his slider; the delivery itself is quite sufficient.

Yet, perhaps because it's the first week of August and we've still had only four days of Ashes cricket, Aussie rhetoric has filled the vacuum that media nature abhors, and what started as a few preliminary throat-clearing exercises from McGrath has succeeded beyond John Buchanan's wildest imaginings.

Hoggard has back-pedalled, Giles has front-pedalled, Bell seems still to be straddling the crease, and Vaughan purports to be feeling good while being bowled for 3 and 4. What will it take to make him feel bad? Jaw-jaw seems to be proving almost as formidable as Waugh-Waugh.

A cricketer brooding about individual rivalry or his personal press, contemplating past failures or anxious about technical weaknesses, is a cricketer only partly involved in the match he is playing – and against the Australians, more than any other team, a clear head is a prerequisite. That counts doubly so for captains. A captain pondering his game when he should be contemplating his next move, or contemplating his next move when he could gainfully be pondering his game, is a captain, and a player, of impaired effectiveness.

This is a two-way street. While, even by their own standards, the Australians have been a talkative lot these past two months, the English have been eager, even masochistic, listeners. It is hard to recall another tour, for instance, where the theories of a supernumerary like Stuart MacGill have been reported at such length and depth as they were in Sunday's papers.

In the Australian approach, two influences play a part. They have long noticed the media's propensity in this country for turning on their own. In his first *Ashes Diary* twelve years ago, Steve Waugh even speculated that the English press enjoyed their team's defeats: 'When it happens, they can create a ridiculous headline, or put their players under the microscope and slowly dissect them until the team members are either sapped of all their confidence or dropped altogether to make way for new scapegoats.'

That, it should be said, does not seem to have been the case on this tour. On the contrary, the press seems to have been generally constructive, last week even defending their XI from wholesale changes that no one seemed to be demanding anyway. Although Ashley Giles might be shopping for one, the only handbags wielded in the tabloids have so far been Australian.

Australians have also noticed, however, the tendency of past English teams to shiver into fragments in adversity, for players to pursue their own goals, and to protect their own places: the mentality of the professional preoccupied with personal advancement, arguably instilled in county cricket by incentives like the cap and the benefit.

Singling players out, as the Australians have, has the effect of separating them from the group, holding individual performances up to scrutiny when ultimately only team performances matter. This English XI pride themselves on being as united as the Three Musketeers. We will learn this summer whether beneath that veneer lurk the Three Stooges.

It's easy to say that players shouldn't be suckered into crossing rhetorical swords before and between engagements, that they should perhaps all follow Brian Clough's advice: 'Say nowt. Win it. Then talk your 'ead off.' That will no longer do. Sport has changed. And these new realities will be pregnant with the danger of mismatch between what one does and what one says.

Yet this cuts both ways. Having been heavily outfought by Larry Holmes one day in Houston, the loquacious Tex Cobb was asked why he'd not tried out his usual trash talk routine. Cobb explained that every time he'd opened his mouth, Holmes had put a boxing glove in it.

Kevin Pietersen followed the Holmes philosophy at Lord's, his bat being more eloquent than any of Warne's barbs and baits, while the 'plan' that McGrath had allegedly had in store for him faded to nothing. The lesson is clear. Don't want to be a target? Don't present one.

MATCH REPORT – LOST AND FOUND

It did not take long after it was finished for the Edgbaston Test to feel slightly unreal, even ridiculous. A game containing more than 700 runs in boundaries won and lost by two runs? Test cricket has no business with results so close. Tight finishes are meant to be the prerogative of one-day and Twenty20 cricket. It's the nature of Test matches that they multiply possibilities and magnify differences. But not, gloriously, over this contest's ten taut sessions in which England made the running but Australia somehow kept tapping them on the shoulder.

Nor were the ten sessions all there was. *The Man Who Wasn't There* was a mediocre Coen brothers film in which Billy Bob Thornton tilted at the world celluloid cigarette-smoking record to evince brooding intensity; the title far better fitted Glenn McGrath, whose absence at Brimingham proved as influential as his presence at Lord's. At 9.15 a.m., during Australia's touch rugby warm-up, McGrath groped for a pass from Brad Haddin and trod on a cricket ball ready for a fielding routine. Word of the Grade 2 ligament strain in his right ankle travelled round England like the good news from Ghent to Aix. Michael Kasprowicz, who had arrived at the ground expecting to wait the drinks, was routed to a date with destiny.

There was another absence too, which might be called *The Pitch That Never Was*. At the time of McGrath's laming, Ricky Ponting was scrutizing Steve Rouse's surface, the subject for the preceding week of all manner of horticultural speculation; the tornado that had cleaved a path through Birmingham on 28 July had interfered with Rouse's preparatory work, and he had been broadcasting some pre-emptive excuses. Ponting had decided to bowl first, did not change his strategy when he received word about McGrath, and walked into his own tornado: sent in, England were 132 for 1 at lunch.

Trescothick and Strauss kicked off with their sixth century opening partnership, and cannot have compiled a more crucial one. Strauss was dropped early by Warne at slip off Lee, Trescothick caught at backward point from a Gillespie no-ball at 13; otherwise they took advantage of bowling that tended to the short, the wide and the delectable, and beyond scuffing at the Ryder Stand end, the pitch offered the bowlers little. Even after Warne bowled Strauss bowling into that rough from round the wicket, England continued to attack, Vaughan ending his cameo with a mishook, Trescothick his best Test score against Australia with a faraway waft. And Flintoff and Pietersen, who have never prospered together, then abruptly clicked, ransacking 103 from 105 balls. Pietersen, who hit ten fours and a six, looked every inch the accomplished Test batsman; Flintoff, who cudgelled five sixes with his six fours, in nearly every detail, including the sightless groping at Warne, embodied the gifted village slogger. Ponting seemed content to await their self-destruction, and paid heavily for his patience. Nor did England's tail dither: 114 runs came in 133 deliveries, including the ninth and tenth sixes of the innings from Harmison and Jones. There was a suspicion that England should have made more than 407, but the significant figure was their 5.13 run per over scoring rate. No one has scored so many runs at such speed in a Test against Australia since cricket's primordial days. It was England's best day's run scoring since the Second World War.

After Hayden's early departure, Australia's reply was almost as sprightly, Ponting striking ten fluent boundaries, and Martyn getting smoothly under way. On the stroke of lunch, however, Martyn dawdled between wickets and was narrowly thrown out by Vaughan at the non-strikers' end. Although Clarke played a poised hand in partnership with the ever-adhesive Langer, England now had the scent of wickets. The reverse swing capabilities of Jones and Flintoff, who jagged the ball in the air after tea when the slow surface was offering the faster bowlers nothing, came to the fore as the tail crumbled around a subdued Gilchrist. In the last hour of today's play, the ground announcer was heard to request the attention of a 'Mr Ivan Milat'. Ah, those jolly Aussie japesters; at least it made a change from another appearance by the well-travelled yet somehow evergreen Mr Hugh Jarse. But England – leading Australia on first innings for the first time since the corresponding Test here eight years ago – were now hot on the trail of cricket's most wanted serial killer.

Warne stole the second day show when he landed a ball in the footmarks, which turned at what the Channel Four protractor-o-meter somehow figured to be 35.8 degrees and went outside Strauss's legs to bowl him: extraordinarily, the spinner's 100th Test wicket in England, a feat unprecedented among non-English bowlers. The next morning was duly Australia's, with Warne teasing as Lee reduced England to 31–4. But Australia's thrust was parried by Pietersen and Bell, who added a cool 41 from 69 balls before getting the wrong ends of some Rudi Koertzen caught behinds, then Flintoff and the tail. Simon Jones in particular lent Flintoff sterling support in a last wicket partnership of 51 in 40 minutes that built England's advantage to 281.

Flintoff was retarded at first by a curious injury to his shoulder, which he wrenched at 7 while trying to force Warne off the back foot. Thanks to the rough, in fact, the Englishman was as judicious with the leg-spinner as he was utterly irreverent with Lee and Kasprowicz. This time he dished out four sixes to go with six fours in his 86-ball 73, bringing England's aerial bombardment to sixteen sixes for the match. When Flintoff finally became Warne's tenth match victim, bowled backing away, it was the end of an enchanting duel – and it wouldn't be their last of the match.

Langer and Hayden made a patient start to Australia's chase – less a chase than a stretch, really, considering that the match in allotted time was barely half over. At an early stage, however, the ball started swinging reverse, and a stampeding Flintoff trampled Langer and Ponting in his first over amid Barmy Army chanting more reminiscent of an FA Cup final; when Jones's reverse swing confounded Hayden, the noise was deafening. The Barmy Army in this match, in fact, were an echo of their own team, undismayed by adversity, inexhaustible in attack. And on this third afternoon, they filled Edgbaston with a patriotic cacophony.

Warne's rough was now the province of Giles, and he used it well. Neither Martyn nor Gilchrist had the patience to fight back. Clarke did, and played with precocious maturity, with Warne almost guiding Australia through the extra half hour that England took. But Harmison, for what would have been the penultimate delivery of the last over, held back a slower yorker over which the young batsman fell. Australia began the last day needing, improbably, 107 runs to win from its last two wickets.

Warne and Lee set out to 'have some fun' that was very little fun for the vast majority of the crowd, breezily playing their shots, missing what they had to, bunting other deliveries into space, despite being on the receiving end of some very hostile bowling from Harmison and Flintoff. Warne gave himself his usual room to slash and loft; Lee was a responsive and courageous partner who wore what he could not work; Vaughan seemed incapable of constraining them. The Australians added 45 from 59 deliveries. When Warne's back foot, groping a long way back, knocked his off stump awry, some order seemed to have been restored. But Lee continued to hit with discretion, happy to loft Giles when the opportunity presented itself, while Kasprowicz took the opportunity to regain some batting touch, and scored with freedom too. When Kasprowicz survived an lbw appeal to umpire Bowden, then guided Harmison in the air to third man where the ball bounced out of Simon Jones' clammy hands, the unthinkable lurched into likelihood.

Lee's partnership with Kasprowicz had been worth a brave 59 from 76 deliveries when Harmison dropped in his last bouncer. Number eleven leaned over, but left his bat and gloves in danger, and Geraint Jones, who had kept untidily and batted unproductively, interposed a glove between the ground and the falling ball. At Bowden's raised finger, the ground erupted, the English players fell on one another in a disbelieving huddle, and the batsmen sagged in disappointment and grief. To complete his wonderful match, Flintoff made a chivalrous gesture, showing the presence of mind to bend down to the stooped Lee and offer his congratulations at a fight well fought. 'The Man Who Wasn't There' remained out of sight, although both Flintoff and Harmison shook Steve Rouse's hand in token of appreciation for his 'Pitch That Never Was'.

Some barrack-room lawyers – perhaps it should be 'dressing-room lawyers' in a cricket context – discerned a chink of daylight between glove and bat handle while poring over the replay from various angles and began uttering the expression 'benefit of the doubt' with the solemnity usually reserved for habeas corpus. This was meretricious reasoning. Critics pedantic about the application of the Law should be prepared to have it pedantically pointed out that the extension of a 'benefit of the doubt' to the batsman has nothing to do with Law. It is simply a custom, unwritten, and stressed to greater and lesser degrees by different umpires: Bowden applied it to his satisfaction and judged accordingly. In any case, if you could not savour this result you were watching the wrong game. This was a classic – and yes, it really happened.

DAY ONE

ENGLAND 407

When 'oooh aaah, Glenn McGrath' took on new meaning at about 9.15 a.m. yesterday, it was a setback for Australia's immediate prospects at Edgbaston, but loomed also as a foretaste of Australia's cricketing future.

Some dread day, Glenn McGrath will donate his last pair of boots, put away that last unblemished bat, and settle for bowling dot balls at his children in the back garden. Even for Australians, apt to live in the here and now, thought of that date with destiny is accompanied by a queasy foreboding.

The summer of 2003–4, when Australia took on India without him, was a feast for connoisseurs of batsmanship, but seriously disturbed the preferred Australian balance of power: that is, one tilted heavily their way. The way McGrath tipped the scales at Lord's, he looked destined to be Ricky Ponting's go-to guy this series also.

No one can accuse Ponting of incuriosity about what tomorrow holds. McGrath's grunts of pain were still fresh in his ears when he inserted England, perhaps partly as a vote of confidence in the rest of his attack. But when Brett Lee began with a big, bold, bounding wide, we were already in a different world.

Ponting's deliberations would have been influenced by the confetti-like permanence of England's second innings at Lord's, and the rest his key bowlers had enjoyed since. Had yesterday been the start of the second of two back-to-back Tests, Ponting might well have batted; instead he speculated on gremlins in the pitch to go with those in the mind.

In fact, Steve Rouse's turned out to be a turgid surface to which Trescothick's very simple method, involving weight transference rather than foot movement, is ideally suited. If you tipped England to be scoring at a run a minute after an hour, you deserved your winnings. At drinks, the toast was: 'To absent friends.'

As they are wont to when bowling to Trescothick, Lee and Gillespie concentrated on off-stump, and wide of it; a dozen of Trescothick's fifteen boundaries duly perforated the cover and point. A power outage around lunchtime at Edgbaston returned cricket to the pre-Edison age, the lights going out, the scoreboard falling mute. There was also a perceptible power outage in Australia's performance.

It wasn't exactly *Hamlet* without the prince; maybe, if you were English, it was *Othello* minus Iago. Michael Kasprowicz, McGrath's replacement, will never be a principal character. He is more a comic foil, a Pistol perhaps. But without Pistols, there are no Falstaffs. It was Kasprowicz whose perseverance was rewarded by the wickets of Trescothick, to probably his most innocuous delivery, and Bell, to perhaps his best, in his tenth over. Otherwise, Lee's pace merely provided something for the batsmen to work with. And Gillespie, apart from claiming his 250th Test wicket, bowled plainly, probably unused to as many as 22 overs in a day.

Then came Flintoff, who got off the mark, as at Lord's, with an airy, absent-minded drive, cuffed rather than hit, and barely clearing mid-off. Some shots were not only not in the coaching manual, but seemed to have been borrowed from the coaching manual for another sport: at 48, he somehow found an untenanted area near extra cover for what resembled a double-handed drop shot on the forehand side.

Open-mouthed beneath his helmet, Flintoff resembled a day-dreaming schoolboy, trying to give the impression of concentrating on the geography lesson while wondering what mum had put in his lunchtime sandwich. Every so often, however, he awoke from his reverie to hoick Warne in the direction of the Birmingham Bull Ring. At least he didn't shut his eyes, although Warne shut his enough for both of them.

McGrath's presence was now missed not merely as a wicket-taker, but as a regulator of run flow. McGrath and Shane Warne not only speak for 1101 Test wickets between them, but concede runs at 2.49 and 2.59 an over respectively. What they can't break, they brake, like very few combinations in the history of Test cricket. Even in adversity, Australia have generally been able to retard their opponent's progress. Yesterday, albeit on an outfield of polished perfection, they could bowl only one maiden between lunch and tea.

Warne can be satisfied with one recent development. The back of his head, a testament to his latest sponsor's techniques, now resembles a tumbleweed, or a hairy coconut. Otherwise, until Billy Bowden wormed his way back onto Warne's Christmas card list by granting him two lbws, his was a day to forget: a hundred off 120 balls would normally be something to celebrate, and it did occasion a hearty cheer, but Warne was yielding them rather than scoring them. Warne was annoyed a couple of days ago to be submitted by the security 'Green Team' to the same searching examination as members of the public. Perhaps they confiscated his slider.

England's 276 runs in boundaries yesterday was a triumph not just for attacking batting, but for the power of the unpressed modern bat, from which the ball rebounds with a sweetness unknown even ten years ago. In days of yore, a batsman had to hit the ball in the region of the middle to benefit from a legitimate boundary. These days, you can slap your way to fifty with a mixture of defensive shots and thick inside edges: yesterday, both Flintoff and Harmison half aborted pull shots and ended up bunting Lee for leg-side sixes.

Batsmen also attempt shots of which they would once never have fantasised. Even in the hands of a number eleven, blows from these bats carry prodigous distances. Yesterday's tenth six, which a firm-footed Simon Jones biffed over mid-off from Gillespie's bowling, was an example of the confidence they instil.

Australia started it, but teams all over the world are now scoring faster than ever, as bats grow sweeter, one-day attitudes attain ubiquity and boundaries are roped in. In McGrath, Australia has had one of the few bowlers in the world capable of standing in that trend's way. But one day, an Australian captain watching his bowlers concede five an over may be overheard muttering wistfully: 'Owww. Errr . . .Glenn McGrath?'

DAY TWO

AUSTRALIA 308, ENGLAND 25–1
(TRESCOTHICK 19*, HOGGARD 0*; 7 OVERS)

One of the vogue texts of modern sport is tennis pro Brad Gilbert's *Winning Ugly*, whose message is that one's methods need not look attractive to be effective. And no international batsman personifies the virtue of winning ugliness more completely than Justin Langer.

While Thursday's hectic events continued at one end yesterday, Langer sponsored a one-man campaign for the restoration of old-fashioned Test match values at the other, a game within a game that made few concessions to aesthetics and was probably best appreciated while he was at the non-striker's end – where he was, with his customary self-deprecation, almost 60 per cent of the time.

If it wasn't attractive, Australia would have been in considerably better heart last night after another innings of similar obduracy. As it is, few episodes of *The Simpsons* can have caused such a chorus of 'd'oh!' as the one screened on Channel Four at 6 p.m. yesterday, which curtailed a game so full of possibility.

The rough out of which Shane Warne has now twice bowled Andrew Strauss with early candidates for Ball of the Twenty-First Century also gave Ashley Giles considerable encouragement yesterday and holds the promise of more, given that Australia will bat last here with four left-handers in their top seven. England would be unbackable favourites in this game if Merlyn had an EU passport.

First, to what has been rather than what might. It was once said that you could tell the English season had begun by the sound of the leather on willow and the thud of the ball on Brian Close's body. Something similar may soon be said of Langer, who wore his third delivery from Harmison roughly where he wore his second at Lord's, as though to ascertain the level of English solicitousness. Curiosity apparently unsatisfied, he then absorbed a blow in the sternum, while his gloves took a veritable pounding all day.

Yet even Langer's attire suggested he had a long entrenchment in mind yesterday: helmeted, sweatered, heavily padded, long-sleeved shirt buttoned to his chin with the collar turned up, he seemed almost encased, in a way that matched his natural limits.

Langer is the original nudger and nurdler. He squirts the ball into gaps rather than punching his own open spaces. He sweats on the cover drive but needs the ball in the slot to stroke it fluently, for his bottom hand takes control when he tries to hit on the up. His get-out-of-jail shot against slow bowling is the slog-sweep, but

Vaughan posted a man to the provinces on the leg side immediately yesterday and eliminated the option.

Australia progressed before lunch at the run a minute that England made de rigueur on Thursday, with an accompanying whiff of danger. Ponting might have run himself out before belting the first of his ten boundaries. Martyn's inside edge just eluded a diving Geraint Jones, and his outside edge through where third slip should have been was the cue for hands on heads as surely as Simon Says.

Langer, meanwhile, was batting almost without trace, not facing his 50th delivery until a quarter of an hour to lunch, and his 100th until 2.25 p.m. Somehow, his 50 was timed at a mere 173 minutes; perhaps they were the kind of minutes experienced on the Northern Line, where one is invited to Morden at the very next tick of the clock yet is somehow still standing there ten minutes later.

Langer even succumbed in a very characteristic way. Like another Australian left-hander in Bill Lawry, whom one almost needed a lawyer to remove from the crease, Langer is hard to budge even when out. Mind you, he wasn't alone in looking askance at Rudi Koertzen's lbw decision yesterday, Hawk Eye suggesting that the stumps would merely have sustained a slight graze.

It wasn't the umpiring that let Langer down yesterday, however, but his fellows. Not least of these were Damien Martyn, who seemed almost as surprised by Vaughan's athleticism at mid-wicket as Vaughan's team mates, and Warne, so mesmerized by the voluptuousness of Simon Jones's curves that he came prematurely at Giles – as *People* might report it.

Even Ponting essayed a shot, the sweep, which is one of the few he has never quite mastered. But the batsman who owed Langer most was his old mucker Matthew Hayden, who shovelled his first ball to extra cover as though still receiving his morning ration of throw-downs.

In 1989, Terry Alderman achieved a celebrated eclipse of Graham Gooch by the expedient of posting a short mid-wicket. Gooch was never caught there, but with a productive gap plugged began losing his usual balance at the crease and stumbled into a nightmarish streak of lbws. The placement of Pietersen at short mid-off about fifteen metres from the bat yesterday, an area through which Hayden favours blazing early in his innings, seemed similarly to cloud Hayden's judgement. With 708 runs in his last twenty-five innings at 28.32, the time he has to clarify his conglomerated thoughts is now diminishing.

To concentrate too much on Australian failures, however, would be to shortchange England, who came at their visitors with the ball as they had with the bat, as though Lord's was just a hallucination. Giles was the pick of the attack, effective to some well-set fields, and undoing Michael Clarke with an inventive seamer he should use more often.

Simon Jones bowled an incisive spell of reverse swing to an unremitting off-stump line, while Flintoff certainly makes a welcome change from the tradition of English all-rounders whose batting and bowling were as well-matched as the halves of a pantomime horse. They subdued Adam Gilchrist yesterday in a corner out of which he has often come fighting.

Under Ponting, Australia has been a resourceful side, capable of feats of Houdini-like escapology. Last year in Sri Lanka, for example, it won three consecutive Tests after trailing on first innings. With Glenn McGrath hors de combat, the calculus of this match now looks very different to that undertaken at 9.14 a.m. on Thursday. Langer doubtless has ample ugliness left in him; the winning, from here, will be very difficult indeed.

DAY THREE

ENGLAND 182, AUSTRALIA 175–8
(WARNE 20*; 43.4 OVERS)

At the start of this tour, Ricky Ponting was invited to speculate on whether any English player might at a pinch feature in a putative Australian starting XI. The only candidate over whom he paused was Andy Flintoff, and then he thought better of it. A pommy among Aussies? Why, he might forget to put the beer in the fridge.

What response would the same question now elicit? Twice Australia held the upper hand yesterday; twice Flintoff prised loose their grip. At the press conference after play, Shane Warne suggested that 'any team' would be happy to have 'a quality cricketer' like Flintoff in their ranks. Unfortunately for Australia, he's well and truly taken.

Flintoff's first intervention was with the bat. With the innings dwindling round him, he masterminded an orderly retreat that turned into a thrilling counterattack, scoring 73 of the last 109 English runs from 86 deliveries. In the first innings, the only sign that he was reading Warne were his eyes spinning counter-clockwise; now, he played Warne like a gnarled county pro, mostly with the pad, while he laid about him in every other direction.

Flintoff then started the second innings on a carry-over hat-trick, having upended Gillespie and Kasprowicz to finish the first innings. He achieved everything but, bowling Langer off an inside edge with the second delivery of his first over, then brushing Ponting's outside edge with the last, going from round the wicket to a left-hander to over the wicket to a right-hander without a flicker of the dial. More than that, the Australians were buffeted by the wave of aggression that preceded him up the wicket. He was fast. He was powerful. He was following through almost three-quarters of the length of the pitch, and it was no affectation. And he was marching back to his mark like a workman in love with his job, accompanied by the Barmy Army bugler's rendition of *The Flintstones* theme.

Once prised open, the Australian innings was undermined further by carelessness. Hayden, who drove at a wide one, and Martyn, who flicked in the air, left with their heads penitentially bowed. And watchers had no sooner grown used to the subversive idea of Giles turning the ball than he produced a straight one to Katich, Trescothick making no mistake at slip.

Even then, Flintoff was the gift that kept on giving. He sent the Barmy Army and its whole ersatz auxiliary corps into noisy raptures when picked out by Gilchrist at mid-on, and pinned Gillespie with the yorker that sufficed in the first innings at Lord's and here. When Harmison bowled Clarke with an outrageous slower ball that barely reached the other end, it ended one of the most extraordinary days of cricket I can remember for at least a week or so. Such hopes as the visitors keep alive now rest on Warne – a name which does not have quite the same reassuring ring as it did only quite recently.

This was cricket in the best Ashes traditions, even if there seemed little traditional about it. On arriving at the ground yesterday morning, I had to wait for my security check while men wearing a koala suit and a pink panther suit were screened by a metal detector: no racial profiling here, *Guardian* readers will be pleased to know. On the other hand, the day was begun by leg-spin of the most classical and beguiling kind with a ball only six overs old.

Shane Warne finished the day with consecutive swept sixes from Giles, which he will have enjoyed. More enjoyment impends, for he also finished with 599 Test wickets after also making headway on his second hundred wickets in England. The first century, which accrued when he dismissed Strauss with Friday's preposterous finale, is a feat without precedent; that an Australian leg-spinner would accomplish such a milestone would have seemed inconceivable as little as fifteen years ago.

Of the leg-break bowlers who have come to England from the antipodes more than once this century, only Warwick Armstrong improved on his overall Test record: his 40 wickets here cost 29.15 versus an all-time, all-venue 33.59. O'Reilly's 50 wickets cost 26.16 (compared to his career bowling average of 22.59), Grimmett's 67 wickets 29.95 (24.21), Mailey's 26 wickets 38.07 (33.91) and Benaud's 25 wickets 39.68 (27.03). Benaud is recalled, of course, for his 1961 Old Trafford coup – with this excluded from his performances, however, the great man's wickets here came at a pricey 48.5 runs each. This is not meant to be a country where wrist spin prospers. But Warne, of course, is *alieni generis*.

Five of Warne's six for 46 were taken from round the wicket – and if a leg-spinner has executed a greater proportion of his victims from round the wicket, I do not know of him. The *pièce de résistance* was Warne's dismissal of Ian Bell, after an innings from the boy batsman of encouraging composure. Bell was batting on leg to guard his stumps from the ball by which Warne likes to circum-navigate his opponents; in response, Warne delivered a shot across Bell's bows whose deviation the tyro could not quite cover. It was reminiscent of the means by which Warne deceived a far more experienced batsman, Michael Atherton, at Trent Bridge four years ago. He might sometimes forget he is married, but Warne never forgets a wicket.

Lee, meanwhile, proved his likeness to the girl with the curl in the middle of her forehead. His opening spell of 7–1–19–3 was made possible by some inadequate footwork and poor judgement from Trescothick, Vaughan and Hoggard, but he was hitting Gilchrist's gloves with a whack that not even the Barmy Army could drown. His best delivery was a lifter that followed Geraint Jones as pitilessly as a bailiff on a bankrupt's trail.

When Simon Jones joined Flintoff, however, Lee could some-how not summon the yorker that he usually produces on demand in one-day cricket. Flintoff found the room to execute an effortless short-armed heave into the Hollies Stand; Lee did not even watch the ball, simply turning on his heel, chastened. He then had an extensive brood when Billy Bowden, quite rightly, denied him an lbw against Jones, followed by a kick at the end of the over like a petulant child demolishing its castle when told to come in from the sandpit.

Australia were fortunate, in fact, that England did not do more to stretch their bowling resources. Gillespie did nothing in his eight overs to suggest that his tour was turning the corner, his innate lugubriousness deepening with every delivery. His Test might have been different had Warne, standing a little deep at slip for a game on such a slow pitch, held Strauss's dying edge on the first morning. But he did himself no favours yesterday, fluffing a simple return catch from a miscue offered by Geraint Jones for which the only explanation was that his cricket life flashed before his eyes – as well it might at the moment. A wicket would have reduced England to 84–7 and Australia's target might have been crucially reduced.

Kasprowicz's three overs certainly hit the bat hard, but only as they were leaving it en route to the Ryder Stand straight behind him. The last of these overs involved nine deliveries and yielded 20 runs, as Flintoff struck poses for which only Botham could have been the model. Botham? You remember him don't you? C'mon: he was The Old Flintoff.

DAY FOUR

AUSTRALIA 279. ENGLAND WON BY 2 RUNS.

The average cricket spectator always wants value for money, and generally considers that the more cricket they see the better. Yesterday at Edgbaston turned that understanding on its head: the crowd found themselves rooting for less entertainment rather than more, with a morning consisting of two deliveries probably the optimum outcome.

The Second Test's first three days had been an XL game with a jumbo pack of incident. There was something deeply stirring, even to an Australian, about Andy Flintoff charging in on Saturday as the Barmy bugler blew *The Flintstones* theme. With wickets under his belt, he was glowing, as if he had just wrung a pay rise out of that notorious tightwad, Mr Slate.

Yesterday, however, less was more. Shane Warne and Brett Lee found themselves in a position, not normally associated with blondes, of partypoopers. It was more than an inconvenience that Australia had two wickets to fall; the crowd, as subdued as they had been boisterous the day before, somehow intuited that they would not come quietly. No one seemed likely to be wondering long about the result. Warne and Lee are batsmen who, as they say in Australia, prefer a good time to a long time, and were favoured by a fast outfield with lots of untenanted space.

In fact, they lasted, Warne nerveless in attack, Lee fearless in defence, and everything began taking far longer than anyone bar Australians wanted. When Lee's hands were so badly tenderised by Harmison and Flintoff that he required treatment, physiotherapist Errol Alcott stayed long enough to offer pastoral advice as well.

It felt perilously like history in the making, at least in its first draft. Devotees of Ashes history will know of the famous teamsheet of the original 1882 Oval Test match which features the names of the England XI in a scorer's hand apparently growing more fragmentary with the tension; the last name, Peate, is written so shakily that it looks like 'Geese'. When Kasprowicz faced that final trouser-filling over yesterday, my own scribblings attained an unintelligibility almost doctor-like. After 'Harmison – Pavilion End', the notation might well read 'Take Two After Meals', or 'May Cause Drowsiness'.

It would be a churlish Australian – a barely thinkable concept, I agree – who would begrudge England their victory. Australians have begun to regard 'a competitive Ashes series' in the same light as Mark Twain saw the weather: something everyone talks of but no one does anything about. Now they have one, they can scarcely complain.

At the post-match press conference, Ricky Ponting was commendably cognizant of the Test's status as instant history, generously agreeing that the game was 'right up there' among those he had played. His insistence that the game contained 'many positives' for Australia, however, was a comment of almost Rumsfeldian optimism.

Listeners had to pinch themselves. It was hard to imagine a sentiment about 'many positives' tripping from the tongue of Steve Waugh under similar circumstances. 'We're not here to make friends, mate,' he memorably told a journalist during the 1999 World Cup. And Allan Border's reaction to Australia's one-run defeat by the West Indies at Adelaide in January 1993 was not to hum 'Always Look on the Bright Side of Life'.

This isn't just an outcome of modern take-no-prisoners professionalism either. 'The Australian plays cricket to win,' noted Neville Cardus. 'He leaves it to Mr Warner to make empire-binding speeches.' After the first Tied Test in Brisbane forty-five years ago, Richie Benaud's initial response was acute disappointment that a victory had gone begging, even when Sir Donald Bradman consoled him that the result transcended the needs of the moment. The Australian aversion to wearing ties isn't just sartorial.

Had Australia overtaken their target yesterday, the Ashes would to all intents have been over. The victors would have felt invincible, the victims would have shaken their fists at the fates. The only positive available to Michael Vaughan would have been that he still had his health.

By the same token, Ponting was quite right to contend that the game was hardly won and lost yesterday. While it isn't quite fair to contend that it was lost at 9.15 a.m. on Thursday morning when Glenn McGrath took his costly tumble, the hours before lunch on the first day when England barged to 132 for one were hugely significant.

Having sought first use of the conditions, the Australians tried too hard to justify their decision. Bowling short here was the most fruitless policy since Kate Hoey sought to ban spitting in football, and Brett Lee took too long working this out.

A perverse outcome of narrow defeat, meanwhile, which often makes it more galling, is that one need only imagine a few incidents turning out otherwise for a whole different scenario to emerge. In Australia's case, it will be the soft dismissals of its batsmen in both innings when set, notably the captain in the first innings, his vice-captain in the second, and Damien Martyn in both.

Anxieties now hover over the form of several Australians, and not just marginal individuals but stalwarts during the team's great ascendancy. Jason Gillespie is purveying the sort of bowling that Geoff Boycott always insists would be meat and drink to his mother. And Matthew Hayden remains so mysteriously short of runs as to invite all manner of speculations.

Some believe that he has taken on too many extra-curricular interests, which culminated in his publication last year of a cook-book. Does he still crave thousands more Test runs, runs the argument, or does he want to become the Naked Opening Batsman?

Hayden may even be carrying an injury. The inimitable Greg Matthews has recently queried his body language: 'It's not as powerful, it's not as prominent . . . I don't feel his aura at the moment.' This may indicate a Grade 2 Aura Strain. Hayden may need an appointment with the metaphysiotherapist.

England, meanwhile, has begun enjoying itself, both the team and its fans. To keep tight its sixteen-year grip on the Ashes, the Australians are just going to have to start cold-bloodedly spoiling everyone's fun.

THE OLD ENEMY?

When Allan Border took over the Australian Test captaincy a little over twenty years ago, he asked his distinguished predecessor Ian Chappell for advice. 'You can do anything you like,' Chappell counselled. 'Just don't lose to the poms.'

On the face of it, defeat at Edgbaston means more than simply losing a Test: it involves breaching what has traditionally been the First Commandment of Australian cricket. The English exist for the purposes of beating and baiting. When they decline to do as we wish, even the Prime Minister has a sulk: 'Here's yer medal, ya dirty pom. Don't wear it in the bath. Not that there's any risk of that.'

The First Test was what is meant to happen, the short-lived spasm of English aggression lending some additional satisfaction to its stifling. If the match had been screened on the BBC, Michael Grade would probably have condemned the broadcast of such an obvious repeat.

The Second Test was a repeat in its own way, too. At Edgbaston, a team biffed its way to 400 on the first day, hemmed in its injury-hit opposition with some excellent pressure cricket to secure a big lead, scored quickly again to set a target and finished the job in little more than three days with reverse swing and spin on a wearing wicket. The difference was that this very Australian *modus operandi* was being applied ... by England. Had Edgbaston been a novel or a film, we might by now have been calling it a pastiche or a homage. And this being so, it might be worth wondering what else has changed about the dynamic of Anglo-Australian cricket relations.

Much thought has been dedicated to the effect on English cricketers of the twenty years since the team last won a home Ashes rubber. Teachers in England are notoriously being asked to redefine failure as 'deferred success'; cricketers in England cricket team have for the last decade and a half been involved in a similar semantic experiment, redesigning success as 'deferred failure'.

This defeatism steadily wrought a toll. In his autobiography, as determined a cricketer as Nasser Hussain confessed: 'I was never involved in a close series with Australia and I went into each one almost with a feeling of "here we go again".' Steve Waugh's advice that England should follow some Australian precepts was, to Hussain, 'like Manchester United telling Bolton they should try to do it their way'. The refreshing generational change in English cricket was conveyed in Andrew Flintoff's reply on Sunday to a question about how Ashes cricket had squared with his expectations: ' 's brilliant, innit?'

It is seldom contemplated what might have been the effect on Australian cricketers of their unbroken phase of success. Australian players always profess to enjoy touring England and to relish Ashes cut and thrust. But is this merely the mouthing of a piety? Is it even, perhaps, the expectation of a few easy pickings? Certainly, it is hard to imagine that competition has quite the same tang as it did for Allan Border and his merry men of 1989.

Indeed, it could hardly be otherwise. A prime directive of not losing to someone must lose meaning if there ceases to be any apparent danger of it. To this team the injunction 'don't lose to the poms' must sound like a tiresome parental admonition, like 'don't talk to strangers' or 'don't chew with your mouth open'.

This goes a little deeper too. Much of John Buchanan's energies since he succeeded Geoff Marsh as Australian coach five and a half years ago have been directed to the motivation of men who might otherwise be sated by success: the eternal challenge of being number one and pursued, rather than number two and pursuer.

Buchanan's strategy for doing so has been to raise the bar of expectation. The Australian coach had not long been in charge when, before a Perth Test against Pakistan, he told the members of Steve Waugh's team that they should be aiming not simply to be a great cricket team but a mighty and self-perpetuating sporting dynasty: something like Manchester United, the Chicago Bulls or Australia's Hockeyroos, whose reputations were such that they won many games before they began.

The mandate continues – thus Buchanan's quest on this tour for Alex Ferguson face time – and has so far failed only in not attracting a takeover bid from Malcolm Glazer. It has even created a kind of ideology, of which countries have competed to partake: just look at the eagerness with which Australian coaches have been headhunted and academies inaugurated. Yet it has also taken Australia into a kind of post-Ashes world, in which their impetus is their own past, and their benchmarks are their own performances: a remarkable achievement, but also a species of sporting solipsism.

No one should be other than circumspect in judging the Australians in adversity, where they have been more than a few times during their hegemony. A lot of what was written about England after Lord's applies doubly to Australia after Edgbaston, especially the truism that no good team goes bad overnight. Nonetheless, even before the Second Test, watching Australia on this tour had been, at times, a slightly puzzling experience. England's summer mission statement has been pretty clear and simple: 'Win the Ashes.' Australia's seems to have been more ambiguous: 'Yeah yeah, let's retain the Ashes and all that. But let's become the Chicago Bulls too.'

Defeat in a Test by England, as a result, is no longer felt viscerally, which is why Ricky Ponting can talk about the 'positives' to emerge from one: all very up-beat, and commendably analytical, but smacking slightly of psychobabble. Defeat registers instead as a check on the spread of Australianism, a doctrine whose manifest destiny is to rule the earth. Time will tell whether this defeat truly ramifies. We might even see a restoration of the old First Commandment of Australian cricket. The Second Commandment too. It was: see First Commandment.

A PLAGUE ON ONE HOUSE
IN PARTICULAR

For years my Melbourne park cricket club has aspired to play cricket like the Aussies. In the early weeks of this Ashes tour, it looked a little like our dream had come true, except that they wanted to play like us, what with the batting collapses, dropped catches, wides and no-balls. A player even turned up to a game still drunk from the night before. The only difference at my club is that we'd not only have let him play but conned him into opening.

Over the last week, the Australians have faced a scenario also familiar to club cricketers: the last-minute unavailability through injury. Since Glenn McGrath's pratfall, Brett Lee has pulled up lame with a knee complaint, and the way Justin Langer keeps ducking into Steve Harmison may shortly make him uninsurable. In the same circumstances, my club usually plays with ten, and simply tries to spread out a bit in the field. The Australians, less used to it, have augmented their sixteen-man squad with Stuart Clark from New South Wales via Middlesex.

This is something that Australian teams have traditionally been loath to do. Even when Craig McDermott was invalided home from the 1993 tour with a twisted bowel, the Australians preferred to simply double Merv Hughes's bowling rations. He showed a heart as great as his stomach, famously losing four kilos in one week and gaining six the next. Times, however, are changing. The great variable of cricket is usually considered to be weather. In fact, weather's period of greatest influence, that of uncovered pitches, is long ago. These days it is injury that strikes, as unpredictably and destructively as a blind giant.

In an era of cricket played with unprecedented intensity and frequency, both its risks and its stakes are higher. The difference between Sri Lanka with Muttiah Muralitharan and Sri Lanka without, for instance, suggests they should close every road in Kandy as he crosses it. New Zealand's Shane Bond has just been welcomed back to the fold after more than two years injured, a period during which there have been times when his country's entire first choice attack has been sidelined. The likes of Mfuneko Ngam and Dean Headley, forced into premature retirement by their infirmities, haven't been even that lucky.

Some bowlers are spending so long on treatment tables these days that they should almost be issued season tickets. During the Twenty20 final, Alex Tudor was seen getting around on crutches: it wasn't clear if he was actually injured or carrying them round in case he was. Some recent series, too, have taken place between virtual second XIs. When the 2003–4 Indian tour of Australia began, the first choice attacks of each team should by rights have pitted McGrath, Lee, Jason Gillespie and Shane Warne against Zaheer Khan, Ashish Nehra, Harbajhan Singh and Anil Kumble. In fact, only Kumble played the whole series; the rest were *hors de combat* all or most of the time.

Generally speaking, Australia has been extraordinarily adept at keeping players fit, its injury management having been as far ahead of the rest of the world as its batting, bowling and fielding. The best-known monument to physiotherapist Errol Alcott is Steve Waugh's comeback hundred at the Oval four years ago, but his life's work has been in preventive medicine. Alcott was the first, for instance, to insist on ice baths for players at the end of each day's play to abet recovery. 'When I first started they put the beers on ice,' Darren Lehmann observed recently. 'Now they put the players on ice.'

It should not be generalized from a few ill-timed injuries that this record is now under threat. But Alcott today is working with older material. The Australians have become specialists at short tours with the bare minimum of first-class cricket besides, almost passing through passport control with their pads on. Yet that also cuts the time available to recover from mishap and illness, and also to rediscover lost form. One false move, like a stray touch rugby pass, and that can be your lot.

Perhaps a new parlour game is in order. Blaise Pascal famously proposed that history would have taken a different course had Cleopatra's nose been shorter, and there could be fun to be had with alternative universes based around cricket injuries. In the 1998–9 Ashes series, for example, Graham Thorpe's back failed him during the First Test at Brisbane, and Steve Waugh's hamstring let him down half-way through the Fifth Test at Sydney.

Yet how might that series have unfolded had the injuries occurred in reverse order, had Thorpe been available for virtually the whole series to counteract Stuart MacGill, and a hobbling Waugh been confined after the Gabba Test to spruiking memorabilia for Channel Nine? Would there now be a public holiday in honour of the day the team led by Lord Stewart of Merton reclaimed the Ashes? There may even be another alternative universe in the making right now. How different might the result of the 2005 Ashes series have been had Brad Haddin thrown that pass to McGrath a little more precisely?

WHAT MAKES A GREAT TEST?

'Great Test matches' is the ultimate cricket fogey topic. To the uninitiated, it must sound like a debate about great brass bands or memorable moments in philately. Even to devotees, such a discussion may seem stale, equivalent to debating the proper role of the sun in cricket. Yes, there have been some great Test matches. Some have been really great. Others have been quite good too. And . . . errr . . . that's it.

Something like Edgbaston 2005, however, inevitably sets the cogs turning. Edgbaston was exciting even before it started.

Personally, I'll never forget arriving in the press box just before 10 a.m. to meet my beaming *Guardian* colleague Mike Selvey. 'Your best fast bowler's scared,' he said. 'He's running away!' With Glenn McGrath's crooked ankle in ice, England ran hot, surging to none for 60 after an hour, and did not stop attacking for three days.

Test cricket usually gives you an hour or two for a snooze, or a read, or even a discussion of 'great Test matches'. Not for a ball could you avert your eyes at Birmingham: if you missed something, it was bound to be a turning point. Then there was *that* finish. Can you have a great Test without an excruciatingly tight result? Yes: think Sydney 1903 or Lord's 1930. But there needs to be plenty of competition before the decisive break. As it turned out, Edgbaston had it all. Had Billy Bowden hesitated over his final deliberation, the Test might by now be known as Warne's match. Well, one of Warne's matches anyway.

One point is worth making from the start. Good Tests are not uncommon. Great Tests are very rare. This article will refer to a score or so, but bear in mind that they have emerged from a list of candidates now nearing 1800 strong.

Cricket can be cruel. The beaten edge, the unplayable ball, the impossible chance that is taken, the straightforward chance that is fluffed, the umpire's inadvertent error: on individuals, cricket inflicts the most exquisite suffering. But for all the blah about glorious uncertainty, Test cricket is utterly, massively, viciously fair.

Over four innings, five days, fifteen sessions and a maximum 450 overs, virtually every player has the opportunity to make an impact, and usually several chances to do so, so that in only the most exceptional circumstances does the superior outfit not prevail. Actual upsets are incredibly rare: New Zealand beating West Indies at Dunedin in 1980, Zimbabwe beating Pakistan at Harare in 1995 and India beating Australia at Kolkata in 2001 spring to mind from the last quarter century, but not many more.

Not all games share this characteristic. Most are more forgiving of inequality. When two apparently mismatched soccer or rugby teams meet, for example, there are many ways whereby, with close marking and defensive formations, the weaker can chip the stronger's advantages away. One-day cricket, too, tends to narrow differences between teams, and even generates upsets, like Bangladesh beating Australia.

Test matches are not like that. They can't be won by a freak goal or try against the run of play. Nor does international cricket have the homeostatic mechanisms, like salary caps, drafts and transfer markets, by which other games counteract the rich simply getting richer and the successful still more successful. Pit Bangladesh against Australia in a hundred consecutive Tests and, even on current form, Australia would win a hundred times.

A great Test, then, needs two very closely matched teams, at perhaps different stages in their cycle to afford a contrast. The mighty series of 1960–1 drew its back story from an established Australian team encountering a rising West Indian team. The cut-throat clash of 1995 cast the same opponents in opposite roles. At some point, too, whether totally or partially, an established order has to be usurped. Great team that they are, it is Australia's defeats over the last decade that have been their most memorable matches: say Melbourne 1998, Bridgetown 1999, St John's 2003, aside from those in India. Exceptions would be Port Elizabeth 1997 and Kandy last year, where the team had to rally stunningly to overthrow South Africa and Sri Lanka respectively. Otherwise, Australia, like the West Indies before them, is like a pantomime villain, coming big and falling hard, amid consternation and glee.

There is no such thing as a great Test that develops only one way. It must fluctuate, the more extremely the better. If it's possible, all must, at some stage, look lost: think Sydney 1894, Old Trafford 1961 or – admit it, you were all waiting for it to be mentioned – Headingley 1981. Botham's barnstorming 118 notwithstanding, Old Trafford 1981 would not have been half the Test without Australia's indomitable, seemingly interminable fourth-innings fight-back. And while individual feats are by definition integral to any great Test, a great Test is not solely constituted by individual feats.

Sydney Barnes taking 17–259 against South Africa in Johannesburg in 1913–14 did not make a match on its own. Laker's match at Old Trafford in 1956 is an instance of solo virtuosity rather than a great Test *per se*. No one remembers Old Trafford 1964, with Simpson 311 and Barrington 256, other than unhappily. When Sri Lanka piled up 952–6 against India at Colombo in 1997, it was not history being made but a particularly sadistic statistic.

Just as not all great Tests are great in the same way, not everything about Test cricket is contained in the cricket itself. Some Tests are made more memorable by the context of the present of which they form part. The first Tied Test seems all the more astonishing for the backdrop of drab, austere cricket from which it afforded such relief; the second for the abrupt change of character that overtook Allan Border on the last morning, persuading him to a soul-stirring declaration. Some Tests are enhanced by the context of the past from which they emerge. The *coup de théâtre* of the Centenary Test was to be decided by the same margin as the game it commemorated. Some very rare Tests gain a grandeur or drama from extramural events. 1953 throws up two contrasting examples: the Oval Test, where England's Ashes triumph was suffused with the afterglow of the Coronation, and the Ellis Park Test three months later where New Zealand's strivings against South Africa took place in the shadow of the Tangiwai rail disaster. The simplest act in an India v Pakistan Test, of course, always seems freighted with significance. There can have been few more geopolitically loaded games, for better and worse, than the Chennai Test of January 1999.

One consideration on which purists might divide where great Tests are concerned is the significance of the result. This might seem incongruous on a matter of grand theory, but cannot be underestimated. Let us grant that great Tests need not necessarily conclude, although any inconclusion must surely be reached in dramatic circumstances, such as Adelaide 1961 and Johannesburg 1995. For all their recent deeds, this England team play a damn good draw: see Durban 2004.

When the result is unexpected, a drawn Test rubber can also feel entirely fitting. South Africa were deemed fortunate to be dignified with a five-Test tour of Australia in 1952–3, but won at Melbourne to tie up the series at 2–2; Pakistan bearded West Indies in their Bourda den in 1987–8, forcing the hosts to a stirring riposte at Bridgetown; the summer of 2003–4 was expected to be a Sinatra-like farewell tour for Steve Waugh, but India became like the support act that steadily attained top billing. Such circumstances, however, like novels or plays memorable purely for character or description rather than for leading to some resolution, are exceedingly rare.

This creates a complication in the interpretation of 'greatness'. Test matches achieve their transcendant quality through being contests between teams bearing the names of nations. But the same sense of allegiance cannot help colouring our thoughts. Australia's 1882 victory against England at the Oval has gradually become important to the cricket history of both countries; but the West Indies' 1950 victory at Lord's, for instance, and India's 1971 victory at the Oval matter far more in the West Indies and India than in England. So don't worry if agreement on the epic qualities of Edgbaston 2005 is not so emphatic down under: it's just that this wonderful game becomes ever so slightly more wonderful when one's own team wins.

THE THIRD TEST
– OLD TRAFFORD

11, 12, 13, 14 and 15 August 2005
Match drawn

THE WARNE FACTOR

When I was growing up in Australia in the 1970s, I overheard cricket people talking about leg-spin, but scarcely grasped of what they spoke. By the time I was playing cricket during the 1980s, the leg-spinner had become cricket's unicorn or gryphon, a mythical species. If occasionally a bowler served what passed for leg-breaks, batsman would queue to partake of the succulent full-tosses and long-hops.

Pragmatists sneered when Victoria picked a raw, roly-poly wrist-spinner in February 1991. 'I think if you bowl leg-spin in this country,' said his own captain, 'they go a bit honky tonk.' Such circumspect initial reviews are now reminiscent of the famous assessment of Fred Astaire's first audition: 'Can't sing. Can't act. Can dance a little.' Shane Warne, the man who single-handedly rescued leg-spin from desuetude and disrepute, arrives at Manchester today poised to become the first bowler to obtain 600 Test wickets.

Think about that. Fred Trueman, bowling's blue riband holder for more than a decade with 307 Test wickets, averred that whoever broke his record would be 'bloody tired'. Warne might turn thirty-six next month and have bowled 45,533 deliveries in international cricket, but his thirst for the game seems unquenchable. It might even, after his recent personal travails, be the most satisfying part of his life.

Coy references to problems in Warne's 'private life', of course, make little sense; virtually nothing about his life has been private. 'I am a cricketer and a human being,' he commented in his auto-biography four years ago, and he has since confirmed the latter little less often than the former.

On the eve of his milestone, however, it's his bowling that cries out for attention. It's inaccurate to say that Warne rediscovered leg-spin. He recast it instead in his own image: bold, bumptious, fun and feisty. When Warne was bowling in his backyard in Melbourne, he did not imitate any wrist-spin role models: Australia's leggie of choice, grey-haired Bob Holland, looked like your geography teacher. He instead imitated Dennis Lillee, in his histrionics, if not his hostility.

Something of this survives in the elaborate dumbshow that accompanies Warne's bowling: the stroking of the chin, the pursing of the lips, the sardonic half-smile, the conspiratorial wink. These gestures used to be the prerogative of pacemen. No fast bowler now pauses so meaningfully or pouts so purposefully as Warne.

Aggression with Warne, mind you, is not of the 'hang the conse-quences' sort; he says instead 'I dare you'. Before Warne, leg-spin was a luxury good. He has made it not only affordable but desirable. Warwick Armstrong famously relieved his googly merchant Arthur Mailey after a single maiden over. 'I have other bowlers to bowl maidens,' he explained gruffly. 'You're here to get wickets.' Warne does it all. Grudging runs at 2.6 an over, he vacuum seals batsmen with accuracy before ripping them open with spin.

There is a quaint obsession in this country with Warne's varieties. Jeremiahs complain that his flipper is a ghost, and his googly a phantom of imagination. Yet the delivery that truly distinguishes Warne – the one that a rival like Stuart MacGill, for instance, cannot bowl – is what might be called 'the sixth ball': that is, he delivers six good deliveries an over, rather than five with a four-ball. It is 'the sixth ball' that fails Warne when he is short of form or fitness, as in India twice after recovering from injury. Otherwise, he is relentless.

Warne has even made us see defence in an offensive light. Before him, for instance, leg-spinners only bowled round the wicket as a negative ploy; when Benaud came round the wicket to bowl Australia to victory at Old Trafford forty-four years ago, it was an act of subversion and desperation.

Warne has reinvented the angle as an attacking option. His tutor was Bob Simpson, who many years ago bowled in this vein to Warne in the nets to illustrate its perplexities. The style and the variety he has achieved in it, however, are Warne's own. 'He seemed to attack from all directions,' wrote Sir Donald Bradman of his great contemporary Bill O'Reilly; the description might suit Warne even better.

Some maintain that Warne is not the spinner he was, that the ball no longer deviates as once it did. If you want to see an example of minimal deviation, though, check his average. Having dipped as low as 22.55 after his only Test hat-trick, it began reverting to the mean, trending as high as 26.7 after some expensive analyses against India. Yet it has since fallen to 25.24, like a final unpredicted bit of backspin.

Certainly he no longer enjoys some of his initial advantages. Batsmen have seen a lot of him. Pitches are flatter and boundaries smaller. In the early stages of his career, too, Australia's order of battle was based round deploying Warne at the pitch's dustiest. Time was when an Australian captain would not have thought twice about batting at Edgbaston on winning the toss.

Warne is no longer centre of Australian plans. His team, moreover, has been tending to win matches too quickly to optimise his effectiveness: he has bowled on only three fifth-day wickets in the last year. Yet, somehow, he is still the bowler to watch; for me, a rumour confirmed and a myth made flesh. Appreciate him; he was a long time coming, and he will be a long time gone.

MATCH REPORT – PHOTO FINISH

The death of cricket has been so freely prophesied in England that the queues round Old Trafford on the last morning of the Third Test might at first have been considered a mass delusion. Maybe people thought there was a home show on, or a pop band playing. Perhaps they'd strayed from the other Old Trafford, locked out from a local derby. But no: they were there for the fifth day of an Ashes Test match in which England held the ascendancy, a corroboration of the powerful race memory of cricket, and also the national genius for queuing. The ten thousand who missed out on the available tickets were admirably good-humoured about it, but perhaps also intrigued by the novelty. England's ascendant did not, in the end, translate into victory, Australia's last pair of Brett Lee and Glenn McGrath negotiating the last two overs. But the result was in doubt until the last ball, amid the sort of fear and trembling more commonly associated with bungee jumping and jet boat racing.

Glenn McGrath had provided the game with its first shock even before it began. The state of his health had been monitored with the attention usually devoted to ailing popes, but there was general surprise when he bowled ten overs at practice the day before the Test, and universal astonishment when he was named in the starting XI at Kasprowicz's expense after another spell just before play. McGrath's second ball of the match reared at Trescothick's throat and took a glove on the way to the third man boundary. Lee then hit Strauss behind the right ear, drawing blood, preparatory to yorking him with a well-concealed slower delivery. But Peter Marron's pitch otherwise proved well worth Michael Vaughan's winning the toss; it was hard, with carry that lasted the whole match, and abrasive, which favoured England's artfulness with reverse swing.

Vaughan's own acclimatization was aided by Ponting's bowling choices: Australia's captain unaccountably spelled Lee after 5–2–6–1 in favour of Gillespie, from whom Vaughan took a string of therapeutic boundaries, and delayed the resumption of Warne's search for his 600th Test wicket until the 34th over at 1.50 p.m. Australia also failed to seize the day when Vaughan was dropped at the wicket and bowled by a no-ball from consecutive McGrath deliveries: a double ration of generosity that it was hard to square with the parsimonious Australians of the past. Trescothick then Bell made admirable foils for Vaughan as his touch came flooding back, including the back foot drives and pull shots he'd paraded in Australia thirty months earlier. After a time, in fact, a century began to seem inevitable. For all this recent travails, Vaughan's conversion rate is unimpeachable: this was his fifteenth hundred for the twenty-seven occasions he has passed fifty in sixty Tests.

Australia's only good news was Warne's landmark, achieved in rather humdrum fashion when Trescothick miscued a sweep and Gilchrist pinched the ball off the back of his bat. Warne celebrated by kissing his 'Strength' wristband, a present from his daughter Brooke, but apparently did not share it with fielders who gave Vaughan two further lives: Hayden dropped him at slip from Warne at 141 and Katich did not peg the stumps at 156. Katich would have been relieved when his full toss was shovelled to McGrath at deep mid-wicket soon after. After the loss of Pietersen and Bell to pull shots late that day and early the next, England's innings was further prolonged by some attractive strokes from Flintoff and Geraint Jones. Flintoff meted out further punishment to the hapless Gillespie, yanking him contemptuously for six over mid-wicket; when Gillespie gave away his 100th run off his 98th delivery, the big screen flashed his photo on the screen, a little sadistically. Warne finally rejoined the attack to sweep aside the remainder.

At tea on the second day, the tourists were comfortably situated at 1 for 73, Bell having caught Langer skilfully at silly point. Australia's problems began at once thereafter, Ponting perishing to the first ball on the resumption, the first of six wickets in a session to spin and reverse swing. Hayden went back instead of forward, Katich did not play when he should have and Gilchrist played when he shouldn't; between times, Martyn fell to an exquisite delivery from Giles that pitched in the left-armer's G-spot before snipping the off-bail. Warne was a bold, sometimes extravagant exception, swinging his bat in generous arcs. But the follow-on loomed with the fall of Clarke, who had spent most of England's innings off the field after suffering irritation in a disc and moved with the freedom of Boris Karloff, which reduced the innings to seven for 201 – still 243 in arrears with three wickets in reserve. A large, happy crowd, streaked with wattle from the T-shirts of visiting Australians, seemed to have witnessed what looked like a turning point in the Ashes campaign.

When the balmy, sun-kissed Friday gave way to a sodden Saturday, however, England's problems began. Only fourteen overs were possible, eight from 4 p.m., six from 6.10 p.m., in which Warne advanced from 45 to 78 and Gillespie from 4 to 7. The former was missed twice by Geraint Jones amid hoots of derision, and the follow-on faded from calculations. Seldom can sixty-four deliveries in intermittent drizzle have seemed so pivotal. Time was now of the essence on a pitch that exhibited few signs of deterioration.

England channelled their aggression better on Sunday, with Simon Jones obtaining the best Test figures by a Welshman, and the best by an Englishman in a Manchester Ashes Test for nearly fifty years; his reverse swing was as unintelligible to the Australians as Bosanquet's googly a hundred years earlier. Warne fell in the 90s for the second time in his Test career to end a stand of 86 from 151 balls with Gillespie. Although Gillespie enjoyed his best moment of the tour when he jabbed Jones for six over mid-on, England's lead had been restored to 206 by the time its first second innings wicket fell. Strauss, who needed only some runs to flesh out the generally good impression he had left this series, finally got among them, zeroing in on his sixth Test century, eventually batting 158 balls in just over four hours for nine fours and two sixes. He had some luck, bisecting the unmoving Warne and Ponting at first and second slip when 1, but it was no less than his courage merited, which was reflected in the dressing on his right ear from his first-innings mishap. Trescothick overhauled 5000 Test runs in an attractive 41, Bell completed a brace of crisp half-centuries in which he got the better of his Lord's tormentors McGrath and Warne, and Geraint Jones clouted 27 not out from a dozen deliveries to speed the declaration. McGrath accumulated five wickets in an innings for the twenty-eighth time and ninth in Ashes Tests, albeit a little sheepishly, as the last four were taken in a spell at the cost of 78 runs in less than ten overs; Warne, despite bowling bravely and patiently, went wicketless.

One culprit for the eventual stalemate that seemed to escape criticism was the ICC, whose Standard Playing Conditions did not allow for time to be made up from Saturday by early starts. The quest for uniformity seems to have taken priority over the idea of maximizing playing time. The conditions further disadvantaged England on the fourth evening when they set Australia 423. Because Australia had bowled its overs with calculating tardiness – even umpire Steve Bucknor, known to bring time to a standstill while adjudicating lbws, was moved to remonstrate – encroaching darkness now forced Vaughan to rely on Giles and himself to stay on the field.

With the Old Trafford pitch in excellent order, the task of taking ten Australian wickets on the last day was a tall one. The day, too, dawned gloomily, cold enough for the English slips to be plunging their hands in their pockets between deliveries. But, after Edgbaston, anything seemed possible. Fans came from far and near to will England on – one party of students drove all the way from Cardiff in search of tickets – and soon had reasons for hope. Langer edged the day's eighth delivery and Hayden was baffled by Flintoff's frequent change of angles and bowled behind his legs. Ponting looked secure immediately, befitting one who was over-hauling Greg Chappell's tally of 7110 Test runs, and at lunch was 41 in Australia's 121–2. England was eight wickets and Australia 302 runs from a series lead.

England made the best of the afternoon, after obtaining a lucky lbw against Martyn. Flintoff roared in from the Warwick Road end, and his reverse swing baffled Katich and Gilchrist. But Giles was disappointingly loose and Ponting calmly acquisitive, playing barely a false shot let alone a dangerous one, and taking tea just nine runs from a deserved hundred reached soon after. When reverse swing thwarted a promising innings from Clarke and a brief one by Gillespie, Warne then emerged to play at his eccentric best, as though convinced that Australia could upset all calculations and win the Test. A ripple of apprehension passed through the crowd: a horrid unforeseen twist in an otherwise conventional whodunit. The light, too, was threatening to peter out, just in case anyone had forgotten that this was an Old Trafford Test; Pietersen may have been slow to pick up a round-the-corner flick from Warne (30) that resulted in his fifth consecutive dropped catch.

As at Edgbaston, though quite against the run of recent form, the player who turned the match was Geraint Jones. When Warne's fast-flying edge bounced off Strauss's knee at third slip, the keeper scooped up the rebound; when Ponting got a glove on a ball down the leg-side, the keeper accepted it with alacrity. He might well have run out the wandering McGrath in the last over, but failed to notice that the Australian number eleven was out of his ground. But there were other events for England to rue too: umpire Bowden was the only person who did not believe Lee (1) was lbw to Harmison, while substitute fielder Stephen Peters from Worcestershire might have entered the Syd Copley Club had he thrown a late-starting Lee out from cover soon after. As it was, neither Harmison nor Flintoff bowled quite the final overs they'd have hoped for, and Australia's last pair survived. Those who contrived to get into the ground for the final day could feel blessed; those who failed could console themselves they had also played a part in the spectacle, which was, after all, about what might have been.

DAY ONE

ENGLAND 341–5 (BELL 59*, 89 OVERS)

Eminem is scheduled to bring his Anger Management Tour to Old Trafford next month. In his tenth over yesterday, Glenn McGrath gave spectators at Manchester a foretaste.

The second ball of the over took off from Peter Marron's hard-topped tarmac and decked away, kissing Michael Vaughan's cut shot en route to first slip. The ball was almost in Shane Warne's hands when Adam Gilchrist's glove parried it wide for the streakiest of boundaries to third man.

The next delivery was like the perfect conversational put-down, puncturing Vaughan's defences to flatten off-stump. But the retort was drowned out by umpire Bucknor's proclamation of no-ball, made into two by some helter-skelter running.

McGrath has been known to shake his head if a seagull in the outfield moves too fine; yesterday he shook his head so hard it almost came free. He said something too. It may have been: 'It's a funny game.' It certainly seemed to have an f in it.

McGrath deserved a little better from the fates after bouncing back so determinedly from his pre-match mishap at Edgbaston, in another testimony to the healing hands of physiotherapist Errol Alcott. Lancashire County Cricket Club were so sure that McGrath was out of calculations yesterday morning that they omitted his name from the scorecard in favour of 'S.C.G. MacGill' and 'M.S. Kasprowicz', while one newspaper implored England not be fooled by 'Aussie mind games' into believing he would play. The announcement of his inclusion on the public address system caused a collective case of Grade 2 credulity strain.

That, however, was the best the day held for McGrath. Gilchrist also let him down in the day's fifth over, missing Trescothick (13) to his left as he had Strauss during the Natwest Series match at

Headingley: Gilchrist, a better athlete than gloveman, sometimes seems surer at full stretch than not. McGrath then had no one to blame but himself for the reprieve of Ian Bell (18) in his sixteenth over. Bell was beaten by a slower ball, McGrath by an even slower return catch.

In general, too, the conditions were unwelcoming. For a man whose ankles owe so much to medical science and physical care, this bone-jarring pitch was no pleasure to bowl on. McGrath came in close to the stumps with his arm as high as ever, but his follow-through ended abruptly and the speedometer that clocked him at 87mph in his first over seemed to have been recalibrated as an act of traditional northern hospitality.

Having enjoyed not so much a slice as a three-tier wedding cake of luck, Vaughan pressed on. It was not merely a personally crucial innings, but a vexatious one for Australians, who often talk, as did the West Indies, of turning up the voltage on opposition skippers.

Empirical evidence suggests they just might. The record of captains against Australia for the last two years has been a modest one indeed; any player acquiring 1153 runs at 26.2 and two wickets at 220.5 would be lucky to hold their place in any side. And that, of course, is the idea. For some reason yesterday, however, Vaughan was welcomed to the crease by some plain, flat and diffident bowling from Jason Gillespie, the emphasis in whose name is currently falling on its last three letters. The ideal helpmate for any batsman trying to play themselves back into form, he hit the bat yesterday with the force of a meringue.

Vaughan enjoyed 61 of Gillespie's 92 deliveries, from which he poached 68. In a spell of four innocuous overs for 42 after tea, Gillespie even reunited Vaughan with his long-lost swivel pull. Gillespie looked to be running from fine leg to fine leg with more purpose than when he was running into bowl. England's captain, meanwhile, received only four overs from Lee, who troubled him at Lord's, bowled him at Edgbaston, and at times yesterday was distinctly sharp, especially with the second new ball.

With Gillespie, the Australians are caught in what Kevin Pietersen once allegedly referred to as a Catch-21 situation. He is less effective since he was relieved of the new ball, but is not bowling well enough to justify getting it back. He needs bowling to recover his form, but ends each spell with confidence lower than before. He is Australia's fifth-highest Test wicket taker, but the sixteen Test wickets he has taken since the start of Pakistan's tour of Australia last December have cost 52 runs each. Perhaps his last hope is to be written off by a newspaper columnist. Jason, you're gone. I hope that helps.

At the time Gilchrist nudged Vaughan's nick for four, there seemed some sort of conspiracy to keep Warne out of the action altogether, maybe for fear of overexposure. He idled until the 34th over. At least he had only to wait until his twenty-ninth delivery for his not-so-long-awaited 600th Test wicket – and as we have all had rather a lot of Warne numbers lately, it may be best to stop there. He does keep telling us he's not a man for statistics.

Nonetheless, after Warne's *coup de théâtre* at Edgbaston, there was altogether more aplomb in the English response to him yesterday. It is unclear whether this was a testament to the wiles of Merlyn, recepient of so much recent publicity as to be almost deserving a ghosted column. But Bell was particularly patient, happy enough to hazard only eight scoring shots at Warne from a total of 76 deliveries.

Warne was also, perhaps less obviously, as much a victim of misfortune as McGrath yesterday. Pietersen miscued him into space on the off, Bell leading-edged him to leg, Hayden spared Vaughan at slip. Warne himself ended the day as dusty as an archivist from his toil in the field, but in good spirits. This is already a Test being played at a more measured pace than Lord's and Edgbaston, and it will repay patience. There will be no point in getting angry; one must aim to get even.

DAY TWO

ENGLAND 444, AUSTRALIA 214–7
(WARNE 45*, GILLESPIE 4*, 56 OVERS)

Around noon yesterday at Old Trafford, Andrew Flintoff groped forward to cover a leg-break from Shane Warne, pulled up slightly short of the pitch of the ball, found it whirling past his outside edge and at once went down on one knee.

Once upon a time, this would have been construed as spontaneous genuflection. In fact, Flintoff was merely tying his left bootlace. The days of England bending the knee and tugging the forelock are behind us. This team comes at you hard, fast, and often without warning.

No better example was seen yesterday than when Ricky Ponting resumed after tea, the Australian captain coming off a couple of starts in this Ashes series without the score that would have established his presence.

Ponting's boyish features belie his decade in the international game, and strong cricket upbringing; his first experience of such a scenario probably dates back to Mowbray 3rds, and he would have come through something like it on numberless occasions.

Ponting's forward press to the first ball has been a trademark, an announcement of his enterprise in 90 Tests and through 22 Test centuries. This delivery from Simon Jones, however, was not a loosener or a sighter: it was distinctly sharp. It got big, foiled Ponting's attempt to surmount the bounce and looped from the shoulder of the bat to gully.

In tennis, it would have been classed a big point; in chess, a crushing gambit. Top-order batsmen in an Ashes rubber receive a maximum of ten innings. Ponting's half-finished series leaves him averaging 23.8, while his numbers against England, 38.73, and in

England, now 38.77, have taken, if not a full-fledged buzzcut, a noticeable clip.

All summer, Ponting has retained a breezy optimism about his and his team's capabilities. The day before the Lord's Test, he cheerfully volunteered that England 'thoroughly deserved' their number two position on the world Test ladder: half a commendation, half a dig, with the hint of a reminder not to forget who was number one.

England, though, have been like one of those weird psychiatric cases that feature in the works of Oliver Sacks, constantly forgetting who they are, and their supplicants' role. Australia has thrice had initiative wrested from it. At Lord's it seized it back, but at Edgbaston it did not, and here it has been listless in the field and fallible with the bat.

One can't accuse the captain of failing to set an example, because he is; the problem is that it's a bad one. Games have been allowed to drift, as though Australia will only deign to play when they are damn good and ready. Setbacks have been dismissed as containing positives with what, if it were not the captain of the world's best team talking, would amount to fortune cookie philosophizing.

Ponting's batting malaise, meanwhile, has not been relieved. Where Glenn McGrath has targeted everyone except Sooty this summer, England have quietly drawn a bead on McGrath's skipper, who with his thrusting front foot and early keenness to put bat on ball has been caught four times either at the wicket or in the cordon. He was dropped in gully a fifth time at Lord's.

Ponting is not the only component of Australia's batting, massively productive in recent years, that has been successfully stopped in its very deep tracks. Another is the opening partnership of Langer and Hayden. It's often said that left-handers are cricket's thoroughbreds or bluebloods, crowned with an innate elegance. The theory finds no support in either of these prolific and seasoned batsmen.

If Langer were a specimen of Australian fauna, with his diminutive figure, bright eyes and marsupial cuddliness, he would probably be a koala. But as any Australian will tell you, the koala secretes a disagreeable odour, emits a ghastly noise and is apt to stick his claws into you. Langer attaches to the crease with a similar avidity.

Hayden, meanwhile, with his lifeguard's chest and bodyguard's desire to intimidate, bullies the ball to the boundary rather than persuading it. He is a nice opponent to get the better of, as England have this summer, because he is a dismaying one by whom to be dominated.

Their partnership yesterday was their best of the series, and recalled for a moment their monumental alliances of the past, when they set about their work with the companionable and happy heartiness of Asterix and Obelix off to twist Caesar's nose. Coming after the capture of the final four English wickets for 11, they promised further renewal for the Australians, perhaps even a resumption of normal service.

In fact, they were cut short again by a combination of Giles and the rough at the Stretford Road end. Hayden in particular kept looking over his shoulder as he retreated. Shome mishtake surely? That's enough wickets – Ed.

The most melancholy figure on the park yesterday, however, was cut by Michael Clarke. Before the Test, Clarke told a newspaper that McGrath was 'good enough on one leg' to bowl for Australia; his youthful ebullience is such that he probably volunteered to push the great paceman in to bowl in a wheelchair.

When he took guard at number eight, however, back pain had transformed bonny Michael Clarke into a version of late-period Michael Atherton, moving about as though he was confined to a tight-fitting body cast. The excruciating hoick that cost him his wicket looked like a blessed relief. Born into this period of Australian plenty, he must find this turn of events difficult to credit, like a sudden change to the end of a favourite fairy tale.

The only relief available to Australia in this match now will be meteorological. It was hard to believe yesterday in the little black cloud split by a thunderbolt in the online weather forecast for today, but this is Manchester, and this is also an Ashes series as fickle as an English climate. The other factors in this series seem less easily changeable, and one wonders whether it is in Australia's power to make England revert to their old submissive ways.

DAY THREE

AUSTRALIA 264–7 (WARNE 78*, GILLESPIE 7*, 70 OVERS)

The day begins with a haiku in my inbox from the poet, biographer and Oxfordshire Amateurs XI representative Simon Rae entitled 'On Enforcing the Follow-on at Old Trafford':

> You don't take your boot
> Off a snake's neck in order
> To stamp on its head.

The weather, however, was fit for neither cricket nor snakes, and the follow-on remained as indistinct as the Pennines. Rain tumbled down; terraces were deserted as the capacity crowd sought shelter; Peter Marron's minions busied themselves in their various duties and errands. One of John Arlott's most famous snatches of commentary was a vivid word picture of the covers being shuffled round the Lord's square; you can find it in David Rayvern Allen's splendid biography. As it's already been done far better than I could, I feel no obligation to match it.

When play then finally began at 4 p.m. for the first of two fleeting interludes, the follow-on quickly faded from calculations. Michael Vaughan, in fact, did not seem to seek it with any eagerness: Simon Jones bowled to the passive Gillespie without a short leg, and to the busy Warne without a second slip. England got one glimpse of the possible when Warne (55) ambled amiably down the pitch to Giles and ended up so far from his crease that he needed almost to mail his bat back. In the end, there was no need; Geraint Jones performed his party trick of palming the ball into space. Warne then sustained a crack in his bat, sought a replacement from his kit, and found a sweet one, hefting three boundaries down the ground to ensure that Australia's record of not following on since the Bicentenary Test remained intact.

The follow-on can be like that: an alternative one would prefer not to have, which is why what used to be compulsory enforcement was eventually made voluntary. It requires a gamble on the fitness and form of bowlers and a belief in the zeal of fielders – rather more of a speculation since the gradual eclipse of the rest day, which used to afford recovery time between innings, but is now considered as archaic as Sabbath observance. Because it is an undertaking to bat last, enforcement of the follow-on also requires a certain trust in a pitch's integrity, and a cross-breeze at Manchester has already stirred up a good deal of dust from this one. England would probably prefer this to be Giles's to exploit rather than Warne's: the snake might be pinioned, but it's still poisonous.

By the close, Jones's keeping had entered the realm of embarrassment. His attempt to catch a straightforward edge from Warne (68) in the penultimate over was a shambles. He can now hardly be trusted to carry a helmet from one end to the other without dropping it. The finish of the Edgbaston Test grows more miraculous with each passing day.

DAY FOUR

AUSTRALIA 302, ENGLAND 280–6D, AUSTRALIA 24–0 (LANGER 14*, HAYDEN 5*, 10 OVERS)

'Whatever happens on this Ashes series,' Australian coach John Buchanan told his interlocutors on Saturday evening, 'we will grow as a group as a result.' This great Australian team is certainly broadening its life experiences, with yesterday's another distinctly unfamiliar one: trying to retard the building of a potentially match-winning lead.

And while they have stormed Gallipoli, visited Villers-Bretonneux, and penned more bad poetry than a tortured teenager, the challenge that Ricky Ponting's side face today is as acute, and for them as novel, as any: batting all day to save a Test.

For Australians in recent years, time has flown; today it might conceivably drag. This Ashes tour has become such compulsive viewing as to outdo reality television. What began as *Celebrity Love Island*, when Shane Warne's private life became public knowledge, has now become an edition of *Survivor*.

There is even talk of a rift in the lute of the Australian team – perhaps inevitably. Steve Archibald, or maybe his literary ghost, came up with a lovely line about team spirit always being 'the illusion glimpsed in the aftermath of victory'. The corollary is that disunity is the impression usually garnered in the event of adversity.

It made for a day that hummed with speculation when it didn't buzz with activity. After an edge from Strauss off Lee bisected Warne and Ponting at first and second slip just before lunch, for instance, there was what seemed a pregnant silence in the Australian cordon. Were they simply disappointed, or contemplating how to blame one another in their tour diaries?

When Ponting tossed Warne the ball for the seventh over of the innings, was it a case of 'let's do it for the baggy green', or 'if you're so clever you bloody win it for us, fat boy'? When Warne wrapped a comradely arm round Ponting's shoulders before bowling an over after tea, was there just the hint of a headlock?

It probably does not matter overmuch. There have been bones of contention in Australian teams on their last few visits: over the form of Mark Taylor in 1997, over the recent omission of Warne in 1999, over the eventual omission of Slater in 2001. Victory, as it were, washed away all sins.

When all is said, done, bowled and batted, an irked Warne turns the ball no less than a cheery one, and a separated Warne is no less formidable than a happily married one. And what Ponting needs are runs, not a relationship counsellor.

The reasons the Australians should mourn their performance at Old Trafford lurk on the field, not off. Despite his 5–115 yesterday, McGrath's selection has not borne the expected fruit. If he was not fully fit, he arguably shouldn't have played; if he was, his threat has been considerably diminished.

Andrew Strauss, whose counterpunching hundred maintained England's advance yesterday, seemed to have grown a cubit in his span since the Natwest Series. The Ian Bell and Geraint Jones who lifted McGrath for irreverent sixes yesterday were certainly not the callow youths of a month ago.

As Jason Gillespie obligingly cleaned the ball for Brett Lee shortly after lunch, it looked suspiciously like a means of justifying his presence. His role otherwise was to provide amusement for spectators with some ungainly boundary fielding. When finally entrusted with the ball in the thirty-sixth over, Gillespie pitched a perceptively fuller length to prevent the pull shots by which England have taken toll of him in their last five innings. But when his third over cost 14 including three consecutive no-balls, he furnished an argument in favour of trapdoors in the outfield down which embarrassed cricketers might vanish and wend their way back to the team hotel.

It fell, predictably, to Warne to be the Australian Horatius. His robust 90 was his second-highest Test innings and probably his most-needed. After he was caught in the country one short of a hundred against New Zealand at Perth in November 2001, he reportedly sat around in his batting clobber for a full half-hour rueing his misfortune; he rolled his eyes when he picked Giles out on the square leg yesterday as though he'd just sent an SMS to the wrong number. Warne then bowled tirelessly and lucklessly, playing tricks with the rough, revealing his charm, and his menace, with umpire Bucknor: an entrancing and inventive spell of defensive bowling.

The captaincy, however, was dilatory, the Australians reduced to the somewhat desperate expedient of dawdling their overs, while the fielding was ragged, the quality of the returns from the outfield being particularly slipshod. Damaging publicity for orange keeping gloves continued with Adam Gilchrist, like Geraint Jones, missing a stumping and catch. At the moment you wouldn't trust either to convey a tray of drinks from one end of a room to the other.

Play begins today at the normal time of 10.30 a.m., as yesterday, despite a Saturday on which all of 84 deliveries were bowled, and on which, to judge from their behaviour on leaving the ground, many spectators drank more pints than they saw overs. They were, mind you, pretty good-humoured about it all, considering they had just watched play end during the best light of the day because of an ICC Standard Playing Condition rivalling the Duckworth-Lewis System for unintelligibility.

The ICC's Code of Conduct is already so complex that one half expects to find that mouth breathing is a Level 2 offence. When Billy Bowden came out to explain the ICC's Standard Playing Conditions yesterday to Mark Nicholas on Channel Four, it sounded like the exposition of a mathematical proof by Paul Erdos. Nicholas candidly admitted that he still did not understand it, perhaps because *The Simpsons* went unmentioned.

Maros Kolpak, then, may not be cricket's first mitteleuropean influence. Kafka's parable 'The Problem of Our Laws' begins with the famous lines: 'Our laws are not generally known. They are kept secret by the small group of nobles who rule us.' The ICC was founded towards the end of the Austro-Hungarian Empire; perhaps its constitution was secretly drafted in Prague. Well, it's a theory.

Today, Australian theory meets practice. Don't miss it. There will be a whole lot of growing going on.

DAY FIVE

AUSTRALIA 371–9. MATCH DRAWN.

The search for the ideal partner, when all that seems on offer are couplings of convenience, has become the defining modern quest. Ricky Ponting might have brought his wife Rianna on this Ashes tour, but yesterday he was like a lonely heart in search of real commitment, condemned by modern mores to serial monogamy.

They came. They went. Perhaps there was something wrong with him – something not even his friends could tell him. But no: he wanted all the things a young man is meant to hope for. Runs. The Ashes. Fast greyhounds. He had to, as they say in those magazines at the supermarket checkout, keep putting it out there.

There'd been some scandalous whispers about Ponting not seeing quite eye-to-eye with Shane Warne. People will talk – but hey, let them. That was then. This was now.

The most impressive feature of Ponting's highest score against England, in fact, was how cut off it seemed from the match's first four days: a thing in and of itself. His team mates did not seem so detached, perhaps mentally still replaying Edgbaston to keep Michael Kasprowicz company.

At about 10 a.m. yesterday, the queues at Old Trafford stretched as far as the eye could see; within half an hour, they stretched almost the same distance in the opposite direction as disappointed fans were deflected by 'full house' signs. England hoped for a similarly quick turn-around.

In fact, Australia scored freely after Langer's early fall: so freely as to nourish idle thoughts of a victory thrust. In Flintoff's first over, Ponting wheeled into the trademark pull that his high hands and early pick-up permit, and scattered the crowd beyond deep fine leg. Like St Augustine, he craved continence and chastity – but not yet.

Hayden also wellied Giles for six to reach his best Test score of the summer, but was nearly bowled by him, and generally less secure. He thrice edged at catchable height through the cordon; he threw his head back when beaten by Flintoff, castigating himself disgustedly.

Losing the habit of run-making is indeed an infuriating experience, like losing the drift of a familiar song; it was as though Hayden was humming and ad-libbing through the missing bits before Flintoff sent him back to consult the songsheet.

There was some misadventure in Australia's innings. When Martyn's pads absorbed a ball from Harmison after lunch, he was as confident of his innocence then as convinced of the injustice as the Winslow Boy. Replays revealed an inside edge too late to quash the conviction.

Others fell between two stools. Gilchrist continued his anonymous series, neither attacking nor defending. Katich, bowled not offering first time around, thrust over-anxiously at Flintoff; Clarke, having shaped as well as anyone, suddenly decided to play no shot. Youth is meant to abound in confidence, but here was full of doubt.

Ponting, meanwhile, showed off the iron-bottomed belief that underlies his batting ability. He contends that his mistakes come from trusting his methods too little rather than too much. His worst setbacks as batsman were in India just over four years ago when he was dismissed by a freak bouncing ball from Harbhajhan Singh in the First Test at Mumbai, and began tinkering with his technique as a result.

A conversation with Steve Waugh after the Lord's Test a few months later convinced Ponting that he should have stuck with his usual game plan for spinners, of playing straight and using his feet. The advice that accords with our own instincts is the advice on which we usually act.

The disciplined, self-denying Ponting was not, after all, that different from the death-before-dishonour strokemaker. Between lunch and tea, he scored 50 of the 88 runs off the bat from 78 deliveries: enterprising batting in advance, let alone retreat. After tea, despite the almost overpowering tension, came 65 from a further 115 deliveries.

In leaving the ball, however, Ponting seemed to bring his bat aloft with a flourish, almost symbolic of the restraint he was prepared to exercise for the greater good: itself a kind of rallying cry, that could not go unheeded forever. Dudley Carew wrote of another great long-distance batsman, Maurice Leyland, that he 'seemed to withdraw himself altogether from the conflict round him and engage in some solitary meditation of his own'. That was not the way of Ponting yesterday. He not only looked for company, he sought to inspire it, to kindle the flame in others. When he reached his hundred with a cover drive off Harmison for his tenth boundary, Ponting focused his celebrations on the Australian balcony: the modern vogue, but usually as a tribute rather than an exhortation.

It was Warne who responded – although, to be fair, the flame in him during this game has needed little fanning. At times on the weekend, the Third Test recalled the famous newspaper poster concerning Bradman: a case of 'Warne v England'.

Warne, as ever, was a law unto himself. As a batsman – and it should be emphasized that it is of his batting I write here – he is a frightful flirt. He intersperses shots of utter conviction with off-balance and open-bladed speculations, which are followed by penitential rehearsals of the stroke he meant to play.

Warne saved an Ashes match for Australia at Sydney with the bat ten years ago, playing strokes in the gloaming while Tim May dead-batted. He has remained true to his methods. He might well have been man of the match last night; without him, there'd have been no match for his captain to save.

In the end, Ponting experienced the epiphany that usually follows unrequited love: that you can only be responsible for yourself. There is vindication in this discovery but also a kind of disappointment, a resignation. Innings of solitary grandeur are not how Australia has built its enviable record, and they are not really a viable means of defending it.

THE MORNING AFTER

There is a children's chant which begins with the want of a nail causing a horse to be lost. The horse, it turns out, is the king's. The king, as kings are wont to, had been expected to lead his men in battle, but won't do it without a horse. What do they expect him to use, a skateboard? So he's lost too, and the consequences are dire. The last line of this parable of the multiplier effect runs: 'For the want of a nail, the kingdom was lost.'

It's an English chant, less familiar to Australians – but now, perhaps, we have the Ashes of 2005. In the Second Test at Edgbaston, there were more than 700 runs in boundaries struck, 54 no-balls and wides called, 26 byes conceded, a dozen overthrows donated and a short run. By almost any measure, it was a wild, profligate game of cricket.

Somewhere in there were two runs by England that Australia failed to match: half a thick outside edge to an unpatrolled third man by England, or alternatively a couple of leg-byes cautiously turned down by Australia. Will these two runs be as the nail to the kingdom, overturning not just a whole summer but an entire hegemony?

Old Trafford was a stupendous Test. But the game of the summer is still Edgbaston. Without those two runs, Old Trafford would have taken place in an entirely different narrative – if, of course, it had taken place at all.

Concern about whether England will suffer some sort of trauma from their inability to prosecute victory at Old Trafford has some empirical support from the drained, dejected attitudes struck by the players amid the aftermath of Monday's play. The photograph of Simon Jones and Kevin Pietersen on the front of yesterday's *Guardian* seemed to say it all.

Perhaps, though, not quite all. There is an element of self-projection to such speculations. Jones may have been thinking: 'Vaughny's just used the expression "putting pressure on Australia" for the 576th time this summer. I'm going to put a leek in his jockstrap if he does it again.' And Pietersen, from what is known of him, may not have been thinking at all, simply visualizing himself with paisley hair, or the tattoo of a Beefeater on his shoulder blade.

In the sober light of hangover, England should recall that it did little wrong at Manchester, and nothing seriously. Vaughan could hardly have declared a moment earlier, and the finish suggested he timed it to a nicety. Strauss, who has looked like a well-organized player all summer, acquired the substance to support the style. Jones the bowler had a fantastic Friday, Jones the keeper a startlingly assured Monday – had he been a racehorse, the stewards would have been calling for a swab. Flintoff? To him momentarily.

Monday's disappointments were a drop, a missed run out, and Giles's errors of length, which forced him to bowl with a sweeper on both sides of the wicket despite having 400-plus to bowl at. Even then, Giles did some useful work, taking an important gully catch, and twice pounding round the boundary in front of the pavilion before lunch and unloading throws that landed by the bails: the kind of fielding that shows off a team's sharpness, and was conspicuously lacking from Australia's desultory efforts on Sunday.

Australia woke up yesterday experiencing the afterglow usually associated with a satisfactory one-night stand. Then would have come the thought: 'But where am I?' The answer, one-all in an Ashes series that should have been virtually wrapped up in Birmingham, would have brought a vague sense of queasiness, like the sound of someone whose name you have forgotten in the kitchen frying eggs.

Their reassurance is that they have wormed out of such situations before, and even come from behind, as in Steve Waugh's first series as captain in the West Indies. The respite afforded by the itinerary, moreover, will be welcome: stuff often comes back to you when you're thinking of something else.

Comparisons between the teams at the moment, however, are unflattering. Were this a boxing match, both fighters would still be on their feet, but England would have led on points in the majority of rounds. Their batsman have passed fifty eleven times, twice proceeding to centuries; versus Australia's six, for Ponting's hundred on Monday. England are scoring their runs faster and taking wickets more quickly too. Only in catching are the teams comparable, being equally bad.

England also look more menacing, partly because they are playing better cricket, but also because of their height and weight advantage. This sounds counter-intuitive: one of cricket's greatest appeals is that the race is not always to the swift nor the battle to the strong, and little spinning Davids have toppled many a bat-swinging Goliath. But in the kind of aggressive, fast-scoring, hard-grinding series we are seeing, size and strength are not to be underestimated as a competitive edge, and Harmison, Flintoff, Giles, Trescothick and Pietersen cast long shadows.

Australians have not only never faced a team better than they are, they can have met few teams physically larger, if at all. In the meantime, their three most sizeable physical specimens have all experienced crucial absences: McGrath of fitness (at Edgbaston), Hayden of form, Gillespie of spirit.

The aftermath of a dramatic Test like Old Trafford is a little like trying to piece together a traffic accident to which one was eye-witness. The memory is insecure, fragmentary, full of impressions that turn out misplaced, and incidents of overlooked significance.

One interlude to which we may well cast our minds back was Andrew Flintoff's *mano e mano* duel with Adam Gilchrist on

Monday. They are the most explosive cricketers in their respective XIs: one great all-rounder, one submitting credentials for the title.

When Michael Vaughan came to offer his go-to guy a break after six fierce overs for the wicket of Katich, Flintoff airily waved him aside. Only microsurgery could have removed the ball from his hand. Most bowlers of the last few years bowling at Gilchrist have thought longingly of not bowling to him. But Flintoff wanted Gilchrist, and wanted Gilchrist to know it. Gilchrist tried to counterpunch, and drove fatally at a ball not quite there.

Flintoff isn't the first bowler to try harrying Gilchrist from round the wicket. Four years ago at Trent Bridge, Darren Gough made a great hue and cry about changing from over the wicket, then was thrice smashed through the covers on the up. Michael Atherton, Gough's captain, looked like Blackadder studying the inevitable result of another of Baldrick's cunning plans.

The shorter Gough, however, tended to slide into Gilchrist's hitting zone. Flintoff's steep bounce creates a third dimension to the change of direction, while his reverse swing adds an element of danger to vertical bat shots. Above all, Flintoff is not trying to contain Gilchrist but to attack him, and 88 balls at his Australian counterpart this series have yielded him three for 61.

This duel is the series so far writ small. The rubber's eventual outcome hinges on such exchanges either continuing to go England's way, or reverting to the type of the last fifteen years.

THE FOURTH TEST – TRENT BRIDGE

25, 26, 27 and 28 August 2005
England won by 3 wickets

THE NEW GOOGLY

History is said to repeat itself so often that it might almost be suffering from a stammer, but the Ashes this week takes a turn with at least some intriguing parallels.

The Australians move to Trent Bridge today still trying to decrypt the mysteries of reverse swing, which they have found unintelligible in the summer's first three Tests. It was on the same ground a century ago that England also won a decisive Ashes Test with a bowling weapon over which they alone had mastery: the googly's progenitor B.J.T. Bosanquet took 8–107 to overwhelm Joe Darling's Australians by 213 runs.

Reverse swing and the googly might not seem to have much in common, but they are essentially fast and slow variations of the same principle: by subverting classical arts, wrist spin and orthodox swing, they seek to turn batsmen's natural mental cues against them.

The action that batsmen see when a googly merchant rolls his arm over, and the shiny side they glimpse with a swing bowler reversing the ball, lead them to one conclusion; the ball then turns traitor. It may even be that history has something to teach Australia's coach John Buchanan, the 1905 Ashes series not having being included as an appendix in *Who Moved My Cheese?*

Bernard Bosanquet was born in October 1877. His distinguished family tree sprang from Huguenot soil, and was festooned with clerics, critics, admirals and archaeologists. But like a googly himself, the Etonian and Oxonian went the opposite way.

Bosanquet's speculations with the rotated sphere began at university, where he played a game called twisti-twosti whose object was to bounce a tennis ball across a table so that it eluded someone seated opposite. Although possessed of a natural leg break, Bosanquet perfected a *mot juste* that involved turning his wrist round further so the ball whirred clockwise.

To alter the axis of a cricket ball's rotation in the same way was hugely difficult. Bosanquet had to be as limber as a contortionist to roll his wrist first over then under the ball so that it seemed to emerge from the back of the hand.

Sometimes the googly came out like a garbled message: the googly's inaugural first-class victim was stumped from a ball that bounced four times. At others, it was the most counter-intuitive code. When Bosanquet first met the Australians for Middlesex in August 1902, he quickly defeated Jim Kelly with what appeared a leg-break but turned wickedly the other way. 'There was a josser out there bowling leg-breaks from the off,' Kelly complained to laughing comrades. 'We changed our tune next day when we all had a turn to face Bosanquet,' recalled his colleague Clem Hill, 'and realized that a new bowling era had begun.'

The new era, however, did not dawn everywhere at once. There was no television, let alone super slo-mo hawkvision with Simon Hughes-o-meter to study Bosanquet from fifty-seven angles including through the umpire's hat in infra-red. For a time, too, the Australians worked on the assumption that Bosanquet would always deliver enough dross to make him an uneconomic proposition. Instead, Bosanquet got better. When he visited Australia with Pelham Warner's 1903–4 MCC team, Bosanquet warmed to form at the crucial moment. Having conceded 451 runs for ten wickets up to New Year, Bosanquet seized 7–168 in a losing cause at Adelaide, then 6–51 to recapture the Ashes at Sydney.

Yet, even then, the sun was setting on Bosanquet. His Trent Bridge bag a hundred years ago was both his finest hour and his last efflorescence: he bowled nineteen more overs for one more wicket in two further Tests, was regarded for much of the rest of his career as a batsman, and for much of the aftermath of his life as a news-reader's grandfather. This may be, in fact, the lesson of Bosanquet's feat for the current Australian side: that their countrymen a hundred years layer were confounded finally not by the googly but by its ghost. Match reports suggest that most at Trent Bridge, perhaps even all, succumbed to leg-breaks. Darling's Australians had veered from under-reaction to over-reaction.

Having reverse swung from wilful ignorance to deep brooding in their efforts to counteract Simon Jones and Andy Flintoff, Ricky Ponting's team might be perpetrating the same mistake. To begin looking for a variation is as potentially unsettling as the variation itself. The flat pitch and lush outfield at Trent Bridge do not, in any case, seem so amenable to reverse swing.

The more cheerful augur for Buchanan and Ponting is that no English slow bowler has been a match winner with the googly in the century since Bosanquet, at least against Australia.

On the contrary, Bosanquet soon became like English cricket's Pandora. Warner's team were routed that winter by a South African side containing no fewer than four Bosanquet disciples, who had learned the trick from close study of their unwitting mentor while touring England.

Only once more did Australians falter against the googly: at the Oval in August 1909, when England boldly chose a schoolmaster from Kent, Douglas 'Daddy' Carr, who had been bowling quickish, round-arm googlies for the likes of the Blue Mantles and the Band of Brothers. After early successes, alas, Carr was overbowled back into obscurity, and the match-winning googly bowler was on the way to becoming English cricket's Snark.

That summer's googly coup was instead Australian. At Lord's, Warwick Armstrong seized 6–35 from twenty-five overs, *The Times* reporting that he 'at times got the off-spin with the leg-break action' which 'had all the batsmen guessing and wondering what was coming next'.

What was coming next, in Armstrong's XL footsteps, were 'Ranji' Hordern, Arthur Mailey, Bill O'Reilly and Clarrie Grimmett, who customized the googly for Australian conditions When they were introduced in England in 1930, Bosanquet is alleged to have studied the wizened Grimmett intently before asking: 'Am I responsible for you?'

Here, then, is the lesson for England of Trent Bridge a hundred years ago: no cricket advantage remains anyone's prerogative for long. History might well repeat itself, but it's not always the same people who do the repeating.

SEEN AND HEARD

Jason Gillespie has given voice to what a number of Australian players feel in this morning's *Mirror*, complaining of the hoarse hostility of English crowds: 'Some of the crowd behaviour is appalling, the insulting things people say. People pay their money to come in and they think it is their right to question your parentage and have a crack at your mother. It's always these guys that abuse you, call you effing this and effing that and ten seconds later they are asking for an autograph for their kids. You say, "Look mate, I'm not going to sign it for you", and all of a sudden you are the worst bloke in the history of the world, so you can't win.'

It's hard to feel much sympathy with such protestations from an Australian, crowds in whose country have become steadily crasser and stupider. The first time I really had an insight into what visiting players put up with was in Perth ten years ago. I have a vivid recollection of sitting in a crowd listening to Phil Tufnell, fielding as a sub, being hounded from pillar to post; it ruined my enjoyment of the day, and I can only imagine what it did to Tufnell's.

I attend most Australian Test matches as a spectator, and the general standard of crowd behaviour, exacerbated by the forces of face-paint patriotism, now ranges, with certain honourable exceptions, from inattentive to abysmal. In the latest Test programme, Simon Jones reminisces of being stretchered off the Gabba with his right knee cruciate and his career in disarray thirty months ago: 'One guy in the crowd called me a "weak pommy bastard" and threw a can of Coke on me. That wasn't nice.' Submerged in a mob, the smallest man can become a hero to himself.

What Gillespie is describing, though, is a general trend, not to increasing partisanhood, because fans have always been partisan, but to diminishing inhibition. It is not altogether accurate to speak of 'spectators' any more, because spectate is often the last thing they do; they crave becoming part of the pageant themselves, like contestants on a reality television show. When sport is sold as a commodity, so is it consumed. And in what the historian Geoffrey Blainey has called 'the rights society' – in which rights, whether to free speech or to bear arms, are not just defended but aggressively asserted – the right to abuse whom one pleases is considered inalienable. Sponsors and ground authorities pander to this, and television is more than a silent witness, making a point of hovering on the most demonstrative crowd members. In sociology, this is known as focusing on oppositional groups. On television, it's called entertainment.

That's not to say I think the audiences this summer have been unusually misbehaved. Frankly, given what it costs to get into an English Test ground, they should probably be free to erect a mobile disco. The Barmy Army, for the most part, provide an enjoyable sideshow. Rounding the Wyatt Stand after the Edgbaston Test, I encountered a game in which Queen Victoria batted to the bowling of Sherlock Holmes while Lord Nelson kept wicket, somehow perfectly in keeping with the atmosphere of the aftermath: it mingles now among my most cherished memories of that marvellous match. But it's a sideshow that should remain there: on the side, rather than trespassing on the action. A philosophy becoming popular in England at the moment is that 'cricket is the new football'. Why would cricket want to be anything like the Augean stable of football, with its millionairhead players, venal administrators and sub-culture of crowd violence? English cricket should be careful what it wishes for.

The first day of the First Test at Lord's sets the scene for a hectic series, crowding in seventeen wickets, 282 runs and a string of body blows from Steve Harmison. Australian captain Ricky Ponting was left dazed by this direct hit on his helmeted head, and by Australia's dismissal before tea.

No sooner had England taken the initiative than Glenn McGrath seized it back, dismissing Marcus Trescothick with the first ball after tea to obtain his 500th Test wicket and gathering another four. At stumps, England were a bedraggled 92 for 7.

England's only batting consolation was the solidity of Kevin Pietersen, whose technique and temperament withstood searching examination during his 57 and 64 not out. His form at Lord's, however, proved almost as deceptive as Australia's.

Glenn McGrath, the key Australian presence at Lord's, was the key Australian absence at Edgbaston. His injury during the warm-ups before the Second Test confounded his captain's plans, and gave his opponents heart.

Andrew Flintoff began his first over of the second innings amid a cacophony of patriotic noise, and struck at once, barging through Justin Langer's defence. When Ponting fell five balls later, the Barmy Army roared the roof off the stand.

Geraint Jones, a byword for fallibility throughout the series, caught the one that mattered: Michael Kasprowicz after an heroic last wicket partnership of 59 had taken Australia to within 3 runs of stealing the match. Kasprowicz dropped to his haunches, as Jones looked toward tormentors in the crowd with which to share the moment.

The first day of the Third Test at Old Trafford pitted two out-of-form players against one another, Michael Vaughan facing Jason Gillespie. Vaughan prevailed, mightily, his 166 the biggest and most serene innings of the series. Gillespie did not play again.

No player on either side advanced as much as Simon Jones, whose mastery of the arcane art of reverse swing undermined Australia's middle order at Old Trafford and Trent Bridge. Such became his importance that his absence, injured, at the Oval was felt a body blow to England's prospects.

There were rumours of a bust-up between Shane Warne and Ricky Ponting after the Edgbaston Test, but no sign of same at Old Trafford. Warne's 90 in the first innings and Ponting's 156 in the second ensured that Australia lived to fight another day.

In dimming light the series hung on every ball of the last four overs. Brett Lee and Glenn McGrath saved Australian blushes by coming through against Harmison and Flintoff; England were left to rue the loss of most of Saturday to rain.

Andy Flintoff began the series as a rusty slogger, but by Trent Bridge was a batsman of power and presence. His 102 in a 177-run partnership with Geraint Jones for the sixth wicket underwrote a match-winning first innings.

Adam Gilchrist's travails continued at Trent Bridge when he was the victim of the catch of the summer – actually, many summers – by Andrew Strauss at second slip from Flintoff's bowling. Soon after, Australia followed on for the first time in an Ashes Test for twenty years.

A direct hit that ran out Ricky Ponting in the second innings reverberated for the next few days, for the thrower was a substitute, Gary Pratt. Exasperated by the comings and goings of English bowlers for the tour, Ponting let loose a tirade about England's use of specialist fielders as 12th men.

Shane Warne again gave England palpitations as they closed on their second innings target at Trent Bridge, and it was left to Ashley Giles to work the winning runs through the leg side, ensuring that Australia had to win at the Oval to retain the Ashes.

Andrew Strauss kept England in the
game on the first day with his seventh
Test hundred but the Ashes did not
feel within England's grasp until a
leonine fifteen overs from Flintoff on
the fourth day were followed by a
drenching rain. When England's
twin nemeses Glenn McGrath and
Shane Warne signed off, after a lifetime of victory, it was as members of
the vanquished.

MATT FINISH

'What a marvellous Test we have had at Nottingham. Who'd have thought that Andy Flintoff's leg-spin bowled off the wrong foot would have proven so effective with a bodyline field? What of Glenn McGrath's 150 with ten straight sixes amid the drama of Errol Alcott's Test debut? And let us not forget Geraint Jones's stumping. It came off his chest, of course, but will do wonders for his confidence . . .'

After the prodigies of the first three Tests, it is tempting to wonder what Trent Bridge might have in store that could possibly sustain the summer's note of surprise. Kevin Pietersen could revert to his natural hair colour. Geoff Boycott could praise Marcus Trescothick's technique. Or Matthew Hayden could make some runs.

Time was when the headline 'Hayden 100 leads Aussie assault' was kept in permanent reserve, such was the frequency of its use. In forty-two Tests from Australia's tour of India in 2001, he scored nineteen centuries amid 4523 runs at almost 70, and briefly held batting's blue riband with his 380 against Zimbabwe at Perth.

At its zenith, at Galle in March last year, Hayden's Test average stood at 62.95: better than Pollock, Headley and Barrington in the rankings of batsmen-other-than-Bradman in cricket's statistical hall of fame. He was ambling out to bat like a cheerful woodsman entering a forest with a sharpened axe, a Paul Bunyan or a Johnny Appleseed, the runs flying like chips as he set about his work.

Over the last year, however, bowlers have sawed away at Hayden himself. Since his last hundred at Cairns he has gone twenty-eight innings without another, a period in which he has averaged a distinctly mortal 31.1. Such is the pile Hayden has already accumulated that he could not make another run this series and still boast a Test average of more than 50. But he would in all likelihood be boasting from outside the Australian team. He turns thirty-four in October. Darren Lehmann needed only a short run-less stretch at the same age to find himself consigned to Australian cricket's outer darkness.

What has gone wrong with Hayden? Perhaps the more pertinent question is what went right? It is illuminating to re-examine the early stage of his career, when Hayden was, at best, a peripheral member of the Australian XI.

The first ball Hayden received in Test cricket, from Allan Donald, broke his knuckles. He was then humiliated by Curtly Ambrose and Courtney Walsh. In his maiden Test hundred at Adelaide in January 1997, his bat seemed to have been physically demiddled. After thirteen tests over nearly seven years, Hayden averaged 24. Queenslanders used to regard Hayden's omissions from the Test side as a dark southern conspiracy, like that daylight saving which made the curtains fade. In fact, he simply wasn't good enough against top-class new ball bowling, of which there was in the mid-1990s a bit around.

Hayden's rise coincided with the worldwide decline of quality pace bowling, worn out by the grind of the Test and the one-day roundabout. In a few years, Hayden was transformed from fag to bully. With his middle-stump guard meaning that he almost obscured the stumps, he pervaded the crease. Bowlers felt the cold as his shadow fell across them. Hayden's swaggering figure, in fact, became a motif of Australian aggression, as the striding 'Man from the Pru' used to evoke Prudential's prudence and purpose.

It was not simply that certain great bowlers had retired. The accent of bowling changed. As 'putting it in the right areas' became the summit of virtue, Hayden learned to enjoy putting it back over bowler's heads and down the ground. The only bowler round of speed was smart-as-a-plank Shoaib Akhtar, whom Hayden learned to wind up so skilfully that he was usually spent in three overs.

What's befallen Hayden over the last year has been as mathematical as technical. Francis Galton gave the phenomenon its name: reversion to the mean. Cricket is replete with forces that ensure what goes up must come down; or, if you're a bowler, what goes down must come up.

England have stopped Hayden driving with impunity, strokes that fed his ego. They have confused him with shrewd field placings and changes of direction, and offered him little of the slow bowling on which he used to gorge. They have made him think – always a challenge for a player of instinct. At Old Trafford, Hayden looked baffled about how to build an innings, perhaps still dreaming of the days when they used to build themselves. Having taken almost two hours over 34 in the first innings and perished going back instead of forward, he smacked a six early in the second, seemed to want to play at everything and was finally bowled behind his legs.

England have also curbed Hayden in this series through doing the same to Justin Langer. Much of Hayden's success has attested the power of two, and he draws immense strength from his pal and partner. Both Hayden and Langer were late bloomers as Test batsmen, have sated their early hunger for opportunity while maturing together, and developed complementary and mutually supportive games.

Their harmony at the crease has been a visible dimension of their partnerships. They stand close together during mid-pitch conferences, nose to chest, as though engrossed in discussing their favourite chapter of *Jonathan Livingston Seagull*. They play the congratulatory glove touch off back and front foot with equal fluency.

Langer, however, has been also been hemmed in during this series and restricted to a single half-century. Their turning over of strike, a feature of their partnerships, has been inhibited: Langer was even run out at Lord's by a direct hit, the partners' first such mishap since they coupled up at the Oval four years ago.

Can this be turned around at Trent Bridge? Hayden has had a paltry ration of good fortune this series. Every chance has stuck. He has snicked rather than missing. That could be the workings of karma after such a long lucky streak; it could portend something big around the corner. What's troubling for Hayden, however, is that he seems to have worked his way out of this series, rather than being in the process of working his way back into it. The probability is that he will offer early chances at Nottingham. Now looking to prevent surprises rather than cause them, England must hope that they do not fly in Kevin Pietersen's direction. Then they can get to work on thwarting McGrath's 150.

COMING SLOON

Australia's Shaun Tait has been cleared for his Test take-off tomorrow at Trent Bridge, predictably at Jason Gillespie's expense. Good judges vouch for his speed. Another aspect of the Australian performance that he will improve is the general standard of nickname. Tait's soubriquet is one of those rare ones that is not a pun or an informalization by the attachment of an '-y', but instead has a story behind it. On his first trip abroad with Australia, to Sri Lanka last year, a hotel clerk could not transliterate Shaun into anything more identifiable than 'Sloon'. It stuck.

Australia might have led the world at cricket over the last ten years, but it has been a dire disappointment to connoisseurs of the nickname. Nicknames as an Australian tradition go back at least to the Golden Age: 'Demon' Spofforth, 'Terror' Turner, 'Paddy' Darling, 'Little Eva' Trumble, 'Lightning' McLeod, 'Clum' Armstrong, 'Mary Ann' Noble, 'Ranji' Hordern, 'Governor-General' Macartney. Who can forget such tight-fitting aliases as 'Jackson' Lindwall, 'Nugget' Miller, 'Ninna' Harvey, 'Griz' Grout, 'Phantom' Lawry, 'Wallaby' Cowper, 'Fot' Lillee, 'Bacchus' Marsh? A personal favourite is Richie Benaud's handle, 'Diamonds', in honour of his luck, which was settled on the great man by a remark of 'Dusty' Rhodes's: 'If you put your head in a bucket of shit, Rich, you'd come up with a mouthful of diamonds.'

The Aussies these days are a motley crew: Punter, Warney, Kasper, Marto, Kato, Haydoszzzzzzzzz . . . Nothing intimate, evocative or even particularly memorable there. But this is a long-term trend. A cricketer as characterful as Ian Healy deserved better than 'Heals'; with so many options, it is amazing team mates came up with something as lame as 'Pistol' Reiffel; Mark Waugh was awarded a far better nickname by his countymen, 'Afghanistan' (the forgotten Waugh), than by his countrymen, 'Junior'. It's ten years now since the last half-decent Aussie nickname: 'Fruitfly' Hughes, the great Australian pest.

The best of the current bad lot is 'Churchy' Gilchrist, stemming from the boy who at Derbyshire in 1997 came seeking the autograph of 'Eric Gilchurch', who now seems like the man who accosted the Duke of Wellington and addressed him as 'Mr Smith'. This is a good nickname because it connects to a particular story, and a moment in Gilchrist's career when his face did not stare from billboards and tour diaries: for Gilchrist to keep it shows both humour and humility. If Tait keeps his nickname after enjoying some success, 'Sloon' may begin to exhibit the same qualities. Otherwise only the coach lands it in the right areas. 'Flanders' so suits Buchanan that he should begin team meetings with the greeting 'hi-del-I-ho cricketereenos'.

Why have cricketers' nicknames become so naff? They are narrower than of yore, because of professionalism. They spend less time off-piste, as it were, at fixtures where they can relax and think about something other than the forward press and the corridor of uncertainty. Their identities are more public. Better a simple, dull epithet than one that might be twisted or parodied: 'Becks' is exemplary in this respect. Above all they are celebrities. Celebrities do not have nicknames. Brad 'Bottomless' Pitt? Jude 'Possession-Is-Nine-Tenths-Of-The' Law? Nope. Celebrities, on their pedestals, permit no such intimacy. Perhaps we shouldn't wish Tait so well. Three-for and he'll probably stay 'Sloon'; five-for and there is a danger he'll become 'Taity'.

MATCH REPORT – BRIDGE OF SIGHS

English cricket for the last quarter-century has been a little like a juke box containing only one song. If rain falls in a Test, the programmers screen Headingley '81. If gloom descends, they talk of Headingley '81. If the situation is hopeless, fans lie back and think of Beefy. If a fightback is attempted, the media invoke the memory of those few crazy days – not least, of course, Beefy himself.

With Trent Bridge '05, English cricket took one small step in the Ashes and one giant leap into the present. Edgbaston may have been a flash in the pan and Old Trafford an anti-climax had Michael Vaughan's team not continued their advance in the Fourth Test. As it was, they ran such rings around Australia as to almost render themselves dizzy and fall over in chasing 129. But their advantage was so insuperable by that stage that they could not blow it; it remained to be seen if the same was true of their series lead.

Shane Warne's pre-match promise of 'something special' from the Australians in this Test took a knock before it had even begun when his chief partner in bowling crime Glenn McGrath could not recover from an elbow injury in sufficient time to take his place in the XI. Michael Kasprowicz was thus spared omission, Jason Gillespie having already made way for the vaunted Shaun Tait. There was, too, very little of special quality from the visitors as Trescothick and Strauss added a hundred for the first wicket for the seventh time, abetted by enough no-balls to tire an umpire's arm, one of which bowled Trescothick. Strauss's dismissal was quite against the run of play, as it was the normal run of events: a miscued sweep ballooned to slip from his boot and a video deliberation was necessary to determine whether it had touched the ground.

After rain prolonged the lunch break, Tait atoned for a tame first spell with a testing second, bowling Trescothick and having Bell caught at the wicket. Vaughan and Pietersen needed to show some patience and care to prevent further inroads, until the captain's methodical half-century was ended in sight of stumps by his rival: Ponting's fifth Test wicket, and probably his best. It was a slightly uneasy and inconclusive day's cricket, always somehow holding something back: it was hard to remember a day on which Shane Warne took the first wicket of a Test yet ended up at stumps having bowled a mere six overs, apparently incommoded by back stiffness. The teams were pretty well deadlocked by stumps: one fewer wicket, and England would have felt satisfied; one more, and Australia could justly have claimed the ascendancy. When Pietersen's attractive innings ended after twenty minutes on the second morning, Australian might well have felt themselves slightly ahead, with England five for 241. Fatally, however, they did not act like it.

As Flintoff and Geraint Jones came together, the field was flung wide. Rather like Allan Border at the Gabba nineteen years ago when he made room for Botham's last Ashes hundred, Ponting eschewed catchers, posted sweepers, and seemed happy simply to quell a riot. He fostered instead a highly effective and increasingly ambitious insurgency, that swelled to become the biggest partnership of the series, worth 177 in 235 deliveries without the ghost of a chance. Despite the defensive formations, the English pair were never quiet, save for a short period as Flintoff approached his first Test century against Australia. Flintoff (102 from 132 balls with fourteen fours and a swept six from Warne) played the eye-catching strokes, but Jones (85 from 149 balls with eight fours) was a far-from-silent partner.

Some annoyingly useful and usefully annoying tail-end runs prolonged England's innings to just before tea after a tired shot and a smart return catch saw off Flintoff and Jones respectively. Australia's reply then began under somewhat darker skies than had prevailed for much of England's innings, and Hoggard at once began to obtain a degree of orthodox swing comparable with that obtained in reverse by Flintoff. Hoggard obtained 3–26 in his first eleven overs: Hayden and Martyn lbw half-forward, Langer caught at bat-pad after a crabbed hour and a half. Ponting succumbed to

Jones between times, and Clarke fell to the day's last ball after some crisp strokes. Australia's plight would have been worse had short leg Bell held a first-ball chance off the face of Katich's bat, but only a captious critic could have found fault with England's unflagging aggression: it was, dare one say it, almost Australian. Adam Gilchrist was the X Factor for overnight contemplation, especially as he promised at the close of play press conference that he would be aiming to recapture his intuitive best the following morning, but the odds on Australian victory might not by this stage have tempted Dennis Lillee and Rod Marsh.

With Katich as escort, Gilchrist did indeed make a belligerent start on Saturday, taking out recent frustrations on Hoggard. But he was greeted also by his nemesis Flintoff, who again cut him off in his prime with the help of a slip catch by Strauss that defied belief even in replay. Gilchrist's forcing shot was wide to the left of and slightly behind the catcher by the time he left the ground, yet the ball somehow sank into his left hand, and survived his return to earth. Time seemed to stand still for half a heartbeat while the impossibility of this catch was mentally converted into certainty. With Katich and Warne also gone by this stage, the cudgels were left for Lee to take up. He did so willingly, taking advantage of what was actually an easy-paced pitch, with some premeditated hitting: three sixes and five fours studded his 47 from 44 balls before his under edge was caught on the third man fence. It was not enough, however, to spare Australia the indignity of their first Ashes follow-on for twenty years; and, amid some surprise, Vaughan enforced it.

Vaughan's decision almost immediately suffered a blow, when Simon Jones, fresh from 5–44, left the field after four overs hampered by ankle pain. Anterior cruciate damage was diagnosed, and Vaughan lost his lucky five-leaf bowling clover. With Harmison in search of his former penetration, the burden of the pace bowling fell on Hoggard and Flintoff. The latter dismissed another favourite rival, Hayden, in an incessant spell from the members' end. But shortly after tea, two and a half hours into their innings,

Australia were 129 for 1, halfway to wiping away their arrears, with Langer and Ponting established.

Giles, finally thrown the ball after 78 overs of Australian batting, made the initial break when Langer thrust at a ball nicely pouched at short leg. Martyn then made England's day complete by calling Ponting for an iffy single to point, and pushing carelessly at Flintoff. Ponting transferred the fury he should have felt with his partner and himself to England because he had been thrown out by eagle-eyed substitute fielder Gary Pratt from Durham, standing in for Simon Jones. Australia's captain remonstrated with English players and snapped at their coach Duncan Fletcher about a custom more than twenty years old of using available specialist utility fielders from counties not engaged in first-class games during the Test. The nature of the protest was taken as more significant than its content: Ponting, it was the consensus view, was losing the thread. The Pratt Intervention, as it would surely have been called by Tom Sharpe, was the talk of the media at close of play, almost to the exclusion of the fascinating match situation. Thanks to an embryonic partnership of 61 between Clarke and Katich, Australia were 37 runs behind with six wickets in hand and two days to play.

The fourth day of the Fourth Test was a modern classic, the teams taking it in turn to impose unrelenting pressure. England were first, steadily exhausting the young Australian pair's scoring options. On 43, Clarke was dropped by Bell off Giles at silly point then edged between slip and keeper; on 46, he played three different shots at Flintoff, all unsuccessful, and miscued into off-side space; on 48, Bucknor gave him the benefit of a tiny doubt after a convincing Giles lbw shout. After 26 balls on the same score, he finally slogged, not altogether convincingly over mid-wicket, to reach a 134-ball fifty. Not until the twentieth over did he register the day's first boundary, an edge to third man off Hoggard; he was trying to repeat the shot just after Australia had crept into the black when he nicked Hoggard to the keeper with only ten minutes to lunch. Though his stand with Katich had been worth 100 in 285 balls over 190 minutes, his fall left much undone.

This brought Gilchrist for another classic duel with Flintoff either side of the adjournment. The great Australian drove through the covers and pulled for fours; Flintoff swerved a ball past his outside edge from round the wicket and stopped to give his opponent a pleasant but pregnant smile. After the break, he beat Gilchrist a couple of times more and followed through into the Australian's eyeline. Hoggard trapped Gilchrist next over, but Flintoff deserved a share. Again it was Warne who loosened the bonds restraining his team, twice hoisting Giles with stiff arms but plenty of bottom hand into the crowd, and working the ball effectively square of the wicket. But he lost Katich, vexed to fall lbw after soaking up 183 deliveries, and was finally lured fatally from his ground. Australia hardly appeared to have enough when England began its chase for 129, and even less when the hosts poached 32 from their first five overs.

Headingley '81, however, was now not being uttered as a benediction but as a curse, with jeremiahs pointing to the parallels: at Leeds, Australia enforced the follow-on, ended up chasing 130, made a good start but bottled it. And Warne might almost have been watching the *Botham's Ashes* DVD as a motivational tool. From the pavilion end where he took 6–33 four years earlier, he bounced into action, his first ball glancing from the face of Trescothick's bat to Ponting at silly point. When Vaughan then attempted to turn the first ball of Warne's second over to leg out of the rough, the Australians began appealing while the ball was still arcing to slip. Suddenly they were stirred – as excited as they had been for their entire tour. Warne ripped another out of the rough to Strauss that just carried to backward short leg, and had 3 for 7 in 29 balls.

It was the Radcliffe Road end that was causing Ponting problems. Although Lee had persuaded Bell to help a short ball down fine leg's throat, he had by now bowled eight overs. Ponting decided to risk Tait. It was a mistake, albeit an understandable one. The young man's first two practice balls eluded Lee at mid-on, sending the crowd into nervous hysterics, and he wasn't much more accurate when confronted by batsmen. His four overs to Pietersen and Flintoff cost a run a ball – the soccer chant of 'Easy! Easy!'

echoed round the ground – and Lee had to come back.

Yet no one was to be allowed to get any big ideas in this innings. The snick was accepted when Pietersen drove hard at Lee's first ball, ending a stand of 46 in 61 balls, and Lee beat Flintoff for pace and reverse swing in his next over. The tension was now palpable, and Warne played on it, endlessly consulting his captain and manipulating his field. Hearts fluttered, one of them Geraint Jones's: with 13 needed, he waltzed down the pitch to Warne and hit high rather than long down the ground. The Australians mobbed the catcher, Kasprowicz, as though he had just netted an FA Cup final penalty. Hands froze in applause, chants died in throats; even in the press box, heads hit desks at the thought of Warne the fox loose in the chicken run of England's lower order. No one wanted to hear a word about Headingley '81. England had just three wickets standing and one of these, Simon Jones, was only doing so with assistance: Strauss was padding up as his runner.

Giles had been dismissed by Warne four times in the series for 8 runs; Hoggard hadn't done much better. Lee was also bowling with tremendous pace. Yet these were the circumstances where a wrong 'un would have been very useful to Warne, and where Ponting might have encouraged Lee with a short leg. As it was, the tail-enders had only Warne's occasional straight ball to fear, and knew they weren't likely to be threatened by anything short. Defending his stumps from Lee, Hoggard was able to slot him through the covers twice; when Warne tried for a little more loop, Giles was able to reach a couple of deliveries on the full toss and work them to leg, the first of which hit short leg Katich but the second of which headed for the mid-wicket boundary to win the match. Giles, in fact, was awarded only two for the shot, because the match was won by the time the ball made the rope. But no pair can have added 13 weightier runs than he and Hoggard in the match's last 23 deliveries.

Winners really were grinners, as Vaughan led his team around the outfield at Trent Bridge to accept the crowd's salute and issue their own. The losers faced realities more prosaic. Ponting and Katich incurred fines from the ICC referee for four-letter responses to their second innings dismissals; Warne and Lee, whose appealing throughout the game contained more histrionics than a tele-vangelist's public confession of adultery, were lucky not to be with them. The lights burned late in both dressing rooms, and in the press box too, with Headingley '81 getting a few mentions but Trent Bridge '05 suggesting that in legend it had come to stay.

DAY ONE

ENGLAND 229–4
(PIETERSEN 33*, FLINTOFF 8*; 60 OVERS)

Before lunch at Trent Bridge yesterday, the Fourth Test might almost have been archival footage from the 1950s. The Australians emerged from the picturesque members' stand wearing their baggy greens to polite applause. There was a bit of swing. There was some leg-spin. And the back-foot no-ball law was in operation.

Except, to Australia's apparent confusion, it wasn't. In their first twenty overs, Australia's pace bowlers were called for overstepping eighteen times, as though they were being levied some sort of value added tax, or experimenting with a new EuroOver involving seven balls rather than six.

It bordered on the inevitable when Brett Lee, in the third over of his second spell, bowled Marcus Trescothick, then 55, off an inside edge with an illegal delivery, and Lee's surly scowl reminded us that was 2005 rather than 1955. The now traditional bogus umpires who sauntered onto the field before play began were charged with 'aggravated trespass'; Lee was lucky to escape a similar charge.

If we're talking luck, it's worth pointing out, Trescothick will shortly be pressing for jammy bastard status. This was his third such reprieve this summer: he was caught at third man early in his powerful hundred during the Natwest Challenge match at Headingley, and taken at backward point early in his 90 at Edgbaston. But Australia can count themselves extremely fortunate that this particular infringement cost them a net ten runs. It's getting to the stage that, to satisfactorily replicate the experience of batting against Australian bowling, England will have to complement Merlyn with a robot extending a mechanical arm once an over.

This is sloppy cricket from Australia; one might even use the 'u' word: unprofessional. But it also smacks of the same kind of arrogance that has the tourists suddenly wracking their brains about reverse swing after a decade in which it has been a significant factor in the game, and profligacy, like lighting cigarettes with fivers. Ricky Ponting complains in his most recent tour diary about fast bowlers in the nets who overstep habitually yet wave complaints aside on the grounds they will get it right on match day. He promised a 'zero tolerance policy' on foot-faulting after Australia's calamity at Cardiff against Bangladesh. Yet his bowlers, and apparently their coach John Buchanan, have continued to treat no-balls as light-heartedly as Colemanballs. Lee and Kasprowicz, as they were again yesterday, have been the worst offenders. Lee has bowled fifty-three no-balls and ten wides on this tour, Kasprowicz sixty-two no-balls and two wides. Just as well the zero tolerance policy was operating, eh?

Kasprowicz, as kindly a man as has played Test cricket for Australia, seems to be labouring under the misapprehension that the Laws of Cricket have been amended to include the Lord's Prayer: 'Forgive us our trespasses, as we forgive them who trespass against us.' The 13 runs he yielded in his eighth over included three transgressions. He would probably have been happy had the return catch he dropped from Pietersen (14) been called a no-ball. But – dammit – it was fair.

For a bowler who apparently left a trail of hoarse umpires across England during his brief spell at Durham a year ago, Tait was surprisingly gentle on officialdom yesterday. He, too, had a 1950s look – with his short hair, fresh face, gentle jog and low arm, he might easily have been answering to Lindsay Hassett – but had apparently been briefed on the law change. After four early no-balls, perhaps on the 'when-in-Rome' principle, he settled in snugly behind the line.

Despite clocking speeds in excess of 90mph, Tait looked to be bowling within himself, kept a respectably full length, and brought both to bear when he held one back to bowl Trescothick after the resumption. He was enjoying such a reverie after this first Test wicket that he began wandering to third man rather than fine leg, apparently forgetting that the left-hander was the one he'd just bowled, until Ponting steered him the right way.

Ponting himself then performed a surprise turn of medium pace, as though to prove that this bowling lark couldn't be so hard, and to demonstrate that he at least was comfortable with the front-foot no-ball law. Instead his first ball should have been called a wide – Steve Bucknor is now giving decisions so languidly that he might have been waiting for Ponting himself to give the signal – and his second was.

Ponting is actually not the worst bowler around. When his first captain Mark Taylor threw him the ball in his second Test, he winkled out Asanka Gurusinha, who had 143 under his belt. He obtained favourable bounce yesterday and a favourable decision against Vaughan. Bucknor will be getting a better captain's report in this match from one skipper than the other.

It was a tense day at Trent Bridge yesterday, in front of a surprisingly subdued crowd, apparently well aware of the stakes. As at Edgbaston and Old Trafford, every ball was potentially inscribed with significance and every event held the possibility of ramifying deep into the match.

Some prior events in this series, in fact, were already reverberating yesterday. Had Trescothick perished cheaply at Headingley and not made his first hundred against Australia, or gone early at Edgbaston rather than top-scoring, would he still have been in the England team? Had it not been a no-ball with which Glenn McGrath bowled Michael Vaughan at 45 going on 166 at Old

Trafford, would England's captain have been the stalwart figure at the heart of England's order yesterday? It's not as simple as saying that, in the end, yesterday's glut of no-balls only cost a few runs. They were part of a continued cycle of errors that has not just cost wickets but relaxed pressure, and unsettled Australia while encouraging England.

In a series as tight as this, situations are bound to fray confidence and induce mistakes. All the more reason, one would have thought, to work night and day on minimizing unforced errors. That's what modern hyper-professionalism is about, isn't it? Or maybe some 1950s thinking has crept into Australian coaching too.

DAY TWO

ENGLAND 477, AUSTRALIA 99–5
(KATICH 20*; 30.3 OVERS)

Australians adore stories about irreverence in the face of eminence and authority. When Dennis Lillee greets the Queen with 'G'day', we crease ourselves with laughter. John Howard would probably win a few votes if he mooned Kofi Annan.

When Australians themselves are the established eminence or authority on the receiving end of the irreverence, the laughs don't flow so freely. This has been Andrew Flintoff's gift to his team in this series. Australians now know what it is to be the butt of one of those jokes we're so fond of telling.

For years, aggression has been the traditional Australian vein, in deed, word and thought. Yesterday, again, what might be called the Flintoff Effect pushed them into an uncomfortable and unfamiliar role, straining to contain, against both their instincts and the grain of their recent experiences.

Brett Lee charged in, and Flintoff pulled magisterially for four. Shane Warne came on to bowl with his familiar pantomime menace, and Flintoff mowed him into the Fox Road Stand. Communing between overs with Geraint Jones, his happy-go-lucky partner in a partnership of 177 in 235 balls, he looked so relaxed that one expected him to start whistling. The only semblance of a chance was a mishit falling just short of Martyn in the covers; fielders always stand slightly deeper for a player of Flintoff's power, so he might be said to have made his own luck.

The coltish Shaun Tait enjoyed a promotion to taker of the new ball when another fell due, although that was the last part of the experience he enjoyed, giving away three boundaries to Flintoff in four balls in his second over: two pulls and a straight drive. The crowd revelled in the sequence, even offering a ripple of applause for the elaborate leave that punctuated it: evidence of discretion made the aggression doubly delicious.

The Australians played their best cricket shortly after lunch, when Flintoff was inching toward his hundred and Jones was momentarily becalmed. With great deliberation, Warne bowled a tantalizing maiden to Flintoff into the leg-stump rough, slipping past a back-foot force, and twice hit a thrusting pad.

When Tait followed with a disciplined maiden to Jones – part of a much improved second spell – it was hard to remember the last time Australia had actually made England wait for a run. Then Flintoff found a helpful leg-side gap to reach his century, and the pressure escaped like the steam from a burst boiler.

A player with the presence of a Flintoff, whose 296 runs this series have come at a strike rate of 79 per 100 balls, creates space and oxygen for others. Geraint Jones made excellent use of his slipstream yesterday, then created turbulence of his own. His 85 in 149 balls was an innings with its own delicious strokes, none more so than a lofted straight drive from Warne that Compton would have been pleased to play let alone Flintoff.

The fields that Ponting then set for Ashley Giles – 42 runs this series at 8.4 – were revelatory. Sweepers on both square boundaries.

A mid-on for the on-drive that Giles never plays. No gully and no third man for the open face shot that Giles does. One slip, which by Ponting's standards of aggression was bordering on felonious assault given that on several occasions he dispensed with slips altogether.

With 477 runs behind him, Matthew Hoggard then ran in like someone whose record against Australia was considerably better than 13 wickets at 47 each. He has grown rusty with disuse during this series, but with the lush outfield preserving the shine here found conditions more to his liking. Forensic examination of the lbw samples in Simon Hughes's lab apparently recovered some wood particles from the verdicts against Ponting and Martyn. Like dogs, however, stump mics detect sounds not generally audible. If you really wanted to be sensible about their use, in fact, you would turn off the one at the striker's end and rely on the one at the non-striker's end: it is the only location where the sound of a nick has any meaning. Mutter this the next time you pass a stump mic; someone with more influence than me might hear you.

The precocious Michael Clarke apart, the Australian batting was hesitant and uneasy, as though having stumps in mind from the first ball. Pads were involved in all five dismissals, suggesting that defence was the default recourse of each player. The Flintoff Effect was, perhaps, in evidence again: it is hard, once assumed, to break out of a defensive crouch.

The most aggressive aspect of the Australian effort all day was the appealing, which suggested a pang of nostalgia for the years when Terry Alderman had only to say 'good morning' to English umpires for them to raise their fingers.

Warne cannot clear his throat these days without it coming out as 'owzat?', and his appeals sometimes seem to be addressed to everyone except the umpire. His first lbw shout against Flintoff yesterday morning seemed either to be stuck on an endless loop or echoing off the Fox Road Stand's space-age roof.

Lee's response to the first ball after lunch, at which Geraint Jones played and missed, cannot really be described as an appeal at all. It was a sort of party invitation to the catching cordon with the promise of balloons and pop, umpire Bucknor being left in no doubt that he was generally being a bit of an old stick by not going along with it.

Not quite two years ago, the Australian team voluntarily signed up to a self-imposed code enshrining its own version of the 'Spirit of Cricket', including an injunction to 'accept all umpiring decisions as a mark of respect for our opponents, the umpires, ourselves and the game'. And although this was also a protocol under which Shane Warne also promised to 'value the contribution and sacrifice' of his family, the Australians have, in general, adhered to it admirably. Last year at Kandy, Ponting was given out twice by Dave Orchard, once lbw batting a metre out of his ground, once off his thigh caught behind, and walked off as though his middle stump had been flattened.

It might be time for this team to refresh their memories as to the contents of this document. The 'Spirit of Cricket' may, of course, contain an unwritten extra clause: 'In case of imminent Ashes defeat, forget all this poofter talk.' Or perhaps here is another old understanding fraying under the force of the Flintoff Effect.

DAY THREE

AUSTRALIA 218 AND 222–4
(CLARKE 39*, KATICH 24*; 67 OVERS)

It was the 97th anniversary of the birth of Sir Donald Bradman yesterday at the venue of his first Test century in England: the sort of historical resonance that usually causes an Australian cricketer's sap to rise, and reach for their favourite verse by Rupert McCall or John Williamson CD.

It did. Australia batted as productively in the second innings as it has since Lord's, and ended the day with Michael Clarke and Simon Katich in harness after the addition of an unbroken 61 runs. Whether this will be enough is another matter. There is peril in writing Australia off even now, but the historical antecedents might equally point England's way.

The last time England enforced the follow-on in an Ashes test was almost exactly twenty years ago: 31 August 1985, when David Gower was England's captain, Margaret Thatcher the prime minister, Hulk Hogan the ruler of *Wrestlemania* and Anatoly Karpov the world chess champion. If these meanderings sound a little disoriented, that is the sort of event that England enforcing the follow-on is.

Katich's batting bookended the day, and it was in both instances purposeful. With Gilchrist, he began the morning's play as though intent on wiping the arrears away by lunch. Hoggard's third over of the day vanished for 22 including two no-balls, three fours and a Gilchrist six beyond long-on. When Flintoff finally bowled a maiden to Gilchrist, it felt like an hour-long lull with piped music in the background.

The partnership had screeched to 58 at a run a ball when Katich went searching for one a little wider from Hoggard's replacement, Simon Jones, and speared it to gully. When the next ball opened Warne up and was miscued to point, the insurrection had been put down.

Flintoff again performed his party trick of snuffing out Gilchrist, from round the wicket. It was a shot Gilchrist need hardly have played, but above all a catch Strauss was hardly expected to reach. In fact, he executed the catch with the aplomb of someone who had been rehearsing it all summer, delayed the leap to his left just an instant, then arching his back like a salmon pushing upstream to stay airborne. The ball lodged in his left hand at the extremity of his reach. Strauss didn't so much thud to earth as bounce from it, as teammates flocked from round the field. When Australians used to take such catches like this, we used to nod sagely and say: 'Well, y'know, that's the world's best cricket team for you, eh?' Perhaps we still should.

Australia's innings was not quite yet done with, for Lee, whose impact on the series with the bat has perhaps been more profound than with the ball, plunged headlong into his highest Ashes score. His first six was into Fox Road, his second toward Radcliffe Road, and his third looked at last sight to be heading to Derby. Lee also manipulated the strike with skill. After Jones had reversed the ball past Kasprowicz's outside edge, Tait had to face only nine of 37 deliveries in the 43-run last-wicket partnership.

The pyrotechnics looked likely to continue when Langer flailed at the first ball of the second innings from Hoggard, which bisected third slip and gully on the way to the third man fence. The reaction, if not the stroke, set the tone of Australia's second innings, which seemed at the outset to be stopping only a micron or two away from harm.

Hayden lurched uneasily around the crease, occasionally toppling over like a tree under the axe. He played one splendid pull shot, then, as at Edgbaston and Old Trafford, began playing almost compulsively at deliveries of increasing width. When Hayden is batting these days, the area outside off stump has become a kind of traffic black spot. One waits with trepidation for accidents to happen – and so, again, one did yesterday. It would be illuminating to eavesdrop on Michael Slater's real thoughts about an opening batsman being selected for an Oval Test after averaging 30 in his last thirty innings.

Langer found himself in the kind of situation suited to his monastic self-discipline, and played with admirable control. He, too, lived a little dangerously. It being the way of these things, Strauss missed a chance a good deal easier than the one he'd taken just hours earlier, albeit at that awkward armpit height where catches sometimes look a good simpler than they are. Otherwise, Langer did not budge, flinch or even twitch. England were relieved when he offered Bell further bat-pad practice in the over after tea.

In the gloaming at Old Trafford, Stephen Peters did not quite seize a chance to make a name for himself by throwing out Brett Lee. In the cooler light of day, Durham's dead-eyed Gary Pratt punished an optimistic call of Martyn's by hitting the striker's stumps direct from cover to find Ponting a foot short.

Ponting stood by the ruined wicket while awaiting the third umpire's analysis in conclave with Aleem Dar, passed the time of day with a few of the fielders, then seemed to suggest to Duncan Fletcher that England's coach might be wanted in his own dressing room. As well he might: a coach never knows when he might be needed to demonstrate the front foot defensive shot.

In truth, of course, England's free use of substitutes has aroused Australian ire since the Natwest Series, when Vikram Solanki was like a bachelor at a ball, his dance card crowded with engagements. In truth, too, everyone takes advantage of the ambiguity of the law regarding substitutes. In 1981 it was Australia, when because of a pre-existing bronchial condition, Dennis Lillee seemed to be allowed to go straight from bowling to his personal sauna and masseuse. In this case, however, Simon Jones seems to have been carrying a genuine injury, as he went to hospital for scans on his ankle at the stage when England would have been glad of his bowling let alone his fielding.

The episode may be more enlightening for what it reveals of the present height of Ponting's dudgeon. He has been out of sorts since the first day, when he rounded on umpire Bucknor for having the temerity to call his second ball a wide; Australia's captain would have preferred something a little more PC, like 'ball of width'.

Ponting's ire might have been better directed today at his partner, who cantered off as though jogging round the block, and himself, who seemed a little surprised by the call because he was watching the ball and as a result was slow to accelerate. In other words, there may have been more than one Pratt involved in this interlude. It was a frightful waste of a wicket. Ponting had until then not made a mistake, and his pull shot for six from Flintoff was as delectable as the one he played on the last day at Old Trafford.

Martyn fell as Martyn does, flat-footed, neither forward nor back, too good to miss, not quite good enough to middle. It was left to Clarke and Katich to take advantage of the comfortable batting conditions: there is life in this match yet, and chasing more than 200 on Steve Birks's pitch against Warne will not be a pushover.

On the day that the *Daily Mail* made official that Geraint Jones's 'ability to score heavily outweighs his keeping foibles', he failed to stump Clarke when the batsman was 35. Press theses aren't usually submitted to such an immediate examination, but here is one to watch. Then, of course, there's that old Bradman spirit. Mind you, as tragics will already have been bursting to point out, Australia lost that Trent Bridge Test in which the Don made his first hundred. And the way this series is going, Hulk Hogan may be of just as much relevance.

DAY FOUR

ENGLAND 129–7. ENGLAND WON BY 3 WICKETS.

For the last three months this Australian team has been about to round a corner, sensing a big one not far off, preparing for something special and glimpsing a light at the end of every tunnel, as if to demonstrate that delayed gratification is always the sweetest.

By some measures yesterday, their performances did lift. Australia's second innings was its biggest, longest, most disciplined and determined entrenchment of the series. Shane Warne and Brett Lee then landed hearty blows on the inside of the coffin lid as the shovelfuls of dirt descended, and almost rose from the grave.

There is no point in restaging the withdrawal from Dunkirk, however, if one has already recreated the retreat from Moscow. For a decade, Australian bowlers, fielders and captains have been the most parsimonious in international cricket, yet England's first innings here proceeded as if unmolested by pressure. There was scarce evidence, likewise, of the Australian batting aggression that has caused the stoutest bowling hearts quail during the same period.

Ricky Ponting saw 'lots of positives' in defeat at Edgbaston, John Buchanan 'lots of good things' in the worse of a draw at Old Trafford. By these standards, the Fourth Test represents bringing home the bacon. In fact, the fat is in the fire: Australia will have to play out of their skins at the Oval to keep custody of the Ashes.

In the positive-accentuating Ponting-Buchanan spirit, however, some saluting is in order. For one thing, Michael Clarke and Simon Katich, with the patience of boys toiling over a complicated jigsaw, pieced together Australia's first hundred partnership since Lord's.

Clarke between deliveries is a hive of activity, as though trialling a new form of airport security involving self-frisking. Every accoutrement is touched, pulled, brushed and checked, often twice: helmet, gloves, pads, sleeveless pullover, even sweatbands. If Clarke was fond of personal jewellery, overs would take ten minutes each.

Yesterday, unusually, these pedantic rituals were the most animated feature of his batting. Having ticked over during his previous seven innings at a carefree 66 per 100 balls, he eked out his runs here at half that rate, giving Geraint Jones plenty of opportunity to hone his glovework when offered sufficient width, and languishing 26 balls on 48. It was, eventually, more than an innately exuberant spirit like Clarke could bear: he pursued a ball from Hoggard identical to scores that he had left and touched it fatally.

In circumstances better suited to his survival instinct, Katich also played his most assured innings for more than a month. He has struggled acutely since Lord's. To find England hooping the ball around in the middle overs normally given over to containment and consolidation has been a shock for him, like the bite of an apple that leaves the proverbial half a worm behind. The task was the intimidating factor here – and the task he could contend with.

Katich has a homespun technique including a stand-to-attention stance, a slice of eighties kitsch, and the shortest of backlifts, barely a flex of the wrists. Not a lot, though, can go wrong with it. He has been defeated by good bowling rather than individual shortcoming, having had to put out an all-points bulletin to ascertain the whereabouts of his off stump.

In this match, the ball has swung less, Katich's judgement has been far more exact, and his brand of crease occupation has shown up the headlong pace of most Australian batting this series: he eked out just 17 runs from 78 deliveries in the pre-lunch session, and his 50 here took as long as the tourists' first innings in the First Test.

Brett Lee again cannot be faulted for his contribution to the Australian effort. Everything he has done since arriving has been with incandescent intensity, even communicating his disappointment. When Shaun Tait exposed all three stumps to Steve Harmison yesterday to end Australia's innings, he looked ready to offer to offer the youngster a locked room and a desk with a pistol in the drawer.

Above all, of course, there was the talismanic presence of Shane Warne. He came out to bat when England must have thought they finally had Australia cornered. Instead, his hitting briefly endangered the Betfair blimp. Australians have lamented Adam Gilchrist's subdued batting series, but they have been lucky to find Warne in such a feisty mood.

His bowling then reflected Warne's deep and abiding disinclination, at least on the cricket field, to lie down. 'I hate losing,' he said during the Edgbaston Test with a conviction as vehement as his spin, and it has somehow become his soundtrack this series. From the moment he dismissed Trescothick yesterday, he orchestrated the occasion. There might have been no crowd, no television, no media, no Ashes. There was only Warne, a ball and a match to win.

Desmond Morris could craft a documentary series out of the difference in body language between Warne and his English slow-bowling counterpart. Giles seems to start each spell already weighed down by none for 100, as though born with original sin, and marks wickets with a look of almost manic relief.

Even when he has none for 100, Warne is the same predatory presence, pursing his lips, narrowing his eyes, moving fielders a yard to the right and a foot to the left for that perfect formation, rubbing his fingers in the dirt for that magic grip. Harold Pinter has nothing on Shane Warne for menacing pauses.

None of it, however, has been enough. It turns out that the decisive session – and one now reads these Tests backwards, like fiendishly complicated whodunits full of red herrings and false assumptions – was probably the first of the second day when Andy Flintoff and Geraint Jones made hay. By stumps that evening, the point of no return had been passed.

A common cricket expression when a good player is failing to achieve his usual level of performance is that he is 'due'. This now applies to more Australian cricketers than it does not. There is no delaying delivery. They have run out of corners, mislaid the big one, found only something passable, and misidentified as a light at the end of the tunnel the oncoming English train.

THE HUNGER

A good but not great Australian slow bowler called David Sincock once explained to me why he had retired young in the 1960s to pursue different interests. It was not the travel, the training, or cricket's relatively poor rewards at the time. What ground him down was the repetition. Having dismissed a batsman, he could not see much point in trying to dismiss him again the following week. Hadn't he done it once already?

Other factors probably also bore down on Sincock, such as the burden of bearing the nickname 'Evildick', but he had a point. Because their deeds are an expression of physicality, athletes obsess over staving off physical deterioration. Yet because no one draws on a bottomless well of motivation, only automata cannot suffer some sort of mental toll from the grind of professional sport.

When Steve Waugh shared his views of the Ashes series on BBC Radio Five Live at the weekend, his gaze fell first on the Australians' desire. 'They don't seem to have had the hunger normally associated with Australian cricket sides,' he said. 'From Australia's point of view, there have been a few injuries, too many statements in the papers leading up to the series. Actions do speak louder than words and they need to perform on the pitch.'

The final platitude aside, this was a damning judgement. Accusing an Australian team of lacking hunger is the gravest of insults, like saying that a marathon runner lacks stamina or a sprinter pace. That inextinguishable appetite for contest and conquest is what is meant to distinguish Australian cricketers from those of all other nations; hunger, too, is the quality that county cricket, the welfare state, warm beer and irony are meant to have sapped from the English psyche.

Does Waugh have a point? 'The hunger normally associated with Australian sides' is something that has started at the very top. Allan Border played fifteen years of international cricket without missing a tour, even a one-day beano in Sharjah. Unlike other captains of their time, Mark Taylor and Steve Waugh would no sooner have complained of too much international cricket than too much sun.

Ricky Ponting's Australians, by contrast, have sometimes looked very sated indeed, like those handsome lions in wildlife documentaries apparently always snoozing on the savannah after gorging on zebra. 'Hunt?' they seem to say. 'For another camera crew? Forget it. I only work for Attenborough.'

Rhetoric has been complacent; practices have looked mechanical; intensity has come and gone, in the occasional session and the odd partnership. With the exception of Shane Warne and Brett Lee, who again hurled themselves into the fray on the last day at Trent Bridge, Australia's cricket has been almost totally devoid of flair.

When heavy lifting has been in the offing, hands have been

scarce. Between victory in the Lord's Test on 25 July and the beginning of the Edgbaston Test on 4 August, for example, Lee, Warne, Damien Martyn, Glenn McGrath and Adam Gilchrist played no competitive cricket; Gilchrist even took his family to EuroDisney.

Leading the 1989 Australians, Border set out not merely to beat the counties but to thrash them, issuing a warning like a leaflet drop over the enemy's trenches. Ricky Ponting's team has cruised; the group that some saw as a threat to the unique clean sheet of Sir Donald Bradman's last tourists has won eight games, lost seven, drawn four and tied another.

If it is the case that the sheer humdrum nature of their task has begun getting to the Australians after a success-saturated decade, it would not be surprising; with a trophy cabinet full to bursting and an apparently permanent lien on the Ashes, what joy could be found in disposing of England again – the ninth time, for heaven's sake? They would, though, be a noteworthy casualty of the tide in the affairs of professional sport.

Big-time sport has been remarkably successful at turning itself into a species of labour – athletes are always promising to 'dig deep', dedicating themselves to 'hard work', and speaking of having 'a tough day at the office' – and far less successful at preserving its participants' spark of pleasure. In its emphasis on repetition, discipline and subordination to the group ethic, in fact, professional sport is not an environment naturally conducive to enjoyment, and can even become inimical to it. As British golfer Peter McEvoy once summed up the necessary attributes of the touring pro: 'You have to be the sort of personality that can make a Coke last four hours and be able to read *Golf Monthly* for the tenth time.'

The standard cliché of retiring athletes that 'the enjoyment has gone' is more meaningful than it sounds. Robert Smith, the National Football Conference's leading rusher in 2000, explained in his autobiography last year why he deserted the Minnesota Vikings aged twenty-eight: 'Meetings, films, chalkboards, practice – it all became very tedious for me. I had never been a big fan of football, and to have to spend all that time preparing to play a game really started to wear on me. It was like being caught in a remedial math class each week.'

Smith saw that an inability to turn up and do it again and again would eventually prevent his transformation from good to great; a version of a similar inability may, in the Australians' case, have dragged the great back to being simply good.

TAKE ME TO YOUR LEADER WRITER

An editorial in this morning's edition of the *Independent* in response to events at Trent Bridge is the latest contribution to on-the-run theorizing about the sudden popularity of cricket in England. It strikes the dispassionate, pragmatic, no-nonsense tone beloved of leader writers the world over: 'No doubt this renaissance will inspire cerebral discussions about what lies behind it and whether it constitutes a part of a wider revival of interest in all things English. We suspect it is less complicated. Cricket has become popular again because the English cricket team has rediscovered the formula for success. Quite simply, everyone loves a winner.'

At the risk of sounding cerebral – heaven forfend – this suspicion of the *Independent*'s seems entirely groundless, even wrong-headed. For one thing, what's happened this summer isn't a case of cricket suddenly becoming popular; it's an instance of the discovery, by some poorly informed people who know no better, mainly in the media, just how popular cricket is. The spectators attending the Tests bought their tickets months ago for a small fortune, and do the same every year: they have merely seen their abiding faith rewarded. If we take Johnny Borrell of Razorlight as our repre-sentative celebrity espousing a love of cricket and thus epitomizing its new fashionability, he discovered the game in 1997 and thus has lived through some very dark summers since, from the horrors of 1999 to the dashed hopes of 2001. There are many easier loves to nurture: if he had simply been looking to latch onto a winner, he'd have adopted the Chicago Bulls. And if winning was all that mattered to sport lovers, all spectators would naturally gravitate to those teams that do – which they demonstrably do not, otherwise the Boston Red Sox would have won last year's World Series amid funereal silence. In fact, the struggle is as meaningful as the winning. Just because the Aussie rules team I support in Australia hasn't won a premiership in my lifetime doesn't mean I'm about to drop them for Man U.

The editorial describes cricket as 'a once universally loved but now neglected national sport', and contends: 'For years it has been a poor relation of football, its decline symbolized by the falling number of children playing cricket at school.' Whether cricket was ever 'universally loved' and whether it is 'now neglected' by comparison, both seem debatable propositions. Football has probably been a more truly demotic sport for almost a century; the comparison is, in any case, flawed because it is of a sport where the loyalties are largely tribal with one where the allegiance is mainly patriotic.

What has failed over the last few decades, furthermore, has been not cricket but England's cricket team: there is a world of difference. The popularity of cricket at the grass roots is sensitive to a host of other factors before a country's fortunes in the international arena: cricket was withering on the vine in the West Indies even as its mighty Test XI thrashed all comers. And even if we are to accept a decline in cricket in England, at least in visibility, dwindling support for cricket at schools seems less likely to be a 'symbol' of it than a contributing factor. Cerebral theorizing has its limits, to be sure. But that is no reason to be as utterly uncerebral as the *Independent*.

DIARY

WEDNESDAY 31 AUGUST

While her father was touring England with the Australians in 1993, David Boon's daughter became increasingly agitated and fretful. 'Where's daddy?' she asked her mother eventually. 'He's been away so long – is he in heaven?' Well no, although he had won the Ashes, so perhaps he was close. In the span of a child's life, of course, periods of months can seem proportionally enormous. But in a cricketer's life they can too. Ashes tours are the longest of all and, even in this age of transcontinental jet transport and tele-communications, they can creep by: the same company and the same objectives inevitably start to pall. They might be travelling, but always toward essentially the same destination. Conrad wrote of sailors: 'Their minds are of the stay-at-home order, and their home is always with them – the ship; and so is their country – the sea. One ship is very much like another and the sea is always the same.' I think the same is basically true of cricketers. If you doubt it, I recommend Glenn McGrath's World Cup diary from 2003, a work as regimented as its author, starting every day with the alarm ('My alarm goes off at 6.30 a.m. for our 7 a.m. departure'. . .'My alarm goes off at 6.45 a.m.' . . . 'My alarm goes off at 6.30 a.m.'), and whose most interesting motif is an almost fetishistic fascination with the author's luggage ('After waking up and getting ready, I take my bags downstairs at 8.45 a.m. to be checked in and identified' . . . 'I wake and finish packing my bags' . . . 'I finished packing my bags and put them outside my door' . . . 'We're leaving for Port Elizabeth and our bags have to be in the foyer by 8 a.m.'). Travel narrows the mind wonderfully.

How does one remain motivated under these circumstances?

Some cricket might help. Australia, however, do not play again until a two-day match at the weekend against Essex, which suffices as their preparation for the Fifth Test. I understand the origins of the Australians' contempt for county games, but they did give a structure to tours, and vary the surroundings and the circumstances. Two-day games, which have been the vogue of this tour, are over before they begin, and amount to little more than a glorified net. They have also been an artefact of Australian arrogance. 'No one is good enough to play against us,' it seems to say. 'We are better off practising amongst ourselves.' The Australians have made this tour more monotonous than it needed to be, and it was monotonous enough to begin with.

THURSDAY 1 SEPTEMBER

Ricky Ponting's complaint about England's use of substitutes is steadily filling the controversy vacuum that the media abhors, and generating more heat than light. But it hinges on a question of cricket ethics that's worthy of remark: who actually determines the 'spirit of cricket'?

Ponting has spoken of a shared responsibility: 'I think it is an absolute disgrace the spirit of the game is being treated like that . . . It's within the rules of the game but it's just not within the spirit of the game, which is what we're all trying to uphold.' He does not elaborate on who 'we' might be. He could mean cricketers in general; he could mean cricketers in this series; he could mean Australian cricketers, because they have subscribed to a document defining the 'spirit' as they see it; he could, for all I know, be using the royal plural, and arrogating to himself the responsibility for moral arbitrations.

In a press conference at Trent Bridge, Duncan Fletcher implied that he subscribed to the view that defining 'the spirit of cricket' was the prerogative of the ICC referee Ranjan Madugalle. As Madugalle had said nothing, he assumed the spirit intact. Yet if a fielder claimed a catch on the bounce, a bowler blocked a batsman's path as he ran between wickets, or a batsman feigned an injury in order to obtain a runner, England's coach would presumably know that the spirit had been breached without having to ring Madugalle up and ask him to check the ICC by-laws.

It's hard to feel much sympathy for either position. In fact, the roles could easily be reversed. It doesn't take much imagination to conceive of a situation in which Ponting, say, defended Shane Warne from the charge of overzealous appealing by saying that only the referee's view mattered; or, indeed, Fletcher complained that Australian time wasting at Old Trafford violated the you-know-what. Morality is a fluid and contingent matter in cricket these days; we subscribe to whatever suits and excuses us.

FRIDAY 2 SEPTEMBER

Today marks a quarter century since John Arlott's last spell at the microphone, during the Centenary Test at Lord's, on the eve, of course, of Richie Benaud's valediction, to English audiences at least, at the Oval. Many would bracket them as the essential commentators of their generations: Arlott 'the Voice of Cricket' on radio, Benaud 'the Face of Cricket' on television. In fact, their commentary careers have been radically different, almost antithetical, to the extent that they seem to embody cricket's evolution and expansion.

Arlott, the policeman, the all-sport writer, the poetry producer, the aquatint collector, did many things; Benaud has been a cricket person man and boy. Arlott loathed travelling, and seldom toured, only visiting Australia once; Benaud hasn't experienced a winter since 1962. Arlott could be grumpy about modern cricket, once famously desisting altogether from commentating on a Sunday League match for several overs on the ground that nothing worth describing was happening; Benaud is a tireless enthusiast for the game of the present. They prospered as commentators, no less than cricketers do, by being in tune with their times and their audiences. Arlott belongs to a cricket embedded in local culture and local identity and conversant with its past; Benaud, a specialist and an internationalist, belongs to a game that has become a world of its own, existing in, to borrow Hobsbawm's phrase, 'the permanent present'. Whoever is the master broadcaster of the next generation will reflect the attitudes of the game and the values of its audience in the same way. Sky must hasten to recruit the members of the Big Brother household: individuals so dull as to make almost any game of cricket sparkle by comparison.

MONDAY 5 SEPTEMBER

To see the yellow shirts of the Fanatics sprinkled like wattle throughout English Test crowds, you would not have thought that this country was short of Australians at present. But so it would seem. In the next week, my diary contains two appointments with Channel Four, and engagements on the World Service, Radio 4 and Radio 5. Why? The answer is always the same: 'Because we are talking about cricket and need an Australian.' It seems like a bad sign if I am the best they can do, but it is also a reflection of the steady dwindling of the visiting press corps. When Ian Chappell's Aussies faced their day of destiny at the Oval in 1972, the travelling troupe of antipodean journos numbered about 30. Thanks to the steady consolidation of media ownership and decades of incompetence and meanness in newspaper management in Australia, only seven of my countrymen are reporting home on Ricky Ponting's Aussies doing the same. The print, radio and television needs of home are covered by Jim Maxwell for the ABC, Chloe Saltau for Fairfax, Rob Craddock and Jon Pierik for News Ltd, John Townsend for the West Australian, Adam Cooper for Australian Associated Press, and freelancer Brenton Speed who provides the news footage used by all the television networks. All of them are very good, all of them are terribly overworked; Cooper seems to be umbilically attached to his laptop. Peter Roebuck, meanwhile, writes for Fairfax when he looks up from filing for the *Independent* and the *Hindu*. And were it not for the *Guardian*, of course, I wouldn't be here at all; the BBC would probably be chasing Germaine Greer for her comments on sledging and the law regarding substitutes.

On Friday night, England's Cricket Writers' Club held their annual dinner at the Hotel Intercontinental. About 250 people attended, not all but the vast majority of them journalists; it was very convivial and very collegial. My *Guardian* colleague Alex Brown, here on a six-month secondment from the *Sydney Morning Herald*, commented that a similar dinner in Australia could be held around a table in a Chinese restaurant. Just remind me: which of our two countries is the sports-mad one with the world champion cricket team?

THE FIFTH TEST –
THE OVAL

8, 9, 10, 11 and 12 September 2005
Match drawn

RICHIE BENAUD – THE ORACLE

It testifies to the excitement generated by this Ashes series that it has overshadowed the knowledge of Richie Benaud's imminent disappearance from British television screens after forty-two years of deep knowledge, dry wit and sartorial idiosyncrasies.

When he seemed set to fade away following Channel Four's capture of cricket broadcast rights in 1999, allies ranging from Piers Morgan to Mick Jagger came together to protest that summer without Richie was unthinkable. This time there's been little fuss, no public campaign, no call for a private member's bill to ensure Benaud's preservation in the commentary box *à la* Jeremy Bentham. Perhaps after the Oval Test, 'morning everyone' will be replaced by mourning everyone, but this summer cricket has taken precedence.

There is no doubt that Benaud prefers it this way. If the master commentator has a motif, it is economy of gesture; as he sums it up in his new book *My Spin on Cricket*: 'Don't speak unless you can add to the picture.' A couple of days after the Trent Bridge Test, he is still pleased by the commentary spell with which he and Mike Atherton closed the match: 'We didn't say much. Didn't have to. Mike Atherton made one observation which was relevant to the situation. Otherwise, there was nothing to add.' When the photographer posing him suggests he imagine he is commentating on a dramatic Test match, Benaud says: 'If it was me, I probably wouldn't be saying anything.'

Benaud also points out that the past six years almost did not happen. When Channel Four won the rights, one way they publicly pledged to 'revolutionize' cricket coverage was by banning 'grey-haired old fogeys'. Benaud wrote in his *News of the World* column: 'I see that Channel Four are not going to have any grey-haired old fogies in the com box. I'm sure David Gower and Tony Lewis can look after themselves in this regard, but who else could they possibly have in mind?' A few months later, Benaud was having dinner in Canberra with his brother John when the phone rang: it was Channel Four, who had realized that even revolutions need some semblance of continuity.

It's Benaud, too, who has made the call about his commentary future, by deciding that he is a 'free-to-air man', and thus, although he will continue to work for Kerry Packer's Channel Nine in Australia, unassimilable into the new world of Sky. The designation 'free-to-air man' is one he cannot really explain. He believes that 'the differences would be considerable' in working for pay-TV, but cannot be specific, and finally concludes: 'Let's just say that at seventy-four, I'm in the mindset that having been free-to-air, I want to stay free-to-air.'

'Mindset' is a word Benaud uses a lot, and not insignificantly: there can be few minds so calmly set. I first met Benaud fifteen years ago, but this is the first time I have interviewed him. He has declined other invitations – with, it must be said, impeccable politeness, and no lack of generosity.

Some years ago, for example, I approached him while writing a social history of Australian cricket in the 1950s and 1960s. He said he would prefer if I submitted him a list of questions. I sent him seven pages' worth, and within the week eleven pages of single-spaced typewritten answers teeming with fascinating detail had arrived. Emboldened, I sent another four pages of supplementary questions; another six pages of answers arrived post-haste. Benaud can appear stand-offish, but I think he is merely careful. He leans forward throughout our conversation, perhaps imagining a microphone in his hand: commentary is so much a part of his life, it may now be his natural vein.

Certainly, Benaud's reliability and integrity as a commentator matter to him deeply. He explains that he relies on a group of close associates led by wife Daphne – whom he met when she was E. W. Swanton's private secretary forty-four years ago – to monitor his performance: 'I have a very small but very good cross-section of people who I trust implicitly. Daphne's one of them. With her background in BBC and in cricket writing and her knowledge of cricket and the English language, she is a wonderful guide to how things are going. There are others. Mr Packer would be very quick to tell me if things weren't going well, because he knows he can ring up and say: "Son, not too sure what was going out there. Perhaps you can advise me what the mindset was."'

The beginnings of Benaud's career, of course, date back to an era when the proprietor was always deserving of his honorific. He experienced his first media urges in the early 1950s when he was a junior accountant in the 'counting house' of the Fairfax media group in Sydney. He would drift upstairs to the offices of *Sporting Life* magazine where Keith Miller held court with three first-class cricketers turned journalists, Dick Whitington, Ginty Lush and Johnnie Moyes. Benaud would think: 'This is the most exciting thing. I'd love to be able to write like all these guys.'

Benaud applied annually for a reporter's job at Fairfax's morning paper, the *Sun*. For six consecutive years, editor Lindsay Clinch turned him down, not weakening until Benaud arrived home from a successful 1956 Ashes tour. Benaud recalls their interview with such evident enjoyment that he even permits himself a profanity.

'I s'pose you've come in to ask about your application to join editorial,' said Clinch.

'Yes, Mr Clinch.'

'When did you get back?'

'Last night.'

'That's pretty keen.'

'I'm pretty keen to do it, Mr Clinch.'

'Why is that?'

'I want to learn to be a journalist.'

'You want to fucking learn to be a journalist. Everyone would like to learn to be a journalist, *particularly some of those who are writing on this paper!*'

For the first few years of his career, Benaud was apprenticed to the paper's star police roundsman, Noel Bailey, chasing fires, car crashes and even the odd murder. Listening to Bailey dictate copy of perfect length from payphones with minutes to edition taught him the importance of not wasting a word: something that still characterizes his plain, spare prose, as well as his concise commentary.

Working as a columnist while he was Australian captain made him the object of some suspicion from a hidebound and parsimonious Australian Board of Control. In an age when Test cricketers seem to be issued a column with their cap, it seems astonishing that Benaud was in his time barred by board statute from writing about any match in which he was involved, even when he dashed off fifteen excited paragraphs for Sydney's *Sun* after the Tied Test.

'I got a letter from Barnesy [board secretary Alan Barnes] in the next post,' Benaud recalls. It said: 'I wish to remind you that you have broken by-law so-and-so by writing about what occurred in a day's play. Please do not do this again or the board will have to take action.'

When freed by retirement from the board's diktat, Benaud made tough calls as a journalist. He was at the forefront of criticism of Charlie Griffith forty years ago; he backed his brother John in a celebrated dispute with the New South Wales Cricket Association over footwear in 1970; he boldly fronted Kerry Packer's breakaway World Series Cricket in 1977. As years have passed, however, his pronouncements on the game have been less trenchant, more Delphic.

Benaud's great hero Keith Miller, thought 'too wild', never led Australia in a Test; Benaud's great friend, the gruff, insouciant Neil Harvey, did it only once in an emergency. How does Benaud feel, I wonder, about the likelihood that the best Australian cricketer of his generation, Shane Warne, will probably not captain his country for reasons that have nothing to do with his cricket ability or his leadership skills? Is cricket too precious about this stuff?

'There's no yes or no answer to that,' says Benaud. 'In 1999, the situation arose where either Steve Waugh or Shane Warne was going to be captain. I thought Warnie captained the Australian team side very well in the one-day games, but Steve Waugh was vice-captain of the Test team, and I saw no reason why he should not become captain. Ian Chappell thought Warne should have been captain, which is something he and I have discussed many times over a glass or two of red.'

But Warne was then Waugh's vice-captain, which must have entitled him to succession in the same way. Do you think his claims have been wrongly discounted?

'I wouldn't be prepared to say that. It would have been very nice to see Shane captain, and where he's had a chance to captain the side he's done very well.'

Warne looks, does Benaud not feel, like the kind of man around whom cricket teams rally?

'You may well be right.'

And there is surely something a little quaint about losing the Australian vice-captaincy for his peccadilloes while representing Hampshire?

'The only way you would find out about that would be to ask the board why they stripped him of the vice-captaincy. Whether you got an answer would probably depend on the libel laws.'

Do you think they were right or wrong?

'I wouldn't be prepared to answer that. You want me to answer that so you can get a headline or a lead-in to a chapter.'

I'm asking because I'm interested in your views.

'I've no views other than those I've given you.'

Such reticence about a subject that may or may not constitute a headline sits a little oddly with Benaud's forty-five years at the *News of the World*, where he bears an increasing resemblance to the pianist in a bordello. Does Benaud read the *Screws*? 'Mmmm. Yes.' What does he think of it? 'It's an interesting paper, particular to someone who's been employed longer than any other freelance contributor.' Care to add anything? 'I think I'll leave it at that.'

Benaud, likewise, is not to be drawn on the subject of relationship between television, inherently sensationalist, and cricket, inherently not. All he will say on the subject of behaviour is that players should mind their p's and q's. 'There are 15 or 16 cameras around now, and 24 or 25 tape machines,' he says. 'The players have to realize that everything will be captured.'

Does he not agree that broadcasters have something of a vested interest in playing up petulance and confrontation – things cricket would like to curb – because it makes good television? 'No. You might as well say it would be good if someone went up and punched the umpire every so often.'

Here, of course, I am missing the point. The game is not short of controversialists. There is only one Benaud. And shortly, in England, there will be none; another reason, if it was needed, not to miss this Oval Test.

EXEUNT OMNES

In early 1984, when the Australian cricket team was shaken by the simultaneous retirements of Greg Chappell, Dennis Lillee and Rodney Marsh, a group of their team mates fell into a dressing room conversation about the optimum timing of the end of a career. Should a player aim simply to go out on top? Should he play on so younger men had the benefit of his experience? How important was enjoyment? Success? Money?

The meandering debate was interrupted by Rodney Hogg, a player of much salty wisdom. What were they talking about? How many players ever enjoyed the chance to choose the time and manner of their leaving the game? Cricket, Hogg commented, would give them away long before they could do the opposite.

The Oval is traditionally English cricket's goodbye ground:

most famously, it was where Donald Bradman received three hearty cheers from Norman Yardley and one killer googly from Eric Hollies. But some less famous Australians will also be leaving it these next few days with a reminiscent glance over their shoulders, wondering if cricket's ongoing interest in them is a match for their interest in cricket.

The longevity of Australian players has been a source of wonder this last decade, with Glenn McGrath and Shane Warne making a specialty of bouncing back from the brink of baggy green bus passes. The team will probably take the field on Thursday with eight of the XI chosen for the corresponding Test four years ago. By the corresponding fixture four years hence, however, more members of this team may be commentating rather than competing.

Some have already fallen by the wayside. Jason Gillespie is known in the Australian dressing room as 'Jamaican Brown', for his preferred treatment in staving off premature greyness. If there is talk of him in the context of 'highlights' this week, it may be safely assumed to be those in his hair.

At his peak, Gillespie was a grand sight: athletic, elastic, hostile, beating the edge consistently even when not taking wickets. Yet no one's descent on this tour has been steeper, or begun earlier. Perhaps the first tell-tale sign that this would not be the tour Australians were expecting was Gillespie's expression as he returned to his mark after being hit for six by Aftab Ahmed in the final over to precipitate Bangladesh's coup at Cardiff. Where one expected anger or resolve, there was confusion. Gillespie looked like a singer whose vocal range had suddenly shrunk, or a comic whose best material was no longer raising a laugh. When Kevin Pietersen took to his bowling the next day at Bristol, the confusion had phased into panic. The Australians kept expecting Gillespie to return to his best; had they looked in his eyes, they'd have realized he'd given it.

Michael Kasprowicz and Matthew Hayden seem to fall into the same category. While Kasprowicz's 47 Test wickets at 24 last year were an unanticipated Indian summer for a justly popular team man, it has, like most Indian summers, been followed by a grim winter.

And if Matthew Hayden is back in four years, it will only be as the host of a cooking show.

If this much we know, some legends of this Australian team would even in the normal run of events be coming to the end of their natural lifespans. Glenn McGrath is unlikely to return; likewise Shane Warne, although the tabloids would probably be pleased to hold a whip-around for his fare. Before the tour, too, Adam Gilchrist admitted that he pondered the question of 'how much longer can this last' on 'an almost daily basis'. He was referring neither to *Neighbours*, nor even Rebecca Loos's celebrity, but to playing into his mid-30s. Gilchrist's wife, son and daughter have accompanied him on this trip, but such a Bedouin lifestyle will not long be feasible.

Lack of continuity between the composition of the Ashes tourists of 2005 and 2009 may no more be bad news than continuity between the teams of 2001 and 2005 has been an unmitigated good. If the team remains dependent on Glenn McGrath and Shane Warne in even two years' time, in fact, it would be arguable that something had gone seriously amiss with cricket in Australia. For this is a bigger story than an XI's comings and goings; Australia's selectors have to ponder how professionalism is affecting the traditional life cycles of their country's cricketers.

Traditionally, Australian teams have been naturally deciduous. Increasingly generous rewards have not made them evergreen. On the contrary, by persuading older players to play longer and compelling younger players to start later, they may be making true of the antipodean game what Australians have often alleged of county cricket.

This has not gone unacknowledged. Trevor Hohns has been an been increasingly interventionist chairman of selectors; since 2001, he and his colleagues have pointed out writing on the wall to the likes of the Waughs, Michael Slater, Darren Lehmann, Michael Bevan and Ian Harvey, and exercised increasing influence on selection on tour, traditionally the prerogative of the players.

The strangest feature of the Australian touring party when it was announced, however, was the presence of an uncapped reserve batsman, Brad Hodge, who turns 31 this year: an age when his countrymen have, in days gone by, usually been closer to concluding their careers than commencing them.

The age of the present team is not nearly so concerning as the ages of those considered its next generation: Simon Katich (30), Martin Love (31), Matthew Elliott (33), Michael Hussey (30), Andrew Symonds (30), Phil Jacques (26), Dominic Thornely (26) and Chris Rogers (28). The best-performing quick bowler outside this touring squad, Brad Williams, is 30; the bowling cover that Australia called up after Edgbaston, Stuart Clark, turns 30 this month.

Whatever happens at the Oval, there are unlikely to be wholesale changes in the Australian team. Part of Australian success has been about resisting impulse and planning transition. But by the Oval in 2009, Australians can expect to have seen considerable attrition in their national XI, natural and not. Some players face hard decisions. Others face having hard decisions made for them.

A MOST INGENIOUS PARADOX

With their flair for paradox on this Ashes tour, Ricky Ponting and John Buchanan have been giving Eco and Calvino a run for their money. Defeat? Full of positives. Possible loss of the Ashes? An opportunity for personal growth. Conceding 500 in a day to a mediocre county? All part of our master plan. As my great friend Alex Ferguson was saying just the other day . . .

Yet they may be onto something. The Ashes of 2005 contains one deep paradox: that despite being outplayed in every respect for a solid month, Australia have only been narrowly beaten, and might by now have retained the Ashes with a favouring breeze. As it is, they go to the Oval with the prospect of prolonging their custody of the urn and sense of innate superiority for at least another two years.

To rewrite the series this way would seem to require not just glass half-full thinking, but the imagination at work in Michael Craig-Martin's glass of water purporting to be an oak tree at Tate Modern. But it can be done: the Oval, then, is not just a Test, or even a series decider, but the key to a whole alternative narrative for the Ashes 2005 – a narrative, moreover, on which the futures of captain and coach may hinge.

Ponting's tour has been torrid for essentially one reason: he has not made his usual shedload of runs. Unlike his predecessors Allan Border, Mark Taylor and Steve Waugh, his authority is built around his productivity as a batsman. When he is not inspiring by deed, his rather formulaic captaincy looms larger. Easily his best day of the tour was the last at Old Trafford when his task was simply to bat, bat and bat. His worst has been every other day, when needs have been more complicated.

As for Ponting's tactics, there are some larger forces at work here. Captaincy is in the process of catching up with the extraordinary acceleration in scoring rates over the last five years, which has made a priority in field placing of reducing boundaries conceded.

As the tenets of one-day batsmanship have infiltrated Test cricket, so have those of bowling and fielding. Patrolling the square boundaries is Test cricket's new black; likewise long catchers to discourage the slog sweep. Catching cordons are more thinly populated. Short legs are waved back more quickly.

Michael Vaughan's cardinal virtue as a captain has been an inclination, even when attending to the priority of economy, to maintain attacking pressure; Ponting, especially when deprived of McGrath, has conceded too much too soon.

In an interview with a Sunday paper, Geraint Jones confessed candidly to an acute attack of nerves when he came in to bat in the first innings at Nottingham. Yet Jones would have experienced more pressure going to buy the paper to read what he'd said than he did in building his match-winning stand with Andy Flintoff, the biggest of the series.

Whatever happens at the Oval, however, Ponting is unlikely to lose his job. Australia does not reduce captains to the ranks, and the last to reduce himself, Kim Hughes just over twenty years ago, did not set an encouraging precedent, making 0, 2, 0 and 0 preparatory to accepting the Bacher shilling. Buchanan's position is less secure – paradoxically so, it would seem, given that the team during his watch has won 53 Tests while losing a mere 10.

Buchanan has tended to shrink a little from the designation 'coach', on the grounds, eminently sensible, that players at Test level do not need much 'coaching' per se; he sees himself as closer to a 'high-performance manager', attending primarily to grand strategy, philosophy and motivation. Players have prospered under a regime that encourages their free expression in different ways.

The question for Cricket Australia – to be asked sooner rather than later because Buchanan's current contract expires next month – is whether an overseer who is more help crafting a rhyming couplet than decrypting reverse swing is apt for a period of generational transformation.

The team on this tour has stumbled over details, like no-balls, that Buchanan apparently finds trifling; it has deteriorated in skill areas, like ground fielding and running between wickets, that seem simply to have been taken for granted; it has been undermined by an attitude that somehow England proposes and Australia disposes.

An Australian player was quoted last week as likening his team's plight to that of Ali during the Rumble in the Jungle – and we all know how that ended, eh? The Australians, the message was, were working to a plan so cunning that Blackadder would have stuck a tail on it and called it a weasel: lull England into a false sense of security by losing two Tests and then . . . well, what exactly? Pull a funny face? Put a whoopee cushion on the chair at Vaughan's next press conference? The clever, clever fiends.

Ponting and Buchanan have been quite right to re-emphasize at intervals that Australia retains a formidable cricket team. Only a formidable team could have come back with such pride and determination at Edgbaston, Old Trafford and Trent Bridge, and the alternative narrative of the series can still obtain endorsement at the Oval.

Australia's is a formidable team, however, with a bigger opponent than England: time. The team has been seen without McGrath this summer, to severe disadvantage; it has been saved again and again by Warne, who turns 36 a fortnight after the Oval. Their eventual absence will not simply rob the team of two great talents; it will irrevocably alter the team's dynamics. Over the last ten years, most particularly, young Australian players have had the good fortune to join a team in which there was no immediate pressure to perform.

An index of how quickly the world is changing can be deduced from the fact that Australia's 391st Test cricketer, Shane Watson, walked out to bat in his Test debut with Australia 471–5, while Australia's 392nd Test cricketer, Shaun Tait, took guard in his Test debut with Australia 175–9, trying but failing to avoid the follow-on. Whatever narrative one chooses for this series, this has been its subtext.

THE BIG BASTARD

Glenn McGrath was always a safe bet to please a lot of people at the Oval this morning. His playing would grant spectators the opportunity of saluting this generation's finest fast bowler on what loomed as his last Test appearance in this country. In the event of his forced omission, English supporters would have felt a great deal closer to the Ashes they covet.

That has been the way of it all summer long. The sensation that McGrath occasions in foreign crowds is that rare and special one of fascinated dread. Mick Jagger has put his name to a few clunkers lately – how bad is 'My Sweet Neo Con'? – but the other day he got England's Australian nemesis exactly right: 'That Glenn McGrath . . . what a bastard.'

Lately among Australians, McGrath has been a cause for a different kind of ambivalence. When playing, he continues to deliver, as he will be expected to today, with the reliability of a milkman dropping off the morning pint. When not, as during the Australian defeats at Edgbaston and Trent Bridge, he provides a window on a looming decade a good deal less promising than the last.

McGrath has been Australia's bowling talisman for almost the duration of his career. No fast bowler has played in more Test victories, 73, or dominated those wins so comprehensively, with 370 wickets at 18.61. Coincidentally, he and Shane Warne have played in exactly the same percentage of Australia's Tests during their respective careers (79.9 per cent); but McGrath has also appeared in 70 per cent of its one-day internationals against Warne's 62 per cent.

The summer of 2005 has demonstrated a corollary of this McGrath Effect. Deprived of his XL bounce and GPS accuracy, the Australian pace attack has had a makeshift look. McGrath's value is not only in the wickets he takes, but the over-ambition he encourages when batsmen try making hay against other bowlers.

The effect of his absence was most pronounced at Edgbaston, when he also encouraged overambition in his own captain. Having designed insertion with McGrath in mind, Ricky Ponting conjectured that it could be redesigned around the rest of the attack when McGrath was injured.

The decision to put England in would have been merely unwise with McGrath; without him, it made as much sense as *Charlie's Angels 2: Full Throttle*. Brett Lee opened with a wide, and Trescothick and Strauss had to play at only a couple of deliveries in the first three overs. Heads clear, arms free, they fetched 60 from the first hour.

The most compelling aspect of McGrath the bowler is that, in a sporting world in thrall to theories, jargon and doubletalk, his methods are so unadorned, so earthy. Asked to describe his technique, Jeff Thomson said: 'I just shuffle up and go wang.' McGrath isn't even that noisy; instead, the ball seems to come out humming, with trademark backspin that makes the seam bite.

There's nothing flash about McGrath's career either. He enjoyed no special favours or armchair rides. His home town of Narromine in country New South Wales mines a rich seam of sporting talent, having also dug up the likes of the sprinter Melinda Gainsford Taylor, rugby league star Dave Gillespie, target shooter Kevin Haywood and archer Jody Webb.

Yet no one sensed that McGrath was a coming man – perhaps he turned sideways at inopportune moments – until Doug Walters spied him bowling as a nineteen-year-old for Dubbo against Parkes and made enquiries.

The Barmy Army who keep querying Jason Gillespie on the whereabouts of his caravan have the wrong man. It was McGrath who occupied one on the shores of Botany Bay when lured to the smoke sixteen years ago to represent Sutherland in Sydney grade cricket; he still answers, occasionally, to the nickname 'Millard', manufacturer of the archetypal Aussie mobile home.

Even now, McGrath seems an unlikely cricketer. Like John McEnroe, he is ungainly and unathletic in repose, and only resembles a sportsman when in motion. In his baggy green at fine leg, he still looks like an overgrown schoolboy dealing with a recent growth spurt.

McGrath's batting, meanwhile, was until very recently the longest-running fantasy since Snoopy stalked the Red Baron. As a boy he scrimped and saved to buy a Stuart Surridge Jumbo in the hope it would make him play like that bat's great wielder, Vivian Richards; he just got out more expensively.

This unlikeliness is, however, part of the trap. Off the field, McGrath is open, relaxed, well-spoken, humorous. In the dressing room, he is playful, daft, and still perhaps the only room mate that Merv Hughes ever complained made too much noise. When he follows through to give a batsman the eye, McGrath still looks like someone who's imitating what they've seen on television rather than venting an inner rage.

Likewise, when McGrath takes a wicket, it is seldom dramatic, with stumps flying or quarry cowering. He always does just enough – and why do more? It's apt that Richie Benaud should be commentating today in his last Test in England, for McGrath is to bowling as his distinguished countryman is to commentary: the maker of small but telling differences.

McGrath is also 36 in February, and already the oldest bowler to take the new ball for Australia since Ray Lindwall in 1959. His chest-on action has preserved his back and his easy run has saved his knees and feet, but he has not been spared limited-overs duties like Shane Warne and Steve Waugh, and his ankles and his right elbow were trouble spots before this tour.

That, however, always made it likelier rather than less that he would play at the Oval. There is nothing like an impending end to instil the attitude that every opportunity must be seized, while Steve Waugh's against-the-odds comeback at the same ground four years ago and McGrath's Oval record of 14 wickets at 15.6 were encouraging auspices. A farewell to English audiences would not be chief among McGrath's priorities; preventing a farewell to the Ashes will matter to him very much indeed.

MATCH REPORT –
THE END OF EMPIRE

In some respects, the summer's climactic Test at the Oval was the fullest and richest cricket match of all. The game was seen in its every faculty and dimension. An excellent pitch was provided. There was sumptuous attacking batsmanship from Kevin Pietersen, plus some immensely skilled defence from Andrew Strauss, Justin Langer and Matt Hayden. There was swing bowling of the first order from Andrew Flintoff and Matthew Hoggard, while Shane Warne's 12–246 was a sublime exhibition of wrist spin. Weather played a leading role, as was always likely in a Test staged in September, and there was no result, so the match obtained the priceless distinction of being entirely inexplicable to Americans. In fact, no result was exactly what most people wanted. Some of the match's most memorable scenes were on the far side of the boundary where, on the second and fourth afternoons, people who had paid hundreds of pounds for their tickets cheered themselves hoarse as play was suspended. English fans waved umbrellas to persuade the umpires to remain off the field; Australians stripped off their shirts to bask in imaginary sunshine. When play resumed briefly on the second occasion, Ricky Ponting's team, wreathed in smiles, came out wearing sunglasses to a man. It was like a Test match staged at Wonderland Stadium, although everyone did not win and not everyone had to have prizes. At the end of it, Australia's hegemonic pretensions had been dashed, and the Ashes were England's after a gap of sixteen years. Writing this even now still has a novelty value. One could learn to like it.

The preliminaries to the Test were overshadowed by the tale of two injuries. Simon Jones was sealed in a hyperbaric chamber to cure his ankle impingement, but remained impinged, and it was decided against risking further impinging. Lancashire's James

Anderson was called up as pace bowling cover, but the selectors preferred to take an extra batsman and superior fieldman in Durham's Paul Collingwood. If not in the Compton's knee and Benaud's shoulder category, meanwhile, McGrath's elbow had become a kind of national vigil; the announcement of his recovery the day after Jones's failure to pass his fitness test seemed to pessimists decidedly ominous. Vaughan reassured them by winning what it had been conjectured was a crucial toss, and Trescothick and Strauss began the match as though to prove just that, sauntering to 82 without looking in the remotest danger. When Ponting threw him the ball at 11.28 a.m., however, Warne was at once the master of the situation, pitching everything in the area where the batsmen wanted it least, mustering close-in catchers like a kelpie. In an hour either side of lunch, he collected the wickets of an overanxious Trescothick, a casual Vaughan, a transfixed Bell and a fretful Pietersen. He was not appealing so much as detonating. Fielders rallied round him at every wicket, patting his back and mussing his hair as though to partake of his lustre. Strauss alone, pressing forward at every opportunity, looked equal to playing him.

At one time, Australia might have charged through such a breach in an English wall. Here they still had Flintoff to contend with. At Lord's, he had hardly looked like a Test match number 6, out of time and out of tune, his only scoring shot for the game an ungainly shovel. Now he brought with him a reassuring sense of solidity, perfectly happy to pay Warne homage, but irreverent enough to use his strength when it mattered. Strauss, who had been subdued, began to enjoy himself too; likewise the crowd. When Warne was finally given a rest after 18–3–52–4, the stand swelled further, to 135 in 220 deliveries of enterprising but controlled batting. Both men had fallen by the close, Strauss for a seventh Test century in three and a half hours with seventeen fours, but there was little in it. After an hour, Australia would have settled for the stumps score; after two, England would have done the same.

Although Geraint Jones played inside Lee's third ball on Friday, Australia were slow to amputate England's tail. Giles played some nice strokes, Harmison took three consecutive boundaries, and Ponting was dilatory in the field, as though quite happy to contain. The same feeling pervaded Australia's response to England's 373. Langer and Hayden, fortunate to survive a torrid spell before and after lunch, were painstaking in their approach, passing 50 in 110 balls, 100 in 181. Langer's only concession to attack was to slog two sixes from Giles's first over; otherwise he kept a low profile. Hayden, playing well within himself, showed the kind of humility he had lacked all tour. When they resumed after tea, they then accepted the umpire's offer of bad light – exactly, one imagines, as Vaughan would have wished them to.

In *Rosencrantz and Guildenstern Are Dead*, the protagonists muse that England might not exist; perhaps it is merely a 'conspiracy of cartographers'. Saturday's play, trimmed to 197 minutes with only 45.4 overs of the allotted 98 being bowled, looked suspiciously like a conspiracy of meteorologists. Langer and Hayden prolonged their stand – easily the most resilient and resourceful Australian batting of the series – to 185 in just under four hours. But the weather kept them in check when England's bowlers could not. Harmison broke through Langer's defence just before a rain break, Flintoff roared in to have Ponting caught fending with the second ball of a new spell and persuaded the batsmen to accept a light offer again. John Buchanan was buoyant at stumps, predicting another day's batting and the compilation of a decisive lead. But this was dependent on there being no further interruptions – rather like betting against Eddie Izzard ad-libbing – and on Sunday everything Australian reverted to its now traditional pear shape.

Flintoff had exhorted his team mates to leave their last ounce of energy on the ground in fighting this game out; like every great player, he made this a case not simply of do as I say but do as I do. He resumed on the fourth morning in murk with a hint of drizzle – and simply did not stop. On Flintoff's only tour of Australia, he arrived unfit, became still less fit, and was finally fit only to go home just after Christmas. His closest friends would surely not have bet on his ability to last this series as a key bowler, let alone finish it with an 18-over spell of 4–38, interrupted by stumps and lunch, that went on like a bottomless cup of coffee. Having seen off a fending Martyn, Flintoff took the new ball and would not let it go, defeating Hayden's drive, Katich's push and Warne's pull. At the moment they wanted to accelerate, Australia were pinioned. The Red Bull ads that kept flashing on the screen seemed the acceptable face of product placement.

There was excitement in the air as well as mist. English disbelievers were coming round; believers were feeling vindicated. Outside Oval tube station yesterday morning stood a lugubrious man holding a card reading 'One ticket wanted for English masochist.' *Le vice anglais* had made a comeback: support for England's cricket team, that is. In fact, for English fans, Sunday proved a day of hugely enjoyable sadism. What Flintoff had started, Matthew Hoggard finished with some splendid swing bowling, and Giles made an awkward running catch on the mid-wicket boundary to finish the innings look easy. Strauss could not cope with the combination of Warne and rough, but the light closed in patriotically at 3.42 p.m. when England's innings was just 13.2 overs old, and play was finally abandoned at 6.15 p.m.

England had a final 98-over day to endure. Vaughan made a firm start, punching the second ball straight for four, but when Warne resumed after two overs from Lee he immediately obtained plumes of dust and prodigious turn from the footmarks. It was McGrath, largely anonymous until now and short of fitness, who gained Australia its first two breaks, exploiting the off stump fallibilities of Vaughan and Bell in consecutive deliveries. But it was Warne and Lee who held Australia's destiny. Like the security Green Team that formed a cordon round the pitch at every interval, they constituted the green and gold team protecting the Ashes.

The hour before and after lunch decided the match's fate. Patient defensive innings by Trescothick, Flintoff and Collingwood were ended by Warne, but Pietersen survived, sometimes stretching credulity as he did so. His first ball travelled to slip from his shoulder – men had been given out in this series with less cause, but Bowden correctly spared him. He was still 0 when narrowly missed off Warne by Hayden at slip, 10 when he just escaped being run out by Clarke's direct hit from mid-on, 15 when he was palpably dropped by Warne himself off Lee. He made Warne regret his error with a kind of messianic self-belief, essaying his step-and-fetch slog sweep twice in an over for six, missing a third attempt, playing a defensive shot as a concession to convention, and calling for a new bat perhaps as a gesture to his sponsors; Pietersen's thoughts are never easy to follow, even to himself. After the break, he was involved in the contest of the match, hooking compulsively as Lee bowled very fast and very short, hitting two sixes and a four which Tait almost turned into an amazing outfield catch. At times, he lapsed into almost monastic restraint, padding Warne away over and over. At others, he was a hyperactive blur, pulling another six from Lee to become the highest scorer of the series and celebrating with another back over Warne's head. Tait removed Geraint Jones with a ball that kept low, but Giles now enjoyed his best day's batting in Test cricket, playing irreproachably straight. Indeed, it is surely some sort of comment on the breadth and depth of cricket character that England should be saved thus: by a gentle introvert from Chertsey who is every inch yeoman stock, and a brash cove from Pietermaritzburg as assimilated into his place of residence as Sir Les Patterson.

Towards the end of a 31-over spell that was almost a sentence, Warne began to tire; finally he retreated toward the third man boundary where he might have cut a rather lonely figure had the crowd not volubly kept him company. In fact, in their moment of defeat, the Australians won many friends with their deportment. There was no truculence, no sullenness; there were many smiles, not at defeat, but at the prodigies of the game they play. Some of them, of course, will not be back. And it was time for some other farewells too: the last dismissal which Richie Benaud commentated on English television was Pietersen's after an innings of fourteen fours, seven sixes, 187 balls and 285 minutes.

Only the whimper-not-a-bang end of this series did not become it: Warne came back to polish off the tail, and the light was too bad for Australia's batsmen once Harmison had bowled three bouncers.

There was a strange wait and a festive buzz while the umpires decided whether play could resume, until finally a huge cheer rent the air as Koertzen and Bowden uprooted the stumps. It seemed to be taking security rather too far to not allow spectators to walk over the field in the game's aftermath, and the few invaders were summarily, if not tactlessly, dealt with. The English players made up for this by visiting every quarter of the ground and reciprocating the crowd's tributes, a process that continued into the next day when tens of thousands turned out to throng the team in Trafalgar Square. It wasn't a bad choice of location for the celebration of an English victory with one crucial difference. Two hundred years ago, England had expected; in 2005, it had hardly dared.

DAY ONE

ENGLAND 319–7 (JONES 21*, GILES 5*; 88 OVERS)

When Australian film-makers churn out their monthly documentary about Sir Donald Bradman, they often make up for the general shortage of archival footage by dwelling on a famous newspaper poster bearing the headline: 'Bradman v England'. Shane Warne has by now more than deserved the same.

The Australians bounded from the Bedser Stand like a team on a mission yesterday – as well they might have. The captain seems to want substitutes to present their passports and drivers' licences before coming on the field. Their coach could not be under more scrutiny had he started checking into hotels as Mr Eric Jones.

Warne, by contrast, has very little to prove – on the cricket field anyway. He could pass away tomorrow, leaving his spinning finger to Lord's and his texting thumb to science, and remain a cricket immortal. Yet the occasion made his competitive sap rise; once he came on after an hour, only dull convention prevented his bowling from both ends.

Warne struck first in his third over, continuing his unusual toxicity to Marcus Trescothick in Tests; unusually for an opener, he has only fallen more often to Makhaya Ntini. Well, not so unusually, given that Trescothick even finds it hard coming forward to the drinks tray.

Michael Vaughan then struck a fearsome blow against the Kansas Board of Education. It was twenty minutes to lunch when England's captain tried tugging a short leg break against the spin, hit it in the air as his regrettably casual habit, and was neatly caught at mid-wicket: no evidence of intelligent design behind that shot; perhaps Yorkshire teaches flying spaghetti monsterism.

When Warne bowled to Ian Bell, there was barely time to remember that the batsman's Test batting average coming into the Lord's Test was 297 before it had been further reduced to 46.8. It took Warne eleven deliveries to trap his young opponent with a straight delivery at Lord's; here it took two. Merlyn's manufacturers will not be turning to Bell for an endorsement.

Three for 11 in twenty-two deliveries: Warne never looks bored on a cricket field, but now he was positively snatching off his hat as each preceding over ended and he headed for the umpire. He polished the ball as though it was a family heirloom. He posed and pursed his lips like he'd taken some lessons from Graham Norton on Monday night.

There is simply no more spellbinding bowler in the game. Warne has, we are often reminded, basically two deliveries – one that turns, one that doesn't. But he no more needs additional variation than the Ramones needed a third chord. Yesterday he came at the batsman from every angle, over and round the wicket, close to the stumps and wide of the crease, with the arm high and low, slower and faster, higher and flatter. He even bowled a string of googlies, including one which turned as slowly as an old watch and elicited a laconic smile from Strauss.

Warne's *jeu d'esprit*, however, was reserved for Kevin Pietersen. Warne greeted his old mucka with two mid-wickets, one-third and two-thirds of the way to the boundary. The first, Katich, soon became short leg; the second, Clarke, remained in place. The slog-sweep, which Pietersen has played so profitably, thus remained an option, but a risk if mishit. On top of this pressure, Warne then fastened the seal of precision. His first over to Pietersen, deadly accurate, was a maiden – in a series in which they have been so scarce, a gauntlet thrown down.

Pietersen did not score from the first dozen deliveries he received from Warne, then in resisting the impulse to hit over the top botched a whip to leg. Warne's thinking was not, perhaps, exceptional; his delivery was not, ultimately, a candidate for ball of the twenty-first century. But if you seek a reason for Warne's 616 wickets, it is the ability to lay a snare like this in the decisive Test of an Ashes series, when others' hands are clammy and trembling.

Warne might have run amok but for Andrew Strauss, who repented earlier misspent days on the back foot to leg spin. Yesterday his first movement to Warne was always forward, pad closely escorting the bat when it wasn't leading the way. If this testifies to its influence, Merlyn deserves at least a Level 2 coaching certificate.

Andy Flintoff, who used to confront slow bowling as though he had just consumed a crate of his Red Bull sponsor's product, also proved to have learned a trick or two. Some cricketers' capabilities fill you with awe; Flintoff makes it look as though you could have a bit of a go at this Test cricket lark yourself. Three consecutive boundaries from Warne were followed by an almost parodic defensive shot and a genial smile, as if to share a joke between them about what a funny old game this cricket can be. When Flintoff just laid a bat on a quicker ball that took a thick inside edge to fine leg, he again smiled at Warne, this time more furtively, acknowledging that the joke had almost been on him.

As Strauss and Flintoff survived the afternoon, Warne's yakka grew harder. On several occasions, he went past the bat and began to jump about like a child on a bouncy castle. His competitive effervescence is such that it spills over at the slightest knock.

When Strauss finally exposed his bat while pushing forward, Warne had taken more wickets in a five-Test Ashes series in

England than any Australian. *Wisden* does not enumerate all the occasions on which a leg spinner has taken three wickets before lunch on the first day of a Test. Warne makes you think of stats nobody records, because they are so extraordinary it never occurred to anyone to keep them.

Three more wickets and Warne will have dismissed more Englishmen than any other bowler. He will get them too. The other newspaper poster on which the documentary makers lovingly dwell is 'Bradman Bats and Bats and Bats and Bats'. By the time he's finished here, Warne will also have deserved the bowling equivalent.

DAY TWO

ENGLAND 373, AUSTRALIA 112–0
(LANGER 75*, HAYDEN 32*; 33 OVERS)

Over the last couple of days, Australians have been mourning the death of Donald Horne, the public intellectual who forty years ago settled on their country the mantle of 'the lucky country'. Horne intended the description as a rebuke; Australians, to his chagrin, basked in it as a compliment.

Ricky Ponting's Australians haven't had much reason to imagine themselves as lucky on this tour, losing Tests by two runs and three wickets. In this game, however, their luck has started to turn. Since losing the toss, they have been ceded advantage by England's top order, gained a couple of poor lbw decisions and escaped experiencing their own, while the catch they dropped cost nothing.

Matthew Hayden might have nicked half a dozen deliveries either side of lunch yesterday, and twice almost dragged pull shots onto his stumps, but has now groped his way to within a few runs of his highest score of the series. Justin Langer might have been caught at the solitary slip when 53, and should have been found out of his ground at 65. Mind you, a Geraint Jones stumping victim these days would wonder what he'd done wrong in a previous life. England's keeper is standing so far back from the stumps to Giles that he almost needs a modem to get the ball back to the bails.

One run later, Giles had what looked to be a good lbw appeal against Langer turned down. Close examination on the press box television revealed that the winner was Sendintank in the 2.45 from Doncaster. If the third umpire relied for his feed on Channel Four, he would probably fill in a form guide rather than a scorecard.

Good luck, of course, is all about the feeling of it, and Langer could hardly help feeling that the Oval was a kind of home away from home. It was here four years ago that he revived his Test career by displacing Michael Slater and scoring a hundred as an ersatz opening partner for Hayden. Their partnership of 158 that day was striking in its belligerence, with both batsmen expediting the celebrity career of Phil Tufnell by sweeping him brutally. Attack became the motif of their pairing, as they turned their improvised arrangement into a permanent coupling.

Their fourteenth opening partnership of more than a hundred, by contrast, was perhaps their most painstaking. While Langer has been in reasonable nick, Hayden has been an ever-shortening shadow of his former self. One factor that has not changed throughout Hayden's run of outs, however, is Langer's belief in him. Even at Trent Bridge, Langer was telling anyone who would listen not to 'write off a champion', and that he had 'seen glimpses' of the Hayden of yore.

People claim to have seen the face of Jesus in a tortilla and of the Virgin Mary in a grilled cheese sandwich, so these visions could not be dismissed out of hand, but they had certainly escaped everybody else's detection. Langer, though, could be thought not only to have the best view of his partner and best insight into his thinking, but the keenest sense of how quickly a batsman's luck can turn around.

Whether the Australians quite deserve a change of luck is another question. Their cricket before noon as England's tail wagged yesterday was ordinary verging on poor, particularly when Rudi Koertzen failed to RSVP his invitation to a caught behind party in which Ashley Giles was special guest. Glenn McGrath, who had come capering down the pitch to have his health toasted by the slips, turned in disbelief, and had a flounce that would not have disgraced a supermodel: a kaleidoscope of bewilderment, consternation, fury, then, incongruously, suppleness, for he finished the performance by bending to touch his toes.

A limber physical specimen, McGrath can actually reach 30cm past his feet. He was, however, so supple as to be able to reach out and accept his cap from Koertzen en route to fine leg as the over ended. One wondered yet again how the ICC polices the size of sponsors' logos so vigilantly, yet allows players to stage demonstrations that rival Camp Casey.

The last twenty-five minutes of England's innings were then marked by some further leaves from Ricky Ponting's edition of *The Art of Captaincy*, which has been bowdlerized of the racy passages regarding attack. The best fast bowler of his generation bowled to Giles with one slip and seven men on the fence. The greatest leg spinner of all time began to Harmison with four men back and no bat pad fielder. Had Vivian Richards been at the crease, deep fine leg would probably have been pushed back into a hospitality suite and the off-side sweeper posted near the Tenison's School bus stop.

Was Ponting trying to flush out a declaration? Did he want to give his fielders some throwing practice? If you could see the sense in this passage of play, you were a very, very deep reader of the game. Or one of those people who sees Jesus in a tortilla.

The biggest variable in this game, as we were always told it would be, is now weather. Some English pessimists would have been quite happy had this Test been scheduled at the New Orleans Superdome.

Here Australia may be misspending their recent good fortune. The time lost after tea will have vexed them. Langer and Hayden probably would not have accepted the light offer had they known it would cost them the rest of the day, but they must also have known it was a risk. Australia is the team needing the result here, yet seemed happy enough to indulge the team that didn't. In a Test in September, it would seem a pretty good rule of thumb to try to continue through any light remotely playable. More severe precipitation today and it won't just be the Ashes that changes hands but maybe the mantle of 'the lucky country' too.

DAY THREE

AUSTRALIA 277–2 (HAYDEN 110*, MARTYN 9*)

Scorelines such as Australia 185–0 and 264–1, incongruous this summer but in their time as routine as 'lbw b Alderman', made a belated reappearance at the Oval yesterday afternoon. But England would also not have been entirely displeased by a day on which eyes were trained as anxiously skywards as they were on the field of play.

Justin Langer and Matthew Hayden recovered some of their former harmony by prolonging their partnership to 185, an Australian record at the Oval and a testament to their understanding. Both scored hundreds. The tide in English luck in this series also continued to ebb: the only person who did not believe that Langer was lbw to the day's first ball and that Ponting was not caught at short leg after tea was the only one who mattered, Billy Bowden.

In the Test overhead, however, the clouds scudded England's way, for a delayed start and three interruptions trimmed the day to 197 minutes, with only 45.4 overs from its adjusted allocation of 98 being bowled. It is almost as though the individual that Shane Warne calls 'the man upstairs' and Bowden calls 'my third umpire' will only accept this series being decided in the last hour of the final day.

Once the early rain cleared, Australia's openers continued their steady progress. In what soon became Australia's biggest partnership of the series, Langer was clearly the senior partner, like daring Dash dragging Mr Incredible into the fray. He punched hard into gaps, flickered fast between wickets, and continued to grow in historic stature: his tenth boundary brought his 22nd Test hundred, his eleventh a 7000th Test run that took him past Sir Donald Bradman's long-standing run benchmark.

Hayden was content to cruise along in Langer's slipstream, secure enough without ever quite finding touch. He pulled Harmison's first ball for a succulent boundary before lunch, and clubbed Hoggard through cover in the air in reminiscent vein a few overs later, but otherwise played within the limits against which he has tended to fight for the last year. He might have been both caught and run out by Collingwood in the first half hour, then on 46 parried Hoggard just wide of Strauss at second slip.

For a time, England looked bereft of ideas, with the Australians content to simply keep Flintoff at bay. England did not sniff a breakthrough until Harmison, who had bowled to the openers as though someone was waving his passport at him, suddenly found a yard. His fifth over of the day had everything: eleven runs including two bouncers called wides, and a third, pedantically, a no-ball. For once, however, Harmison did not begin pining for his fireside and village pub; he became faster with each succeeding ball, and finally barged through Langer's defence, like a nightclub bouncer bursting through a crowd.

Then came the rain, if not in the copious quantities one had been led to expect by climatologists, but quite sufficient for England's needs, and a growing impediment to Australia's hopes. Usually under these circumstances, crowds grow restive; for fairly obvious reasons, onlookers at the Oval looked most cheerful when their umbrellas were open. Some had written 'Bad Light?' on the reverse of their '4' and '6' cards.

Neville Cardus wrote a piece for the *Spectator* in 1964 where he described the changing humours of the crowd at the summer's Lord's Test. All the while play was in progress, they bleated and bickered about the appalling standard of England's cricket, the dreadful strokes and abysmal bowling through which they were suffering. Rain was no intrusion; on the contrary, it was a welcome respite from workaday care. Everyone cheered up. People talked to their neighbours. Conversation turned to happier matters. Cardus claimed that he had not seen Londoners so united since the Blitz and, struck by the contrast, fantasized of cricket grounds where it would be guaranteed that no play would take place, with perhaps a band to provide a cheery soundtrack. At last, perhaps, Cardus's idea has taken root.

The break also allowed the security Green Team to reinvade the square, where they have developed a curious habit of remaining until not only the fielders are in position but the batsman have arrived in the centre. One almost expects them to run a metal detector over the umpires and demand that the batsmen account for those suspicious bulges. 'Thigh pad? Turn it up. That's what all the holy warriors say.' While everyone is bound to feel safer for the protection of the thin green line, the risk of suicide streakers might be felt to have fallen since the weather got colder. Perhaps the Green Team could be redeployed more gainfully guarding the man-of-the-match votes and the upright urinals – bound to be considered profane by extremists because of their savour of democracy and bodily secretions.

While the rain was a welcome opportunity for England's four-man attack to recharge, its effect on the outfield was to reduce the chance that reverse swing would be a factor. Hayden duly picked up the pace after the interruption, and began to look more like the batsman who averaged 70 for forty-two innings in the middle of his career rather than one who had not reached 70 for his last thirty innings. Harmison was pulled eagerly. What used to be the most damaging sweep in the world reappeared. The luck continued. In the same over as Bowden failed to detect a thick inside edge onto Ponting's pad caught by Bell at silly point, Hayden's outside edge bisected keeper and slip. Giles, in fact, did rather well to contain himself: had Warne been the bowler, the stump mics might have to have been muted for the next half-hour.

Flintoff finished the day with its best spell, breaking 90mph, and proving that Martyn possesses the quietest edge in international cricket: those off the inside of the bat went undetected at Old Trafford and Trent Bridge; the outside is apparently just as muffled, for not even the slips picked up the fine nick to the keeper when the batsman was 7. Flintoff's hostility had one reward, however, encouraging Hayden and Martyn to come off for bad light at 6.25 p.m. with 6.2 overs remaining. Given that this has been a series of such fine differences, turning on single decisions and handfuls of runs, the batsmen's was a strangely unambitious decision. The scoreline of this series is still wide open, but Australia's ability to alter it diminishes ever so slightly with each passing minute.

DAY FOUR

AUSTRALIA 367, ENGLAND 34–1
(TRESCOTHICK 14*, VAUGHAN 19*; 13.2 OVERS)

In his exclusive column in the *Observer* yesterday morning, Australian coach John Buchanan revealed his team's battle plan for the rest of the match in intimidating detail. The two days' play remaining would be divided thus: 30 overs to overhaul Australia's 96-run deficit, 60 overs to pile up a 300-run lead, 90 overs to bowl England out in plenty of time to fire up the barbecue and enjoy a few quiet ones. 'I'd say our position is getting stronger, no doubt,' he concluded.

This is what happened instead: Australia lost 7 for 44 in 90 balls, yielding England a six-run lead that they had built to 40 with nine remaining wickets by the premature close, when the light closed in patriotically at 3.42 p.m. when England's innings was only 13.2 overs old. Mystic Meg's job is safe; Buchanan's looks less and less so.

Australia certainly stuck to its scheme, Matt Hayden and Michael Clarke electing to continue batting at 11 a.m. in light barely good enough for a dark satanic mill let alone a cricket match. This was another battle plan, however, that did not survive contact with the enemy, for Duncan Fletcher and Michael Vaughan had hatched a rival compelling in its simplicity: (1) keep throwing it to Fred; (2) And, errrr, that's it.

It was a little more cunning than that, of course, for part of its cleverness lay in the appearance of having sacrificed a five-man attack by including Paul Collingwood for Simon Jones. It turned out that Flintoff, thanks to the cool weather and refreshing rain breaks, could do the work of two.

Amid Australia's subsidence, the vital wicket, and in some ways a motif of the series, was again that of Adam Gilchrist. Gilchrist was the key to a decisive Australian lead. His containment was the essence of England's effort to thwart it.

Cast your mind back. Seldom has a team seemed so powerless as England to curb Gilchrist in 2001. In his autobiography, Mike Atherton recalls sitting in England's dressing room during the corresponding Test four years ago and looking across at Duncan Fletcher's clipboard with its tactical summaries of how to bowl to Australia's batsmen; next to Gilchrist's name was a question mark.

By the start of this summer, this might well have straightened into an exclamation mark. Gilchrist came into the Lord's Test with 1253 runs in his last twenty dismissals at 62.65. Most recently against New Zealand, he had played a brand of one-man Twenty20 cricket in what was advertised, and otherwise played, as a Test series.

Yet for the last two months, Gilchrist's form has been an ellipsis. He is the spectacular never staged, the news story that never happens. Each innings has been much the same: he has trailed banners to the crease, accompanied by the flourish of trumpets that his reputation demands, then retreated not so much later to the sound of his own feet. Only his scoring rate has maintained its usual headlong pace: a convivial 69 per hundred balls. Yesterday, however, was an innings of a piece with his series: a bold but brittle 23, the same as his summer's Test average.

Flintoff, the Australian's chief foeman this season, had been hard at work for an hour and a half when Gilchrist came to the wicket yesterday; his first ball cut the new batsman in half anyway. Gilchrist cover drove four in retaliation, then wafted Hoggard through gully. But Collingwood also reduced a certain boundary to a single with an acrobatic trap at cover, and Flintoff raised an enquiring arm, followed by an impish smile, when he went past Gilchrist's outside edge in the next over.

Gilchrist's eagerness to attack this summer has smacked more and more of desperation. It was Hoggard who exploited it yesterday, in the same way as Trent Bridge with a ball holding its line that Gilchrist tried impatiently to work to leg. It was a stroke of accumulated frustration, at both paucity of runs and inability to fulfil his normal team role.

The eclipse of Gilchrist, in fact, has affected the whole balance of the Australian team. For their top order, his presence has always been relaxing, like money in the bank or petrol in the tank; he has also provided someone for the lower echelons to rally round. Without runs from Gilchrist, Australia's batting has lacked that core of stability. Nor have the selectors been comfortable about the option of omitting a batsman for an extra bowler.

If anyone heard a tearing sound coming from the Australian dressing room after Brett Lee holed out to cow corner yesterday afternoon, it can only have been that of Buchanan filing his latest battle plan. The only approach viable now was the one the Australians have kept in a cabinet marked 'in case of emergency break glass', and applied previously just once, in the fourth innings at Trent Bridge: attack.

It is surprising, in fact, that battle plans such as Buchanan's had not already gone by the board. The only Australian cricketer who has thrived this summer is the one who does not indulge in anything like them, not even a jocular '5–0'; Shane Warne's motto, indeed, is: 'Expect the unexpected.'

When Warne came on to bowl the fourth over of England's

innings, he bubbled over with lures and baits. Even the suncream on the end of his nose suggested an effort at deceit; where everyone else might have seen gloom, he saw sun. He also saw footmarks outside the left-hander's off-stump freshened by the damp and used them at once to remove Strauss, whooping it up even as the ball looped to short leg from bat and pad.

Warne on the cricket field today is a study in proprietorship. He places his field with the same air as a baron of business walking through his factory, or a director strolling round his film set. He motions men here and there, falls into sotto voce conversations with those who are his colleagues and casts withering glances at those who are not, subtly controlling the pace of the game with every gesture. When he is not bowling, the question seems to be when he will; when he is, the straightforward has a way of complicating exponentially.

Not even Warne, however, can master the weather. When the umpires took England's batsmen off for a second time at 3.45 p.m., he briefly masqueraded as King Canute, standing at the end of his mark as though he could compel the tide of players and officials heading for the pavilion to return by sheer force of will.

If Buchanan mentions battle plans today, someone should just give him a sudoku and tell him to amuse himself: the Ashes will be retained only by individual genius. But that barbecue sure looks in jeopardy.

DAY FIVE

ENGLAND 335, AUSTRALIA 4–0. MATCH DRAWN.

When, in the Australian vernacular, an event is classified 'good for cricket', it usually means that the national team has lost, and is almost invariably said through gritted teeth. In light of the first occurrence, there will be being a lot of 'good for cricket'-ing across Australia as you read these words. There is, however, little need for the grudging tone.

It was hard to watch England retrieve the Ashes yesterday, but only because the fingers of one's hand tended to obscure the view, as the teams presented another gift of a game that just kept on giving. It was a drama, thriller and comedy rolled into one, though not a tragedy. Nothing much is genuinely tragic in sport, least of all an end of sixteen years' one-way traffic.

For the duration of Australia's dominance, Ashes cricket has been like the Giant's Causeway: worth seeing but seldom worth going to see. This series would have justified taking out a second mortgage to witness, while its last instalment was at least worth pawning the family silver.

No one arrived at the Oval entirely happy yesterday morning. With ninety-eight overs to play, even signs of confidence seemed grotesquely misplaced. The *Sun*'s 'Ashes Coming Home' bus has been the ghost at the feast these last five days, its banner potentially as collectible as the newspapers that announced Dewey had beaten Truman.

Perhaps it will now be decreed that it was 'The Sun Wot Won It', but after forty minutes that bus looked like it bore the destination 'Hubris'. McGrath and his elbow, far from fit in this game, took time to warm to their tasks, but then found that traditional nagging length. Vaughan followed one that went away to send a tremor through his team, and Bell responded to his first delivery as though he had been passed the 'black spot'.

By that time, too, after two exploratory overs from Lee, Warne was in harness. In the inaugural Ashes Test at the Oval in 1882, it was Fred Spofforth who assured his colleagues that 'this thing can be done' before going out and doing it; it was tempting to ascribe the same sentiments to Warne.

Like the volatile, mephistophelian Spofforth, Warne wears his heart on his sleeve and his cricket on his face. He has at least as many guises as he has deliveries, from pent-up fury to barely suppressed hilarity. Though he leaves the crossing to Hayden, there is even pious Warne. During the pre-lunch session, he regularly returned to his mark with eyes upturned, mouthing imprecations to the individual he calls 'the man upstairs' – a phrase ambiguous when he was on Kerry Packer's payroll, but now more obviously aimed heavenwards.

Trescothick, meanwhile, resembled a London bobby trying to quell a riot, somehow retrieving his equilibrium each time a breach of his defensive line was threatened. It is no discredit to Trescothick that it never looked an equal contest. Could Warne's unearthly chaos ever have been contained by the forces of law and order? From round the wicket at the extremity of the crease, with his arm at the same elevation as Clarrie Grimmett's, Warne almost appeared to be bending reality, the ball deviating as though passing through a prism. Warne turned one delivery out of the footmarks so far that it was almost a breach of the spirit of cricket – by the standard unit of measurement, it spun a Double Gatt, and would have ended up at backward square leg had the batsman's pads not been struck a micron or two outside off stump. From this point, Trescothick's fall was almost foretold: another Double Gatt, and umpire Koertzen almost did not need to be asked. The wicket was Warne's 168th against England: no one has taken more, and it will be a long time before anyone else does.

Warne had no more left-handers to bowl to, but did have Pietersen, whom he'd devoured in the first innings like Hannibal Lecter. Pietersen again looked like a juicy morsel. But for a touch of Gilchrist's gauntlet, his under edge would almost certainly have been swallowed whole by Hayden at slip. The eyes that closed all over the Oval when he played his first slog sweep may have included Pietersen's own.

Warne's chief impact on Pietersen's innings, however, was to prolong it. Pietersen was a skittish 15 when he edged face-high to his Hampshire captain, almost infallible in the position this season. There was no time for a vertical petition and the ball went to ground. The roles had been reversed at Old Trafford, Pietersen dropping Warne in the gloaming; Pietersen couldn't have asked for cricket to be the great leveller at a more telling juncture.

Warne flashed predatory eyes at Pietersen for the rest of the day, twice removing the bails at the bowler's end when he went wandering down the pitch in mid-over, perhaps only half-jokingly. As he stood rather forlornly at third man after tea, stretching his sore and weary fingers, he was, as ever, the toast and the bait of the crowd, whose choruses alternated between 'There's only one Shane Warne' and 'Warnie dropped the Ashes.' The first is beyond contradiction, a tribute to the bowler and haunting thought for Australians. The second is unsupportable: with 40 wickets at 19.93 and 249 runs at 28, it is arguable he made them. 'We wish you were English' sounded much more like it.

The contest between Lee and Pietersen was perhaps the day's leading indicator. At first, Lee treated him as a punch bag, pounding his body from short of a length. Especially after gloving one short ball over the catching cordon, Pietersen looked grateful for the asylum of the non-striker's end.

Pietersen's retaliation was, in its own way, still harder to watch: a face-to-the-wall rather than a backs-to-the-wall effort. He hooked thrillingly, crazily, just millimetres each time from having his head turned into a turnip by the tabloids. Collingwood's involvement in their 60-run partnership was so minimal that he might have been tempted to a chorus of 'Eng-ger-land Eng-ger-land Eng-ger-land' just to feel more part of the action.

In the end, however, Lee had one of those days where he mistakes shortness of length for hostility of intent. On the Test's driest day, he had the ball reversing at 95mph when he pitched it up. The opportunity to turn England's best weapon against them, however, was lost in the backwash of testosterone.

With Tait too callow for lifting this heavy, too much labour was left for the unflagging Warne and the unfit McGrath. With Giles a loyal sentry, Pietersen stood guard over England's series lead until it was impassable. A fifth bowler might have been handy, although perhaps only if his name had been Lillee or O'Reilly.

In any event, there will be time for inquests later. For the moment, an Australian gives thanks. For years, my countrymen have publicly pined for a 'competitive Ashes series', without perhaps something so competitive in mind, but no ground for complaint exists. A sporting rivalry is only a rivalry if there is the danger of defeat; England have not only won the Ashes but reflated the whole currency of Anglo-Australian cricket. That is, unambiguously, good for the game.

AFTERMATH

THE PRESSURE VALVE

In the preliminary exchanges ahead of the 2005 Ashes series, Michael Vaughan made a counter-intuitive remark that proved remarkably prescient: Australia, he decided, would be 'under more pressure' than England in the forthcoming summer.

At the time Vaughan's proposition seemed a little like saying that the most dangerous ball in cricket is the long hop on leg stump, because everyone *expects* you to hit it for four. But Vaughan stuck to the idea: 'putting pressure on Australia', in fact, became to Vaughan as 'my dear old thing' is to Blowers, something that seemed to tumble from his mouth unbidden. And it turned out he was onto something.

Australia came into this series with a claim to Test supremacy that brooked no argument: victory at Lord's meant that the team had triumphed in fifty-four of its preceding seventy Tests, and was surrounded by an aura of excellence and entitlement. It was built on expectations, of themselves and of opponents, that games could be won without deviating too far from the tested formula. In hindsight, Australia was supremely well equipped to dispose of mediocre opposition, and rather less so for a rival that stood up to them.

How Australia lost this series is a conundrum set to tax us for some time yet, for teams have internal dynamics to which we are not privy. My own feeling from watching them this summer is that, in thrall to the mighty victory machine they had created, they could not cope when signs of malfunction or need for adjustment arose. They kept trying to assure themselves that everything was normal – they were insisting even at the Oval that this was 'just another

Test match' and that everything gone before was 'irrelevant' – as circumstances became less and less so.

In a sense, this is bred in the bone. The first commandment of Australian cricketers of the Border era and beyond has been the injunction to 'back yourself', regardless of events, and sometimes even of results. It builds confident cricketers, who trust their talents and put failures behind them quickly, but this tour may have revealed the corollary: that these same cricketers tend to rigidity and predictability when challenged. It has been said of the press that they always fight the next war with the weapons of the last; the Australians were similarly slow to sense the obsolescence of their former methods.

Repeat offenders in this respect were Australia's two most effective offensive batsmen, Matthew Hayden and Damien Martyn, who like adolescents resenting adult responsibilities bridled at the sudden constraints on their ability to do as they pleased. Hayden finally, belatedly, adapted his game at the Oval; Martyn never did.

Martyn is troubled by the same affliction as David Gower, a naturally good technique and ease of movement that make dismissal look self-inflicted, and a premeditated effort to spoil the spectators' day. He receives less credit for application and more blame for carelessness, because he walks out to bat radiating as much intensity as someone toddling to the newsagent for the *Racing Post*. But one also detected in him the same attitude as characterized Mark Waugh on his second tour here, that nobody was quite good enough to bowl to him. The players who really worked at their games on this tour were all English. The Andrew Strauss and Andrew Flintoff who partnered so profitably at the Oval, for example, were unrecognizable improvements on those the Australians had seen at Lord's.

For this, the can must be carried by the Australians' unshakeably deadpan coach John Buchanan, who this summer put the confusion in Confucius. Buchanan's performance at the Oval – where his belief that one can only 'control the controllables' led him to dismiss as trivial the uncontrollable of weather – was a classic of its kind. Sun Tzu must have said somewhere that one should always aim to do what most discomfits one's opponent – and if he didn't he should have. By going off for light on Friday afternoon, the Australians granted England a solace whose value is not to be underestimated.

Steve Waugh has come to his old team's defence in the aftermath of their defeat, commenting that they have not become bad cricketers overnight. Quite so: no one called for wholesale changes to Frank Worrell's West Indians after they narrowly lost the glorious series of 1960–1. The question is not so much whether Australia is a good team now, but how good a team it will be in two years' time.

Waugh's diary of Australia's tour of the Caribbean a decade ago, the one on which they bearded the West Indies in their den and established themselves as Test cricket's glass of fashion, begins with a charming story. Standing around Mascot Airport neat in their blazers and ties, they were approached by an elderly woman. 'Excuse me,' she asked. 'To which school do you lads go?' The average age of that Australian team, Ricky Ponting's first, was less than 27; the average age of the team on its way back to Australia is almost 31, and you would no more mistake them for schoolboys than the Rolling Stones for the Rakes. Michael Clarke and Shaun Tait, too, do not as yet appear the basis of a new dynasty.

Quite what fate awaits the team in Australia is far from clear. The ICC Super Series follows quickly, and memories are fleeting: short-term redemption may await. Longer term, the dilemmas remain. There is talent in Australian first-class cricket but it is maturing later. What can be surmised is that, as in Lampedusa's Sicily, things will have to change if they are to stay the same. Australians are accustomed to their team winning efficiently; Australian cricketers believe in methods tried and true. The match between performance and expectation has lasted so long that its undoing will be messy and protracted, precisely because the pressure is of the team and the game's own making.

ALL OUT

At about 4.30 the morning after England's victory at the Oval in the Fifth Test of the Ashes of 2005, opening batsman Marcus Trescothick was seen sitting by himself in the lobby of the team hotel in London. He was, he explained quietly, awaiting the morning papers. He had ordered them all. Oh, he was happy all right. But he could not quite bring himself to believe what had happened until he read it in print.

If they read the morning papers at all themselves that day, Ricky Ponting's men probably stuck to the sudoku. They prepared to wend their way home as something not known for twenty years: an Australian team defeated by England. Defeated narrowly – in the end, only 2–1 – but defeated justly. If anything the margin flattered them, reflecting grit in adversity rather than competition on equal terms.

They didn't see it coming. Nor did many of the rest of us. The Ashes summer of 2005 will go down as one of history's most extraordinary and effervescent. The middle three Tests went to the wire; the first and last contained passages of play that made them minor classics. The games unfolded at breakneck pace, yet also had time for moments of decency and sportsmanship one had almost ceased to associate with the game. Even Ponting called the series 'the best I have played in'. It was certainly the best that almost everyone had watched.

The rubber contained two titanic performances. Man-of-the-series Andrew Flintoff had come back from his tour of South Africa injured and in need of an operation. He played almost no first-class cricket before the First Test at Lord's and scored only three rusty runs. From that point, however, he towered over almost every exchange in which he was involved, with his power-packed batting and strength-through-joy bowling.

Flintoff's batting matured during the series. He was sound in defence and judicious in attack. In the Second Test at Edgbaston, he hit brutally, and dished out as many as nine sixes; by the Fourth at Trent Bridge, he was capable of a century as serene and poised as any seen in recent years. With the ball he was a revelation, regularly achieving pace in excess of 90mph, and the master of reverse as well as orthodox swing. Above all, he impressed with his physical prowess, at the Oval bowling eighteen consecutive overs in which the last ball was as fast as the first. On the field, he was a joy to watch, infectiously enthusiastic, hugging his team mates not as a footballer might but with unfeigned warmth and affection. He might be named for Fred Flintstone, but he is more the scion Bam-Bam: natural, unaffected, chock-full of fight and fun.

In any other summer, Shane Warne's 40 wickets at 19 and 255 runs at 27 would have guaranteed some individual award. It carried, indeed, its own badge of distinction. Warne, for long a great player in a grand side, was here seen in a new guise: Australia's best, last and sometimes only hope. Time and again he redeemed Australia's cause on his own, apparently by sheer force of will. In the only Test in which he did not clean up with the ball, at Old Trafford, he hefted 90 and 32. Warne's lead-up to the series had been what might euphemistically be called less than ideal; in particular, publicity of a new round of sexual peccadilloes finally drove off his long-suffering wife. Yet once on the field, he sunk himself entirely in his task. The crowd at the Oval paid him warm tribute with a chant of 'We only wish you were English' – taking the words, as it were, from the tabloid newspapermen's mouth. As Chesterton said of Dickens: 'The critics blustered but the people wept and cheered.'

Warne's workload, however, was itself a confession of Australian weakness. With Glenn McGrath absent from two Tests, and at impaired effectiveness in two others, shortcomings in Australian bowling glimpsed during the Border-Gavaskar Trophy of 2003–4 became clear as day. Brett Lee toiled manfully, and sometimes bowled very fast indeed, but without the variety or finesse of his great contemporaries. Without the pressure exerted by their stars, the auxiliary members of the attack, Gillespie,

Kasprowicz and Tait were markedly less effective.

Watching the Australians bat, meanwhile, was sometimes a little like watching a club side. There was always, somehow, the hint of wickets in the offing, with only three partnerships of more than a 100 runs achieved. The captain enjoyed only one major innings, a brave 156 to save Australia's bacon in Manchester. The obstinate Langer appeared to enjoy the fight and Michael Clarke had his moments; but Matt Hayden, Damien Martyn, Simon Katich and even Adam Gilchrist were barely more conspicuous than the Bradleys Haddin and Hodge. Gilchrist, hemmed in from round the wicket and confronted by Flintoff's brazen aggression, could not decide whether to play with or against his own attacking grain. As a result he did neither, not lasting long enough for a single half-century.

Where the Australians impressed least, however, was in the leadership. Ponting off the field said many of the right things, but on the field was depressingly stereotyped in his thinking. His bowling changes seemed at times to be being recited by rote – witness his decision to spell Lee with 5–2–6–1 at Old Trafford when the out-of-form Vaughan came to the crease – and his field settings were defensive bordering on defeatist. His long consultations with bowlers suggested a man who took too much counsel. Coach John Buchanan, so impressive in maintaining Australia's motivation in his six years extracting from the excellent the better yet, suddenly found the team failing in matters of detail, which he seemed either unwilling or unable to remedy. One sometimes needed a Babel Fish simply to understand him. Australia's bowlers, for example, were not instructed to sort out their own no-ball problems; they were asked to 'implement self-management processes'. Not that any of this was Buchanan's fault: 'I'll certainly take accountability for it, but I can't take responsibility for it.' To which the temptation was to reply: 'Yes, minister.' Nor, with an average age of 31, was this a hard-working Australian team by the standards of the sweat-soaked tracksuited training junkies of the past. Key players barely played outside the Tests. Its county fixtures had been reduced to a derisory two days each. Its fielding routines looked especially tired, and its throwing was ragged. Australia clearly expected England to capitulate after the Lord's Test: thus Ricky Ponting's decision to field after winning the toss at Edgbaston even when McGrath had turned an ankle that morning, which if it does not haunt him should.

This was a quality in Vaughan's team – a group of good cricketers who genuinely liked one another and who were clear about their objective – almost universally underestimated. In hind-sight the period that mattered was when almost no one was watching: immediately after the First Test, when England somehow convinced themselves they could still compete, and Australia persuaded themselves that England could not. The Australians dispersed, playing barely any cricket before the Second Test; the English wrote the First off to experience and came back twice as hard. They were none for 60 after an hour, one for 130 at lunch, and a lickety-split 407 all out in a day. It was like watching your favourite grandpa suddenly decide to play chicken on a motorway; the Australians looked askance. Flintoff's first over of the second innings, in which he overthrew Langer and Ponting as the crowd bayed for blood, was then perhaps as shattering as Jack Gregory's brutal, dismaying over at Trent Bridge in 1921.

England would have won comfortably at Old Trafford but for rain's exactions, and only won narrowly at Trent Bridge because of Warne's unearthly genius. Deprived again of McGrath's services by injury at the latter, Australia seemed simply to be trying to hold the line. There was no coherent plan for victory, merely progressive formations of defence. When Warne was not bowling, England seemed to bat under no pressure at all. As Flintoff and Geraint Jones put on 177 in 235 balls in the first innings, it was like watching the middle overs of a one-day international, with the field devoid of catchers as deep fielders prowled the boundaries.

Vaughan looked a better captain for the dilatory nature of his rival. He also made mistakes, probably taking his foot off Australia's throat on the third day at Old Trafford, and his bat was muted aside from his 166 at Manchester. But he was firm, decisive, canny, clearly popular, and enjoyed an excellent rapport with his coach Duncan Fletcher. England kept, moreover, taking leaves from the Australian playbook, resisting discretionary changes to their starting XI even when there seemed logic to them because of the value inherent in an unchanged unit. England's attack, as a result, cohered rather than simply adhering. The decision to include a fifth bowler and promote Flintoff to number six was an inspired piece of selection – very nearly rescinded after Lord's – for Simon Jones turned out to be as effective as any of the other four. His and Flintoff's mastery of reverse swing, which made the middle overs of each Australian innings compulsive viewing, also relieved Giles from the pressure of being England's key stock bowler.

Dr Johnson said that much could be made of a Scotsman, if caught young. The same might be true of a South African. Kevin Pietersen is perhaps the most fascinating member of the team, with a technique built around keen eye, rubbery wrists and awesome bat speed using one of the daintiest bits of willow in the game. He looked like a powerful batsman when he felt the gods were with him, with the possibility that when he felt they were not it could all go terribly wrong. No one would have been entirely surprised had he been swept away by the wave of aggression of Warne and Lee in the second innings at the Oval. In fact, he met it head-on, with a string of slog sweeps and crazy-brave hook shots. Once upon a time, a match situation like this fifth day would have been a pretext for the deadest of bats and the dourest of tempers. Pietersen gave us a 21st-Century Draw, correctly intuiting that time could be stolen from the Australians two ways: by its absorption, and by the compilation of runs that would take getting.

Above all, England seemed to want this victory more. They were more dogged, more desperate, more diligent. They did not talk in riddles; their goal was compellingly simple, and individual egos were entirely subordinate to it. They did not simply try to stop Australia; they tried to beat them, to dominate them. Australians talked above enjoying the challenge, but often gave the impression of balking it.

It was, nonetheless, too early to be prophesying an English

dynasty. They have the best all-round cricketer in the world in Flintoff. They have an excellent opening pair in Trescothick and Andrew Strauss, with the patience to survive and the power to retaliate. The loss of any of these three, however, would be costly. They have one opening bowler, Steve Harmison, who gets homesick if he has to trundle down to the off-licence; they have another, Matthew Hoggard, who when the conditions do not suit swing bowling looks all dressed up with nowhere to go; they have a third, Ashley Giles, who seems to begin wrestling with personal demons when batsmen get the better of him. Vaughan's technique is disconcertingly frail; Ian Bell was against Australia fighting out of his weight range; when the coltish keeper-batsman Geraint Jones was observed carrying the series trophy round at the end of the Fifth Test at the Oval, one hoped that the insurance premiums were current. One trusts that Trescothick enjoyed his reading; one trusts, too, he took it all with a cellarful of salt. Publicity is a wonderful thing, but the last thing one should do is believe it.

SCORECARDS

FIRST TEST: Lord's 21, 22, 23 and 24 July 2005

TOSS: Australia   **AUSTRALIA** won by **239** runs

AUSTRALIA 1ST INNINGS			R	M	B	4	6
JL Langer	c Harmison	b Flintoff	40	77	44	5	0
ML Hayden		b Hoggard	12	38	25	2	0
*RT Ponting	c Strauss	b Harmison	9	38	18	1	0
DR Martyn	c GO Jones	b SP Jones	2	13	4	0	0
MJ Clarke	lbw	b SP Jones	11	35	22	2	0
SM Katich	c GO Jones	b Harmison	27	107	67	5	0
+AC Gilchrist	c GO Jones	b Flintoff	26	30	19	6	0
SK Warne		b Harmison	28	40	29	5	0
B Lee	c GO Jones	b Harmison	3	13	8	0	0
JN Gillespie	lbw	b Harmison	1	19	11	0	0
GD McGrath		not out	10	9	6	2	0
EXTRAS	(b 5, lb 4, w 1, nb 11)		21				
TOTAL	(all out, 40.2 overs, 209 mins)		**190**				

FoW: 1-35   (Hayden - 7.6 ov)   2-55   (Ponting - 12.5 ov)

       3-66   (Langer - 14.4 ov)   4-66   (Martyn - 15.1 ov)

       5-87   (Clarke - 21.5 ov)   6-126   (Gilchrist - 28.3 ov)

       7-175   (Warne - 36.1 ov)   8-178   (Katich - 36.3 ov)

       9-178   (Lee - 38.4 ov)   10-190   (Gillespie - 40.2 ov)

BOWLING	O	M	R	W	
Harmison	11.2	0	43	5	
Hoggard	8	0	40	1	(2nb)
Flintoff	11	2	50	2	(9nb)
SP Jones	10	0	48	2	(1w)

ENGLAND 1ST INNINGS			R	M	B	4	6
ME Trescothick c Langer		b McGrath	4	24	17	1	0
AJ Strauss	c Warne	b McGrath	2	28	21	0	0
*MP Vaughan		b McGrath	3	29	20	0	0
IR Bell		b McGrath	6	34	25	1	0
KP Pietersen	c Martyn	b Warne	57	148	89	8	2
A Flintoff		b McGrath	0	8	4	0	0
+GO Jones	c Gilchrist	b Lee	30	85	56	6	0
AF Giles	c Gilchrist	b Lee	11	14	13	2	0
MJ Hoggard	c Hayden	b Warne	0	18	16	0	0
SJ Harmison	c Martyn	b Lee	11	35	19	1	0
SP Jones		not out	20	21	14	3	0
EXTRAS	(b 1, lb 5, nb 5)		11				
TOTAL	(all out, 48.1 overs, 227 mins)		**155**				

FoW: 1-10 (Trescothick, 6.1 ov) 2-11 (Strauss, 6.5 ov)
3-18 (Vaughan, 12.2 ov) 4-19 (Bell, 14.3 ov)
5-21 (Flintoff, 16.1 ov) 6-79 (GO Jones, 34.1 ov)
7-92 (Giles, 36.6 ov) 8-101 (Hoggard, 41.4 ov)
9-122 (Pietersen, 43.4 ov) 10-155 (Harmison, 48.1 ov)

BOWLING	O	M	R	W	
McGrath	18	5	53	5	
Lee	15.1	5	47	3	(4nb)
Gillespie	8	1	30	0	(1nb)
Warne	7	2	19	2	

AUSTRALIA 2ND INNINGS			R	M	B	4	6
JL Langer	run out (Pietersen)		6	24	15	1	0
ML Hayden		b Flintoff	34	65	54	5	0
*RT Ponting	c sub (JC Hildreth)	b Hoggard	42	100	65	3	0
DR Martyn	lbw	b Harmison	65	215	138	8	0
MJ Clarke		b Hoggard	91	151	106	15	0
SM Katich	c SP Jones	b Harmison	67	177	113	8	0
+AC Gilchrist		b Flintoff	10	26	14	1	0
SK Warne	c Giles	b Harmison	2	13	7	0	0
B Lee	run out (Giles)		8	16	16	1	0
JN Gillespie		b SP Jones	13	72	52	3	0
GD McGrath		not out	20	44	32	3	0
EXTRAS	(b 10, lb 8, nb 8)		26				
TOTAL	(all out, 100.4 overs, 457 mins)		**384**				

FoW: 1-18 (Langer, 5.3 ov) 2-54 (Hayden, 14.4 ov)

3-100 (Ponting, 27.3 ov) 4-255 (Clarke, 61.6 ov)

5-255 (Martyn, 62.1 ov) 6-274 (Gilchrist, 67.2 ov)

7-279 (Warne, 70.2 ov) 8-289 (Lee, 74.1 ov)

9-341 (Gillespie, 89.6 ov) 10-384 (Katich, 100.4 ov)

BOWLING	O	M	R	W	
Harmison	27.4	6	54	3	
Hoggard	16	1	56	2	(2nb)
Flintoff	27	4	123	2	(5nb)
SP Jones	18	1	69	1	(1nb)
Giles	11	1	56	0	
Bell	1	0	8	0	

ENGLAND 2ND INNINGS (TARGET 420 RUNS)			R	M	B	4	6
ME Trescothick c Hayden		b Warne	44	128	103	8	0
AJ Strauss		c & b Lee	37	115	67	6	0
*MP Vaughan		b Lee	4	47	26	1	0
IR Bell	lbw	b Warne	8	18	15	0	0
KP Pietersen		not out	64	120	79	6	2
A Flintoff	c Gilchrist	b Warne	3	4	11	0	0
+GO Jones	c Gillespie	b McGrath	6	51	27	1	0
AF Giles	c Hayden	b McGrath	0	2	2	0	0
MJ Hoggard	lbw	b McGrath	0	18	15	0	0
SJ Harmison	lbw	b Warne	0	3	1	0	0
SP Jones	c Warne	b McGrath	0	12	6	0	0
EXTRAS	(b 6, lb 5, nb 3)		14				
TOTAL	(all out, 58.1 overs, 268 mins)		**180**				

FoW: 1-80 (Strauss, 26.3 ov) 2-96 (Trescothick, 29.2 ov)
3-104 (Bell, 33.1 ov) 4-112 (Vaughan, 36.2 ov)
5-119 (Flintoff, 39.3 ov) 6-158 (GO Jones, 50.3 ov)
7-158 (Giles, 50.5 ov) 8-164 (Hoggard, 54.6 ov)
9-167 (Harmison, 55.3 ov) 10-180 (SP Jones, 58.1 ov)

BOWLING	O	M	R	W	
McGrath	17.1	2	29	4	
Lee	15	3	58	2	(1nb)
Gillespie	6	0	18	0	(2nb)
Warne	20	2	64	4	

SECOND TEST: Edgbaston 4, 5, 6 and 7 August 2005
TOSS: Australia   **ENGLAND** won by **2** runs

ENGLAND 1ST INNINGS			R	M	B	4	6
ME Trescothick	c Gilchrist	b Kasprowicz	90	143	102	15	2
AJ Strauss		b Warne	48	113	76	10	0
*MP Vaughan	c Lee	b Gillespie	24	54	41	3	0
IR Bell	c Gilchrist	b Kasprowicz	6	2	3	1	0
KP Pietersen	c Katich	b Lee	71	152	76	10	1
A Flintoff	c Gilchrist	b Gillespie	68	74	62	6	5
+GO Jones	c Gilchrist	b Kasprowicz	1	14	15	0	0
AF Giles	lbw	b Warne	23	34	30	4	0
MJ Hoggard	lbw	b Warne	16	62	49	2	0
SJ Harmison		b Warne	17	16	11	2	1
SP Jones		not out	19	39	24	1	1
EXTRAS	(lb 9, w 1, nb 14)		24				
TOTAL	(all out, 79.2 overs, 356 mins)		**407**				

FoW: 1-112 (Strauss, 25.3 ov)   2-164 (Trescothick, 32.3 ov)
3-170 (Bell, 32.6 ov)   4-187 (Vaughan, 36.6 ov)
5-290 (Flintoff, 54.3 ov)   6-293 (GO Jones, 57.4 ov)
7-342 (Giles, 65.1 ov)   8-348 (Pietersen, 66.3 ov)
9-375 (Harmison, 69.4 ov)   10-407 (Hoggard, 79.2 ov)

BOWLING	O	M	R	W	
Lee	17	1	111	1	(3nb, 1w)
Gillespie	22	3	91	2	(3nb)
Kasprowicz	15	3	80	3	(8nb)
Warne	25.2	4	116	4	

AUSTRALIA 1ST INNINGS			R	M	B	4	6
JL Langer	lbw	b SP Jones	82	276	154	7	0
ML Hayden	c Strauss	b Hoggard	0	5	1	0	0
*RT Ponting	c Vaughan	b Giles	61	87	76	12	0
DR Martyn	run out (Vaughan)		20	23	18	4	0
MJ Clarke	c GO Jones	b Giles	40	85	68	7	0
SM Katich	c GO Jones	b Flintoff	4	22	18	1	0
+AC Gilchrist		not out	49	120	69	4	0
SK Warne		b Giles	8	14	14	2	0
B Lee	c Flintoff	b SP Jones	6	14	10	1	0
JN Gillespie	lbw	b Flintoff	7	36	37	1	0
MS Kasprowicz	lbw	b Flintoff	0	1	1	0	0
EXTRAS	(b 13, lb 7, w 1, nb 10)		31				
TOTAL	(all out, 76 overs, 346 mins)		**308**				

FoW: 1-0 (Hayden, 1.1 ov) 2-88 (Ponting, 19.5 ov)
3-118 (Martyn, 24.5 ov) 4-194 (Clarke, 44.2 ov)
5-208 (Katich, 49.4 ov) 6-262 (Langer, 61.3 ov)
7-273 (Warne, 64.5 ov) 8-282 (Lee, 67.1 ov)
9-308 (Gillespie, 75.5 ov) 10-308 (Kasprowicz, 75.6 ov)

BOWLING	O	M	R	W	
Harmison	11	1	48	0	(2nb)
Hoggard	8	0	41	1	(4nb)
SP Jones	16	2	69	2	(1nb, 1w)
Flintoff	15	1	52	3	(3nb)
Giles	26	2	78	3	

ENGLAND 2ND INNINGS			R	M	B	4	6
ME Trescothick c Gilchrist	b Lee	21	51	38	4	0
AJ Strauss	b Warne	6	28	12	1	0
MJ Hoggard c Hayden	b Lee	1	35	27	0	0
*MP Vaughan	b Lee	1	2	2	0	0
IR Bell c Gilchrist	b Warne	21	69	43	2	0
KP Pietersen c Gilchrist	b Warne	20	50	35	0	2
A Flintoff	b Warne	73	133	86	6	4
+GO Jones c Ponting	b Lee	9	33	19	1	0
AF Giles c Hayden	b Warne	8	44	36	0	0
SJ Harmison c Ponting	b Warne	0	2	1	0	0
SP Jones	not out	12	42	23	3	0
EXTRAS	(lb 1, nb 9)	10				
TOTAL	(all out, 52.1 overs, 249 mins)	**182**				

FoW: 1-25 (Strauss, 6.2 ov) 2-27 (Trescothick, 11.2 ov)
3-29 (Vaughan, 11.5 ov) 4-31 (Hoggard, 13.5 ov)
5-72 (Pietersen, 24.6 ov) 6-75 (Bell, 26.5 ov)
7-101 (GO Jones, 33.6 ov) 8-131 (Giles, 44.3 ov)
9-131 (Harmison, 44.4 ov) 10-182 (Flintoff, 52.1 ov)

BOWLING	O	M	R	W	
Lee	18	1	82	4	(5nb)
Gillespie	8	0	24	0	(1nb)
Kasprowicz	3	0	29	0	(3nb)
Warne	23.1	7	46	6	

AUSTRALIA 2ND INNINGS (TARGET 282 RUNS)			R	M	B	4	6
JL Langer		b Flintoff	28	54	47	4	0
ML Hayden	c Trescothick	b SP Jones	31	106	64	4	0
*RT Ponting	c GO Jones	b Flintoff	0	4	5	0	0
DR Martyn	c Bell	b Hoggard	28	64	36	5	0
MJ Clarke		b Harmison	30	101	57	4	0
SM Katich	c Trescothick	b Giles	16	27	21	3	0
+AC Gilchrist	c Flintoff	b Giles	1	8	4	0	0
JN Gillespie	lbw	b Flintoff	0	4	2	0	0
SK Warne	hit wicket	b Flintoff	42	79	59	4	2
B Lee		not out	43	99	75	5	0
MS Kasprowicz	c GO Jones	b Harmison	20	60	31	3	0
EXTRAS	(b 13, lb 8, w 1, nb 18)		40				
TOTAL	(all out, 64.3 overs, 307 mins)		**279**				

FoW: 1-47 (Langer, 12.2 ov) 2-48 (Ponting, 12.6 ov)
3-82 (Hayden, 22.5 ov) 4-107 (Martyn, 26.1 ov)
5-134 (Katich, 31.6 ov) 6-136 (Gilchrist, 33.5 ov)
7-137 (Gillespie, 34.2 ov) 8-175 (Clarke, 43.4 ov)
9-220 (Warne, 52.1 ov) 10-279 (Kasprowicz, 64.3 ov)

BOWLING	O	M	R	W	
Harmison	17.3	3	62	2	(1nb, 1w)
Hoggard	5	0	26	1	
Giles	15	3	68	2	
Flintoff	22	3	79	4	(13nb)
SP Jones	5	1	23	1	

THIRD TEST: Old Trafford 11, 12, 13, 14 and 15 August 2005

TOSS: England   **MATCH DRAWN**

ENGLAND 1ST INNINGS			R	M	B	4	6
ME Trescothick c Gilchrist		b Warne	63	196	117	9	0
AJ Strauss		b Lee	6	43	28	0	0
*MP Vaughan	c McGrath	b Katich	166	281	215	20	1
IR Bell	c Gilchrist	b Lee	59	205	155	8	0
KP Pietersen	c sub (BJ Hodge)	b Lee	21	50	28	1	0
MJ Hoggard		b Lee	4	13	10	1	0
A Flintoff	c Langer	b Warne	46	93	67	7	0
+GO Jones		b Gillespie	42	86	51	6	0
AF Giles	c Hayden	b Warne	0	11	6	0	0
SJ Harmison		not out	10	13	11	1	0
SP Jones		b Warne	0	7	4	0	0
EXTRAS	(b 4, lb 5, w 3, nb 15)		27				
TOTAL	(all out, 113.2 overs, 503 mins) **444**						

FoW: 1-26   (Strauss, 9.2 ov)   2-163   (Trescothick, 41.5 ov)
     3-290   (Vaughan, 74.3 ov)   4-333   (Pietersen, 86.2 ov)
     5-341   (Hoggard, 88.6 ov)   6-346   (Bell, 92.1 ov)
     7-433   (Flintoff, 109.2 ov)   8-434   (GO Jones, 110.2 ov)
     9-438   (Giles, 111.4 ov)   10-444 (SP Jones, 113.2 ov)

BOWLING	O	M	R	W	
McGrath	25	6	86	0	(4nb)
Lee	27	6	100	4	(5nb, 2w)
Gillespie	19	2	114	1	(2nb, 1w)
Warne	33.2	5	99	4	(2nb)
Katich	9	1	36	1	

AUSTRALIA 1ST INNINGS			R	M	B	4	6
JL Langer	c Bell	b Giles	31	76	50	4	0
ML Hayden	lbw	b Giles	34	112	71	5	0
*RT Ponting	c Bell	b SP Jones	7	20	12	1	0
DR Martyn		b Giles	20	71	41	2	0
SM Katich		b Flintoff	17	39	28	1	0
+AC Gilchrist	c GO Jones	b SP Jones	30	74	49	4	0
SK Warne	c Giles	b SP Jones	90	183	122	11	1
MJ Clarke	c Flintoff	b SP Jones	7	19	18	0	0
JN Gillespie	lbw	b SP Jones	26	144	111	1	1
B Lee	c Trescothick	b SP Jones	1	17	16	0	0
GD McGrath		not out	1	20	4	0	0
EXTRAS	(b 8, lb 7, w 8, nb 15)		38				
TOTAL	(all out, 84.5 overs, 393 mins)		**302**				

FoW: 1-58 (Langer, 15.5 ov) 2-73 (Ponting, 20.1 ov)
3-86 (Hayden, 23.3 ov) 4-119 (Katich, 32.1 ov)
5-133 (Martyn, 35.3 ov) 6-186 (Gilchrist, 48.1 ov)
7-201 (Clarke, 52.3 ov) 8-287 (Warne, 76.2 ov)
9-293 (Lee, 80.4 ov) 10-302 (Gillespie, 84.5 ov)

BOWLING	O	M	R	W	
Harmison	10	0	47	0	(3nb)
Hoggard	6	2	22	0	
Flintoff	20	1	65	1	(8nb)
SP Jones	17.5	6	53	6	(1nb, 2w)
Giles	31	4	100	3	(1w)

ENGLAND 2ND INNINGS			R	M	B	4	6
ME Trescothick		b McGrath	41	71	56	6	0
AJ Strauss	c Martyn	b McGrath	106	246	158	9	2
*MP Vaughan	c sub (BJ Hodge)	b Lee	14	45	37	2	0
IR Bell	c Katich	b McGrath	65	165	103	4	1
KP Pietersen	lbw	b McGrath	0	3	1	0	0
A Flintoff		b McGrath	4	20	18	0	0
+GO Jones		not out	27	15	12	2	2
AF Giles		not out	0	4	0	0	0
EXTRAS	(b 5, lb 3, w 1, nb 14)		23				
TOTAL	(6 wickets dec, 61.5 overs, 288 mins) **280**						
DNB: MJ Hoggard, SJ Harmison, SP Jones.							

FoW: 1-64 (Trescothick, 15.3 ov)   2-97   (Vaughan, 25.4 ov)

   3-224   (Strauss, 53.3 ov)   4-225   (Pietersen, 53.5 ov)

   5-248   (Flintoff, 59.1 ov)   6-264   (Bell, 61.1 ov)

BOWLING	O	M	R	W	
McGrath	20.5	1	115	5	(6nb, 1w)
Lee	12	0	60	1	(4nb)
Warne	25	3	74	0	
Gillespie	4	0	23	0	(4nb)

AUSTRALIA 2ND INNINGS (TARGET 423 RUNS)			R	M	B	4	6
JL Langer	c GO Jones	b Hoggard	14	42	41	3	0
ML Hayden		b Flintoff	36	123	91	5	1
*RT Ponting	c GO Jones	b Harmison	156	411	275	16	1
DR Martyn	lbw	b Harmison	19	53	36	3	0
SM Katich	c Giles	b Flintoff	12	30	23	2	0
+AC Gilchrist	c Bell	b Flintoff	4	36	30	0	0
MJ Clarke		b SP Jones	39	73	63	7	0
JN Gillespie	lbw	b Hoggard	0	8	5	0	0
SK Warne	c GO Jones	b Flintoff	34	99	69	5	0
B Lee		not out	18	44	25	4	0
GD McGrath		not out	5	17	9	1	0
EXTRAS	(b 5, lb 8, w 1, nb 20)		34				
TOTAL	(9 wickets,108 overs, 474 mins) **371**						

FoW: 1-25 (Langer, 11.1 ov) 2-96 (Hayden, 29.4 ov)
3-129 (Martyn, 42.5 ov) 4-165 (Katich, 49.3 ov)
5-182 (Gilchrist, 57.4 ov) 6-263 (Clarke, 75.2 ov)
7-264 (Gillespie, 76.5 ov) 8-340 (Warne, 98.2 ov)
9-354 (Ponting, 103.6 ov)

BOWLING	O	M	R	W	
Harmison	22	4	67	2	(4nb, 1w)
Hoggard	13	0	49	2	(6nb)
Giles	26	4	93	0	
Vaughan	5	0	21	0	
Flintoff	25	6	71	4	(9nb)
SP Jones	17	3	57	1	

FOURTH TEST: Trent Bridge 25, 26, 27, and 28 August 2005
TOSS: England   **ENGLAND** won by **3** wickets

ENGLAND 1ST INNINGS			R	M	B	4	6
ME Trescothick		b Tait	65	138	111	8	1
AJ Strauss	c Hayden	b Warne	35	99	64	4	0
*MP Vaughan	c Gilchrist	b Ponting	58	138	99	9	0
IR Bell	c Gilchrist	b Tait	3	12	5	0	0
KP Pietersen	c Gilchrist	b Lee	45	131	108	6	0
A Flintoff	lbw	b Tait	102	201	132	14	1
+GO Jones	c & b Kasprowicz		85	205	149	8	0
AF Giles	lbw	b Warne	15	45	35	3	0
MJ Hoggard	c Gilchrist	b Warne	10	46	28	1	0
SJ Harmison	st Gilchrist	b Warne	2	9	6	0	0
SP Jones		not out	15	32	27	3	0
EXTRAS	(b 1, lb 15, w 1, nb 25)		42				
TOTAL	(all out, 123.1 overs, 537 mins)		477				

FoW: 1-105 (Strauss, 21.4 ov)   2-137 (Trescothick, 30.5 ov)
3-146 (Bell, 34.1 ov)   4-213 (Vaughan, 55.2 ov)
5-241 (Pietersen, 64.1 ov)   6-418 (Flintoff, 103.2 ov)
7-450(GO Jones, 112.5 ov)   8-450 (Giles, 113.1 ov)
9-454(Harmison, 115.1 ov)   10-477 (Hoggard, 123.1 ov)

BOWLING	O	M	R	W	
Lee	32	2	131	1	(8nb)
Kasprowicz	32	3	122	1	(13nb)
Tait	24	4	97	3	(4nb)
Warne	29.1	4	102	4	
Ponting	6	2	9	1	(1w)

ASHES 2005

AUSTRALIA 1ST INNINGS			R	M	B	4	6
JL Langer	c Bell	b Hoggard	27	95	59	5	0
ML Hayden	lbw	b Hoggard	7	41	27	1	0
*RT Ponting	lbw	b SP Jones	1	6	6	0	0
DR Martyn	lbw	b Hoggard	1	4	3	0	0
MJ Clarke	lbw	b Harmison	36	93	53	5	0
SM Katich	c Strauss	b SP Jones	45	91	66	7	0
+AC Gilchrist	c Strauss	b Flintoff	27	58	36	3	1
SK Warne	c Bell	b SP Jones	0	2	1	0	0
B Lee	c Bell	b SP Jones	47	51	44	5	3
MS Kasprowicz		b SP Jones	5	8	7	1	0
SW Tait		not out	3	27	9	0	0
EXTRAS	(lb 2, w 1, nb 16)		19				
TOTAL	(all out, 49.1 overs, 247 mins)		**218**				

FoW: 1-20 (Hayden, 9.3 ov) 2-21 (Ponting, 10.3 ov)
3-22 (Martyn, 11.1 ov) 4-58 (Langer, 19.3 ov)
5-99 (Clarke, 30.3 ov) 6-157 (Katich, 39.2 ov)
7-157 (Warne, 39.3 ov) 8-163 (Gilchrist, 42.2 ov)
9-175(Kasprowicz, 43.2 ov) 10-218 (Lee, 49.1 ov)

BOWLING	O	M	R	W	
Harmison	9	1	48	1	(3nb)
Hoggard	15	3	70	3	(4nb)
SP Jones	14.1	4	44	5	(1nb)
Flintoff	11	1	54	1	(8nb, 1w)

AUSTRALIA 2ND INNINGS (FOLLOWING ON)			R	M	B	4	6
JL Langer	c Bell	b Giles	61	149	112	8	0
ML Hayden	c Giles	b Flintoff	26	57	41	4	0
*RT Ponting	run out (sub [GJ Pratt])		48	137	89	3	1
DR Martyn	c GO Jones	b Flintoff	13	56	30	1	0
MJ Clarke	c GO Jones	b Hoggard	56	209	170	6	0
SM Katich	lbw	b Harmison	59	262	183	4	0
+AC Gilchrist	lbw	b Hoggard	11	20	11	2	0
SK Warne	st GO Jones	b Giles	45	68	42	5	2
B Lee		not out	26	77	39	3	0
MS Kasprowicz	c GO Jones	b Harmison	19	30	26	1	0
SW Tait		b Harmison	4	20	16	1	0
EXTRAS	(b 1, lb 4, nb 14) 19						
TOTAL	(all out, 124 overs, 548 mins) **387**						

FoW: 1-50 (Hayden, 13.4 ov) 2-129 (Langer, 33.6 ov)

3-155 (Ponting, 44.1 ov) 4-161 (Martyn, 46.1 ov)

5-261 (Clarke, 94.2 ov) 6-277 (Gilchrist, 98.5 ov)

7-314 (Katich, 107.3 ov) 8-342 (Warne, 112.3 ov)

9-373(Kasprowicz, 119.2 ov) 10-387 (Tait, 123.6 ov)

BOWLING	O	M	R	W	
Hoggard	27	7	72	2	(1nb)
SP Jones	4	0	15	0	
Harmison	30	5	93	3	(1nb)
Flintoff	29	4	83	2	(9nb)
Giles	28	3	107	2	
Bell	6	2	12	0	(3nb)

ENGLAND 2ND INNINGS (TARGET 129 RUNS)			R	M	B	4	6
ME Trescothick	c Ponting	b Warne	27	24	22	4	0
AJ Strauss	c Clarke	b Warne	23	68	37	3	0
*MP Vaughan	c Hayden	b Warne	0	8	6	0	0
IR Bell	c Kasprowicz	b Lee	3	38	20	0	0
KP Pietersen	c Gilchrist	b Lee	23	51	34	3	0
A Flintoff		b Lee	26	63	34	3	0
+GO Jones	c Kasprowicz	b Warne	3	25	13	0	0
AF Giles		not out	7	30	17	0	0
MJ Hoggard		not out	8	20	13	1	0
EXTRAS	(lb 4, nb 5)		9				
TOTAL	(7 wickets, 31.5 overs, 168 mins)**129**						
DNB: SJ Harmison, SP Jones.							

FoW: 1-32 (Trescothick, 5.1 ov)   2-36   (Vaughan, 7.1 ov)
     3-57 (Strauss, 13.5 ov)   4-57   (Bell, 14.1 ov)
     5-103 (Pietersen, 24.1 ov)   6-111   (Flintoff, 26.4 ov)
     7-116 (GO Jones, 27.6 ov)

BOWLING	O	M	R	W	
Lee	12	0	51	3	(5nb)
Kasprowicz	2	0	19	0	
Warne	13.5	2	31	4	
Tait	4	0	24	0	

FIFTH TEST: The Oval 8, 9, 10, 11 and 12 September 2005
TOSS: England　　　　　　　　　　　　　　**MATCH DRAWN**

ENGLAND 1ST INNINGS			R	M	B	4	6
ME Trescothick	c Hayden	b Warne	43	77	65	8	0
AJ Strauss	c Katich	b Warne	129	351	210	17	0
*MP Vaughan	c Clarke	b Warne	11	26	25	2	0
IR Bell	lbw	b Warne	0	9	7	0	0
KP Pietersen		b Warne	14	30	25	2	0
A Flintoff	c Warne	b McGrath	72	162	115	12	1
PD Collingwood	lbw	b Tait	7	26	26	1	0
+GO Jones		b Lee	25	60	41	5	0
AF Giles	lbw	b Warne	32	120	70	1	0
MJ Hoggard	c Martyn	b McGrath	2	47	36	0	0
SJ Harmison		not out	20	25	20	4	0
EXTRAS	(b 4, lb 6, w 1, nb 7)		18				
TOTAL	(all out, 105.3 overs, 471 mins) **373**						

FoW: 1-82 (Trescothick, 17.3 ov)　　2-102　　(Vaughan, 23.5 ov)
　　　3-104　　(Bell, 25.6 ov)　　4-131　(Pietersen, 33.3 ov)
　　　5-274　(Flintoff, 70.1 ov)　　6-289 (Collingwood, 76.3 ov)
　　　7-297　(Strauss, 79.4 ov)　　8-325　　(Jones, 89.3 ov)
　　　9-345 (Hoggard, 100.2 ov)　　10-373　　(Giles, 105.3 ov)

BOWLING	O	M	R	W	
McGrath	27	5	72	2	(1w)
Lee	23	3	94	1	(3nb)
Tait	15	1	61	1	(3nb)
Warne	37.3	5	122	6	
Katich	3	0	14	0	

AUSTRALIA 1ST INNINGS			R	M	B	4	6
JL Langer		b Harmison	105	233	146	11	2
ML Hayden	lbw	b Flintoff	138	416	303	18	0
*RT Ponting	c Strauss	b Flintoff	35	81	56	3	0
DR Martyn	c Collingwood	b Flintoff	10	36	29	1	0
MJ Clarke	lbw	b Hoggard	25	119	59	2	0
SM Katich	lbw	b Flintoff	1	12	11	0	0
+AC Gilchrist	lbw	b Hoggard	23	32	20	4	0
SK Warne	c Vaughan	b Flintoff	0	18	10	0	0
B Lee	c Giles	b Hoggard	6	22	10	0	0
GD McGrath	c Strauss	b Hoggard	0	6	6	0	0
SW Tait		not out	1	7	2	0	0
EXTRAS	(b 4, lb 8, w 2, nb 9)		23				
TOTAL	(all out, 107.1 overs, 494 mins)	**367**					

FoW: 1-185   (Langer, 52.4 ov)   2-264   (Ponting, 72.2 ov)

     3-281   (Martyn, 80.4 ov)   4-323   (Hayden, 92.3 ov)

     5-329   (Katich, 94.6 ov)   6-356   (Gilchrist, 101.1 ov)

     7-359   (Clarke, 103.3 ov)   8-363   (Warne, 104.5 ov)

     9-363 (McGrath, 105.6 ov)   10-367   (Lee, 107.1 ov)

BOWLING	O	M	R	W	
Harmison	22	2	87	1	(2nb, 2w)
Hoggard	24.1	2	97	4	(1nb)
Flintoff	34	10	78	5	(6nb)
Giles	23	1	76	0	
Collingwood	4	0	17	0	

ENGLAND 2ND INNINGS			R	M	B	4	6
ME Trescothick	lbw	b Warne	33	150	84	1	0
AJ Strauss	c Katich	b Warne	1	16	7	0	0
*MP Vaughan	c Gilchrist	b McGrath	45	80	65	6	0
IR Bell	c Warne	b McGrath	0	2	1	0	0
KP Pietersen		b McGrath	158	285	187	15	7
A Flintoff	c & b Warne		8	20	13	1	0
PD Collingwood	c Ponting	b Warne	10	72	51	1	0
+GO Jones		b Tait	1	24	12	0	0
AF Giles		b Warne	59	159	97	7	0
MJ Hoggard		not out	4	45	35	0	0
SJ Harmison	c Hayden	b Warne	0	2	2	0	0
EXTRAS	(b 4, w 7, nb 5)		16				
TOTAL	(all out, 91.3 overs, 432 mins)		**335**				

FoW: 1-2 (Strauss, 3.4 ov) 2-67 (Vaughan, 22.4 ov)
3-67 (Bell, 22.5 ov) 4-109 (Trescothick, 33.1 ov)
5-126 (Flintoff, 37.5 ov) 6-186 (Collingwood, 51.5 ov)
7-199 (Jones, 56.5 ov) 8-308 (Pietersen, 82.5 ov)
9-335 (Giles, 91.1 ov) 10-335 (Harmison, 91.3 ov)

BOWLING	O	M	R	W	
McGrath	26	3	85	3	(1nb)
Lee	20	4	88	0	(4nb, 1w)
Warne	38.3	3	124	6	(1w)
Clarke	2	0	6	0	
Tait	5	0	28	1	(1w)

AUSTRALIA 2ND INNINGS (TARGET 342 RUNS)		R	M	B	4	6
JL Langer	not out	0	3	4	0	0
ML Hayden	not out	0	3	0	0	0
Extras	(lb 4)	4				
Total	(0 wickets, 0.4 overs, 3 mins)	**4**				
DNB: *RT Ponting, DR Martyn, MJ Clarke, SM Katich, +AC Gilchrist,						
SK Warne, B Lee, GD McGrath, SW Tait.						

BOWLING	O	M	R	W	
Harmison	0.4	0	0	0	

ASHES 2005 AVERAGES

AUSTRALIA BATTING AND FIELDING											
	Mat	I	NO	Runs	HS	Ave	SR	100	50	Ct	St
JL Langer	5	10	1	394	105	43.77	58.63	1	2	2	-
RT Ponting	5	9	0	359	156	39.88	59.63	1	1	4	-
MJ Clarke	5	9	0	335	91	37.22	54.38	-	2	2	-
GD McGrath	3	5	4	36	20*	36.00	63.15	-	-	1	-
ML Hayden	5	10	1	318	138	35.33	46.97	1	-	10	-
SK Warne	5	9	0	249	90	27.66	70.53	-	1	5	-
SM Katich	5	9	0	248	67	27.55	46.79	-	2	4	-
B Lee	5	9	3	158	47	26.33	65.02	-	-	2	-
AC Gilchrist	5	9	1	181	49*	22.62	71.82	-	-	18	1
DR Martyn	5	9	0	178	65	19.77	53.13	-	1	4	-
MS Kasprowicz	2	4	0	44	20	11.00	67.69	-	-	3	-
SW Tait	2	3	2	8	4	8.00	29.62	-	-	-	-
JN Gillespie	3	6	0	47	26	7.83	21.55	-	-	1	-

AUSTRALIA BOWLING											
	Mat	O	M	R	W	Ave	Best	5	10	SR	Econ
RT Ponting	5	6	2	9	1	9.00	1-9	-	-	36.0	1.50
SK Warne	5	252.5	37	797	40	19.92	6-46	3	2	37.9	3.15
GD McGrath	3	134	22	440	19	23.15	5-53	2	-	42.3	3.28
B Lee	5	191.1	25	822	20	41.10	4-82	-	-	57.3	4.29
SW Tait	2	48	5	210	5	42.00	3-97	-	-	57.6	4.37
SM Katich	5	12	1	50	1	50.00	1-36	-	-	72.0	4.16
MS Kasprowicz	2	52	6	250	4	62.50	3-80	-	-	78.0	4.80
JN Gillespie	3	67	6	300	3	100.00	2-91	-	-	134.0	4.47
MJ Clarke	5	2	0	6	0	-	-	-	-	-	3.00

ASHES 2005 AVERAGES

ENGLAND BATTING AND FIELDING											
	Mat	I	NO	Runs	HS	Ave	SR	100	50	Ct	St
KP Pietersen	5	10	1	473	158	52.55	71.45	1	3	-	-
ME Trescothick	5	10	0	431	90	43.10	60.27	-	3	3	-
A Flintoff	5	10	0	402	102	40.20	74.16	1	3	3	-
AJ Strauss	5	10	0	393	129	39.30	57.79	2	-	6	-
SP Jones	4	6	4	66	20*	33.00	67.34	-	-	1	-
MP Vaughan	5	10	0	326	166	32.60	60.82	1	1	2	-
GO Jones	5	10	1	229	85	25.44	57.97	-	1	15	1
AF Giles	5	10	2	155	59	19.37	50.65	-	1	5	-
IR Bell	5	10	0	171	65	17.10	45.35	-	2	8	-
SJ Harmison	5	8	2	60	20*	10.00	84.50	-	-	1	-
PD Collingwood	1	2	0	17	10	8.50	22.07	-	-	1	-
MJ Hoggard	5	9	2	45	16	6.42	19.65	-	-	-	-

ENGLAND BOWLING											
	Mat	O	M	R	W	Ave	Best	5	10	SR	Econ
SP Jones	4	102	17	378	18	21.00	6-53	2	-	34.0	3.70
A Flintoff	5	194	32	655	24	27.29	5-78	1	-	48.5	3.37
MJ Hoggard	5	122.1	15	473	16	29.56	4-97	-	-	45.8	3.87
SJ Harmison	5	161.1	22	549	17	32.29	5-43	1	-	56.8	3.40
AF Giles	5	160	18	578	10	57.80	3-78	-	-	96.0	3.61
PD Collingwood	1	4	0	17	0	-	-	-	-	-	4.25
IR Bell	5	7	2	20	0	-	-	-	-	-	2.85
MP Vaughan	5	5	0	21	0	-	-	-	-	-	4.20